T0330066

The Forces of Economic Growth

The Forces of Economic Growth

A TIME SERIES PERSPECTIVE

Alfred Greiner,
Willi Semmler, and
Gang Gong

PRINCETON UNIVERSITY PRESS
PRINCETON AND OXFORD

Library of Congress Cataloging-in-Publication Data

Greiner, Alfred.
The forces of economic growth: a time series perspective/Alfred Greiner, Willi
Semmler, and Gang Gong.
   p. cm.
Includes bibliographical references and index.
ISBN 0-691-11918-X (cl: alk. paper)
   1. Economic development—Mathematical models. 2. Time series
analysis—Mathematical models. 3. Investments—Mathematical models.
4. Human capital—Mathematical models. 5. Education—Economic
aspects—Mathematical models. 6. Research, Industrial—Economic
aspects—Mathematical models. I. Semmler, Willi, II. Gong, Gang, 1959– III. Title.

HD75.5.G752 2005
330′.01′51955—dc22   2004044534

British Library Cataloging-in-Publication Data is available

I cannot perceive the present situation as final for humanity.... Only so far as I can consider it a transition to a better one, is it valuable for me.

—Johann Gottlieb Fichte (German philosopher, 1762–1814)

Contents

Figures

Tables

Preface

The endogenous or new growth theory has directed new attention to an old and important problem in economics: What are the forces of economic growth and how can public policy enhance them? Over the last two hundred years, countries have varied greatly in their growth performance. While the welfare of numerous nations has increased, per capita income across countries, and across groups within countries, has remained widely disparate. By now it seems certain that there is no all-encompassing theory of economic growth. Rather different sources of economic growth appear to be relevant for different stages of economic development. In our book we study some major forces of growth and how they may contribute to particular stages of economic development. Therefore, the focus of the book is on a time-series perspective of economic growth, which requires dynamic and time-series methods. Although this book employs recent tools from dynamic analysis and dynamic econometrics, this is not a book about methods. There are a number of books on sophisticated dynamic methods in growth economics. Our book attempts to use these tools to draw out significant economic results within a unified framework rather than to focus on the exposition of those dynamic methods. Although the book requires some formal training in quantitative methods, the chapters are not too demanding. A short summary of the dynamic methods used in the book are given in the technical appendix. Computer programs are not included in the book but can be obtained from the authors upon request.

The material of this book has been presented by the authors at several universities. Chapters of the book have been presented as lectures at Bielefeld University; University of Augsburg; Foscari University, Venice; St. Anna School of Graduate Studies, Pisa; University of Technology, Vienna; University of Aix-en-Provence; Columbia University, New York; and New School University, New York. Some chapters of the book have also been presented at conferences of the American Economic Association, European Economic Association, International Institute of Public Finance, Society for Computing in Economics and Finance, German Economic Society, Society of Nonlinear Dynamics and Econometrics, and Society of Economic Dynamics. We are grateful for comments by the participants of those conferences. We are also grateful for comments from Phillip Aghion, Toichiro Asada, Jess Benhabib, Buz Brock, Carl Chiarella, Ray Fair, Stefan Mittnik, James Ramsey, Reinhard Selten, Malte Sieveking, Gerhard Sorger, and colleagues of our universities. We are in particular thankful to Jens Rubart for research assistance in collecting the data set used for the estimations of the models in chapters 4–5 and 7. We also want to thank Almuth Scholl, Mark Meyer, Chih-Ying Hsiao, and Uwe Köller for research assistance and Gaby Windhorst for editing and typing the manuscript. We are in particular grateful to several anonymous referees who read an earlier version of the manuscript and helped the book become better. Financial support from the Ministry of Education, Science, and Technology and from Deutsche Bundesbank, Hauptverwaltung Düsseldorf, as well as research assistance from the CEPA of the New School University, New York, and from the Center for Empirical Macroeconomics, Bielefeld University, are gratefully acknowledged. Portions of chapter 3 have appeared as "Externalities of Investment and Endogenous Growth: Theory and Time-Series Evidence" in *Structural Change and Economic Dynamics* 12: 295–310. Portions of chapter 4 and of chapter 7 are forthcoming as "The Uzawa-Lucas Model without Scale Effects: Theory and Empirical Evidence" in *Structural Change and Economic Dynamics* and as "Economic Growth, Skill-Biased Technical Change, Wage Inequality: A Model and Estimations for the U.S. and Europe" in *Journal of Macroeconomics*. Our thanks go to Elsevier for granting its permission to include this material here.

The Forces of Economic Growth

CHAPTER 1

Economic Growth in Historical Perspective

1.1 HISTORICAL PERSPECTIVE

Over the past two hundred years, countries have varied widely in their patterns of economic growth. In the nineteenth century, the United Kingdom was the leading industrialized country, with Germany and France catching up, and then the United States leapfrogged the European countries around the turn of the century. In the period after World War II, per capita income in Japan and Germany increased dramatically. Out of these spurts of growth emerges a long-term historical trend: the United States and other countries that now belong to the Organization for Economic Cooperation and Development (OECD) have seen a persistent increase in per capita income of roughly 2 percent per annum over the last century. Yet during the same period, other countries have continued to languish in poverty. This marked difference in economic performance is not accidental, for in some countries major forces of growth were set in motion that were lacking in other countries.

The problem of economic growth has been studied for as long as economics has been a recognizable discipline. In the eighteenth century, Adam Smith (1976) saw that the forces of growth were released by freeing market agents from external restrictions. He predicted that the increasing size of markets, as well as increasing returns and externalities due to a rising division of labor, would spur development. Early in the nineteenth century, David Ricardo (1951) emphasized investment in machinery as a cause of the increase in per capita income. Karl Marx (1967), following Ricardo, also saw investment in machinery and capital accumulation as major sources of growth. John Stuart Mill (1900), by contrast, emphasized education and the sciences as engines of growth. All of the classical authors understood that economic activity, carried out by private agents in markets, must be complemented by social and public infrastructure.

The classical economists also knew that the development of market forces and economic growth would likely be accompanied by inequality. As economies expand, traditional sectors and traditional methods of production are rendered obsolete, the workforce is deskilled, and the income of some groups is depressed—while other agents grasp opportunities, create wealth, and accumulate fortunes. Joseph Schumpeter (1935) in particular perceived economic growth as a process of "creative destruction" in which some actors gain and others lose.

In addition to recognizing the divergence in income between sectors and groups, the classical economists (as did Schumpeter) conceived growth as a process that converges in the long run toward a stationary state of per capita income. In the modern period, after John Maynard Keynes (1936), growth theory was furthered by the seminal contributions of Roy Harrod (1939, 1948) and Evsey Domar (1946, 1957) and then of Robert Solow (1956, 1957) and Trevor Swan (1956) and of Nicholas Kaldor (1956, 1961, 1966). Kaldor (1961), taking a position contrary to the classical economists, was the first to state that persistent growth of income per capita is one of the major stylized facts (that is, phenomena that can be observed in a number of countries over a long period) of advanced countries. The revival of growth theory, with important contributions by Hirofumi Uzawa (1968), Robert Lucas (1988), Paul Romer (1986, 1990), and Robert Barro (1990), has taken roughly the same view as Kaldor in identifying the causes of persistent economic growth. Classical forces of growth have been rediscovered and presented in formal models by building on intertemporal behavior and the dynamic optimization of economic agents.

As Angus Maddison (2001) shows, forces of economic growth were set in motion in western Europe a long time ago through its encounter with parts of the world where high cultures had developed. The major sources of growth since the Renaissance, as Maddison demonstrates, have been learning from others, education, collecting and diffusing technological knowledge, and improvement of scientific methods. The diffusion of new knowledge and new technology was, in western Europe, accelerated by the interaction and institutionalized cooperation of scientists in institutions of higher learning and scientific academies, which encouraged discussion, collection, and publication of theoretical and practical research. In European countries this was always a matter of public discourse and public policy.

It is well understood by now that different forces of economic growth characterize each stage of development. This book takes a time series perspective on development, employing dynamic and time series methods to study the major sources of growth. We concur with recent criticism of cross-country studies that maintain that the forces of growth are the same at all times and in all countries. In taking a time series perspective, we support the view that in earlier stages, learning from others, externalities, and increasing returns are major sources of economic growth. At a later stage, education and the build-up of human capital are important, as growth effects are visible that appear to be proportional to efforts devoted to education.

However, such scale effects of education and human capital may not hold for still later stages of development. Nonlinearities now seem to be at work, since educational efforts show less than proportional effects on growth rates in advanced countries.[1] A growth model with human capital, such as the Uzawa-Lucas model, might be an appropriate one to describe the stage of development at which the creation of human capital is effective in increasing per capita income. At a later stage, the creation and diffusion of knowledge and new technology through research and development (R&D) spending and a high proportion of scientists and engineers in the total working population seem to become important. Only countries at the forefront of such efforts may be successful in keeping growth rates high. The Romer model, which analyzes some of these forces, seems to be suited to describe this stage of growth. Social and public infrastructure appears to be important for all stages of growth, yet each stage may need specific social and public infrastructure. Last, the connection between economic growth and inequality, to which a great many theorists, both classical and contemporary, have alluded (see Aghion 2002), appears to be an important factor at all stages of development.

Basing our conclusions on a time series perspective and allowing for nonlinearities, we will discuss the implications of our study for policy. We note, however, that economic growth may not only increase potential per capita income for future generations but may also create negative externalities by reducing renewable and nonrenewable resources, as well as by degrading the environment.[2] Although this is an important problem in the context of a study on economic growth, it will be left aside here. Finally, in taking a time series perspective in our modeling and estimation strategy, we are very much aware of thresholds in development and growth. Only countries that have crossed those thresholds may enjoy the stages of growth sketched above.[3]

1.2 NEW GROWTH THEORY AND CROSS-COUNTRY STUDIES

As we have mentioned, important studies of the persistent growth of per capita income were provided by Harrod (1939, 1948),

---

[1] The view that growth models should allow for nonlinearities has recently also been put forward by Solow (2003).

[2] For an empirical approach to the estimation of the stock of nonrenewable resources in the context of a growth model, see Scholl and Semmler (2002).

[3] An early theoretical study of this problem can be found in Skiba (1978); see also Azariadis and Drazen (1990). More recent empirical studies include Durlauf and Johnson (1995), Bernard and Durlauf (1995), Durlauf and Quah (1999), Quah (1996), and Kremer, Onatski, and Stock (2001).

Domar (1946, 1957), and Kaldor (1961, 1966). Harrod and Domar were primarily concerned with the stability of the steady-state growth path. The knife-edge problem stated by Harrod and Domar was contested by Solow (1956), who, assuming smooth factor substitution, could demonstrate global stability and convergence toward the steady-state path. Kaldor (1966) obtained stability results by referring to different saving rates from class income with changing income levels. However, the growth theory of the 1950s and 1960s did not sufficiently identify the major sources of growth. In Solow, growth of per capita income occurs only because of exogenous technical change. Modern growth theory, by contrast, attempts to explain economic growth endogenously.

The new growth theory started with Romer's 1986 paper. This model explains persistent economic growth by referring to the role of externalities. This idea had been formalized earlier by Arrow (1962), who argued that externalities, arising from learning by doing and knowledge spillover, positively affect the productivity of labor on the aggregate level of an economy. Lucas (1988), whose model goes back to Uzawa (1965), stresses the creation of human capital, and Romer (1990) and Grossmann and Helpman (1991) focus on the creation of new knowledge as important sources of economic growth. The latter authors have developed an R&D model of economic growth. In the Romer model, the creation of knowledge capital (stock of ideas) is the most important source of growth. In Grossman and Helpman, a variety of consumer goods enters the utility function of the household, and spillover effects in the research sector bring about sustained per capita growth. A similar model, which can be termed Schumpeterian, was presented by Aghion and Howitt (1992, 1998). In it the process of creative destruction is integrated in a formal model; the quality grades for a product are modeled as substitutes; in the extreme case the different qualities are perfect substitutes, implying that the discovery of a new intermediate good replaces the old one. Consequently, innovations are the source of sustained economic growth. Perpetual growth can also arise due to productive public capital or investment in public infrastructure. This line of research was initiated by Arrow and Kurz (1970), who, however, only considered exogenous growth models. Barro (1990) demonstrated that this approach may also generate sustained per capita growth in the long run.[4]

Numerous empirical studies have been generated by the new growth theory. The first round of empirical tests by and large focused on cross-country studies. There are a great many cross-country empirical estimations of recent growth theory, using either an extended Solow-based

---

[4] See also Futagami, Morita, and Shibata (1993) and Greiner and Semmler (2000).

approach or endogenous growth theory.[5] Here we do not exhaustively survey the cross-country studies on endogenous growth theory. Their success or failure is reviewed by Sala-i-Martin (1997) and Durlauf and Quah (1999). However, we have to point out that criticism has been raised against cross-country econometric studies. It has been demonstrated that these studies, by lumping together countries at different stages of development, may miss the thresholds of development (Bernard and Durlauf 1995). Moreover, cross-country studies rely on imprecise measures of the economic variables involved, and the results are amazingly nonrobust (Sala-i-Martin 1997).

In addition, cross-country studies imply that the forces of growth, as well as technology and preference parameters, are the same for all countries in the sample. When estimating the Solow growth model using a sample consisting of, say, one hundred countries, the obtained parameter values are identical for each country. However, if the countries in this sample are highly heterogeneous in their states of development, different parameter values will characterize their technology or preferences.

It is also to be expected that different institutional conditions and social infrastructure in the countries under consideration will affect estimations and will make the countries heterogeneous, leading to differences in the estimated parameters. Brock and Durlauf (2001) therefore argue that cross-country studies tend to fail because they do not admit uncertainty and heterogeneity of parameters into the model.

An influential cross-country study that assumes an exogenous growth model is the paper by Mankiw, Romer, and Weil (1992), who augment the Solow-Swan exogenous growth model by integrating human capital. The production function then is given by

$$Y(t) = K(t)^{\psi} H(t)^{\omega} (A(t)L(t))^{1-\psi-\omega},$$

with $Y(t)$ aggregate output, $K(t)$ physical capital, $H(t)$ human capital, $L(t)$ labour, and $A(t)$ the level of technology, which grows at an exogenously determined rate. Physical capital and human capital are formed by saving a certain fraction of output, which is then devoted to the formation of these capital stocks. Denoting with s_k and s_h, $s_k + s_h < 1$, the constant fraction of aggregate output in the formation of physical capital and human capital, the evolution of the capital stocks is given by

$$\dot{k}(t) = s_k \, y(t) - (n + g_A + \delta)k(t)$$

$$\dot{h}(t) = s_h \, y(t) - (n + g_A + \delta)h(t),$$

[5] For the former, see, e.g., Mankiw, Romer, and Weil (1992); for the latter, see Barro and Sala-i-Martin (1995).

where $y(t) = Y(t)/A(t)L(t)$, $k(t) = K(t)/A(t)L(t)$ and $h(t) = H(t)/A(t)L(t)$ give quantities per effective unit of labor. n is the exogenous growth rate of the labor force; δ is the depreciation rate of physical and human capital, which is the same for the two stocks; and $g_A = \dot{A}(t)/A(t)$ is the exogenous growth rate of technology.

Assuming diminishing returns to scale in physical and human capital, that is, $\psi + \omega < 1$, this economy converges to a steady state, which is defined as a rest point of the two equations $\dot{k}(t)$ and $\dot{h}(t)$. Setting $\dot{k}(t) = \dot{h}(t) = 0$ and solving these equations simultaneously gives the steady-state values for k and h as

$$k^* = \left(\frac{s_k^{1-\omega} s_h^{\omega}}{n + g_A + \delta} \right)^{1/(1-\psi-\omega)}$$

$$h^* = \left(\frac{s_k^{\psi} s_h^{1-\psi}}{n + g_A + \delta} \right)^{1/(1-\psi-\omega)}$$

Inserting k^* and h^* in $Y(t)$ and taking logarithms yields an equation that gives aggregate per capita output at the steady state. This equation is given by

$$\ln\left(\frac{Y(t)}{L(t)} \right) = \ln A(t) + \frac{\psi}{1 - \psi - \omega} \ln s_k + \frac{\omega}{1 - \psi - \omega} \ln s_h$$
$$- \frac{\psi + \omega}{1 - \psi - \omega} \ln(n + g_A + \delta).$$

Mankiw, Romer, and Weil (1992) estimate this equation using a cross-country sample of ninety-eight countries. They assume that all economies are at their steady-state position. The result is that the augmented Solow model explains almost 80 percent of the variation in income in the countries of their sample. The implied physical capital, human capital, and labor shares are about one-third each. Mankiw, Romer, and Weil conclude that these findings cast doubt on endogenous growth models and claim that the augmented Solow exogenous growth model is able to explain much of the cross-country differences in income.

Yet in this analysis, structural parameters are posited to be the same, independent of whether a highly industrialized country or developing country is considered. This aspect is taken into account by Durlauf and Johnson (1995), who use the same data set as Mankiw, Romer, and Weil (1992) but allow for different aggregate production functions depending on 1960 per capita incomes and on literacy rates. Durlauf and

Johnson use a regression-tree procedure[6] in order to identify threshold levels endogenously. They find that the Mankiw, Romer, and Weil (1992) data set can be divided into four distinct regimes: low-income countries, middle-income countries, and high-income countries, with the middle regime divided into two subgroups, one with high, and one with low, literacy rates. The result of this study is that different groups of countries are characterized by different production possibilities, implying different coefficients on inputs in the aggregate production functions. Further, in contrast to Mankiw, Romer, and Weil (1992), initial conditions matter for long-run incomes, a result that is in line with endogenous growth models but in contrast to exogenous growth models. This outcome questions the empirical validity of the augmented Solow growth model, implying that cross-country differences in income cannot be explained entirely by differences in the rates of growth of physical capital, human capital, and population.

The contribution by Mankiw, Romer, and Weil (1992) is also criticized by Klenow and Rodriguez-Clare (1998) and Hall and Jones (1999). Hall and Jones show that differences in social infrastructure play an important role in explaining the difference in output per worker across countries. By social infrastructure these authors mean institutions and government policies that determine the economic environment. Proper social infrastructure favors the accumulation of physical and human capital and leads to high output per worker. In particular, Hall and Jones demonstrate that differences in physical capital and educational attainment can only partially explain differences in output per worker. Instead, there is a large residual that varies considerably across countries. They claim that these differences in per capita income can be explained if the effects of social infrastructure are taken into account.

Klenow and Rodriguez-Clare (1998) also reexamine the study by Mankiw, Romer, and Weil (1992). They take the same aggregate production function as Mankiw, Romer, and Weil and write it as follows: $Y/L = A X$, with A the level of technology, as above, and X a composite of the physical and human capital intensities. According to Klenow and Rodriguez-Clare, the two variables A and X are correlated. This holds because countries with policies that favor capital accumulation are also likely to have policies that lead to higher values for A. As a consequence, there is no unique decomposition of the variance of $\ln(Y/L)$ into the variance of $\ln X$ and $\ln A$. Klenow and Rodriguez-Clare propose to split the covariance term and give half to $\ln X$ and half to $\ln A$. This is equivalent to estimating the coefficients by independently regressing $\ln X$ and

---

[6] For a description see Breiman et al. (1984).

$\ln A$ on $\ln(Y/L)$, respectively. With this assumption, the authors then estimate the same equation Mankiw, Romer, and Weil estimated and, in addition, make some further modifications.

A first modification made in the empirical estimation is to resort to that part of physical capital and human capital which is employed only in the production of aggregate output. The results are slightly different from the ones obtained by Mankiw, Romer, and Weil but the differences are not quantitatively important. With this change, a 1 percent increase in Y/L is expected to go along with a 76 percent increase in X and a 24 percent increase in A, compared to a 78 percent increase in X and a 22 percent increase in A in Mankiw, Romer, and Weil (1992). Klenow and Rodriguez-Clare then again estimate the model but take aggregate output per worker as the dependent variable instead of aggregate output per capita. Their results are basically the same as those obtained by Mankiw, Romer, and Weil.

The third modification undertaken by Klenow and Rodriguez-Clare (1998) is to estimate the regression equation with three enrollment rates, namely with primary, secondary, and tertiary schooling. This modification causes large differences: now a 1 percent increase in Y/L goes along with a 40 percent increase in X and a 60 percent increase in A. The reason for this result is that primary enrollment rates do not vary as much across countries as secondary enrollment rates. Therefore, primary schooling does not vary as much with Y/L across countries as secondary schooling does. So if one focuses on secondary schooling in explaining differences in Y/L, one overstates the percentage variation in human capital across countries and its covariance with per worker output.

The last modification, finally, is the use of different proxies for human capital. Klenow and Rodriguez-Clare (1998) argue that the technology for producing human capital is more labor intensive than the technology for producing goods. They cite a study by Kendrick (1976) suggesting factor shares of 10 percent, 40 percent, and 50 percent for physical capital, human capital, and raw labor in the production process for human capital. Constructing data for human capital using a Cobb-Douglas production function with these factor shares drastically changes the outcome of the empirical estimation. The estimation now results in a split of 33 percent $\ln X$ versus 67 percent $\ln A$, while the original decomposition in Mankiw, Romer, and Weil (1992) was 78 percent $\ln X$ and 22 percent $\ln A$.

Another line of criticism of Mankiw, Romer, and Weil (1992), similar to the last modification made by Klenow and Rodriguez-Clare, is offered by Dinopoulos and Thompson (1999). They show that the results obtained by Mankiw, Romer, and Weil are not robust as concerns the proxy used for the human capital variable. Mankiw, Romer, and Weil resort to the secondary school enrollment rate as a proxy for the saving rate determining that part of aggregate income which is invested in the formation of human capital. Dinopoulos and Thompson suggest two other proxies for human capital: the first is an input-based index that relies heavily on school enrollment rates;[7] the second is an output-based index constructed by Hanushek and Kimko (2000). The latter index tries to directly measure the quality of the labor input from performances on six internationally comparable mathematics and science test scores. Those tests were taken at different points in time, and each test had a different number of participating countries.

The empirical estimation of the augmented Solow model using these alternative proxies for human capital can still explain about 70 percent of the international variation in income per capita. However, the implied coefficients are no longer plausible. The physical capital share now is 0.44 and 0.48, respectively, which is a little high but acceptable. The human capital share, however, is 1.62 and 0.73, implausibly high figures.

Another point of criticism raised by Dinopoulos and Thompson (1999) is that the Mankiw, Romer, and Weil (1992) study assumes that technology is the same for all countries in the sample, a point we have already mentioned. Therefore, they test the alternative assumption that a country's technology level depends on its endowment of human capital. The estimation of the model shows that the null hypothesis of a common technology is rejected. Instead, there is strong evidence that the levels of human capital are positively correlated with the level of technology. This evidence implies that the assumption of a common technology available to all countries in the sample is not supported by the data, since human capital differs in the countries under consideration.

Durlauf and Johnson (1995) and Dinopoulos and Thompson (1999) demonstrate that the outcomes of cross-country studies that assume the same technology and preferences for all countries must be considered with caution. However, we do not assert that such studies are useless. Roughly the same stylized facts, which are often seen as a starting point for discussions about economic growth, are observed for numerous countries. Therefore, it is to be expected that these countries share some common structure that can explain the facts. Nevertheless, this does not mean that all countries have identical aggregate production functions and preference parameters, for example. This point should be kept in mind when cross-country studies are considered.

Why, then, are cross-country studies so numerous in the literature on economic growth? The answer is that cross-country studies have some advantages over time series analysis. One advantage is that the growth

---

[7] For details see the appendix in Dinopoulos and Thompson (1999).

rate in cross-country studies is taken over long time periods. For example, when one wants to estimate the effect of some predetermined variables on the growth rate, one may take the average growth rate over ten years, which then is posited to depend on the variables at the beginning of the period under consideration. This method permits the elimination of effects of business cycles that may dominate fluctuations in economic variables at a higher frequency. Because growth theory is primarily concerned with long-term development, this property of cross-sectional studies can be a great advantage.

Further, because the time horizon is rather long, cross-country studies are less susceptible to structural breaks. If one takes the growth rate as the average over ten years, a structural break leading to different parameters in the production function will have less drastic effects than in a time series study, in which the parameters are assumed to be time invariant. Another practical advantage of cross-sectional studies is that data are available for several countries for short periods of time, whereas long-term time series data for single countries are difficult to obtain. Although the data for a larger number of countries may be of lower quality, data for several countries over a time period of, say, twenty years is easier to obtain than high-quality time series data for one country for, say, fifty years.

1.3 TIME SERIES PERSPECTIVE AND ECONOMETRIC ISSUES

To overcome the disadvantages of cross-country studies, recent research has shifted toward a time series perspective. Jones (1995a, 1995b, 1997) in particular has directed attention toward the time series predictions of endogenous growth models. Jones shows that, by confronting endogenous growth models with facts, one is faced with the prediction that a rise in the level of an economic variable, such as an increase in human capital or knowledge capital, implies strong and lasting effects on the growth rate of the economy. This property is referred to as a scale effect. In fact, in the Lucas model (1988) and in the original Romer (1990) model, which takes labor input and human capital as fixed, the growth rate is predicted to monotonically increase with educational attainment or with the level of human capital devoted to R&D. These permanent growth effects of human capital are present in the models by Lucas (1988), Romer (1990), Grossmann and Helpman (1991), and Aghion and Howitt (1992). As stylized facts show, however, measures of human capital or research intensity in most advanced countries have dramatically increased, usually beyond the increase in gross domestic product (GDP). Yet growth rates have remained roughly constant. Why have growth rates not increased? This is a serious question, indeed, since a country would like to know if it can expect a higher growth rate by spending more resources on creating human capital, on increasing its stock of knowledge, or on increasing its stock of public infrastructure.

In this book we pursue a time series approach. By estimating the preference and technology parameters of the various models with time series data, we want to help answer the question of which endogenous growth models are compatible with empirical observations. Further, we intend to modify these endogenous growth models by allowing for nonlinearities so that the property of scale effects disappears, and then test whether the modified models are compatible with time series evidence. For some stages of growth, the scale effect may indeed be operative, whereas in later stages nonlinearities become relevant.

As we have already indicated, current literature on economic growth has advanced a variety of endogenous growth models. In this book, however, we will consider only basic models of endogenous growth. We proceed in this manner because these models have been most influential in the new growth literature and because they seem to capture the major forces of economic growth. The models in question are: (1) growth models with positive externalities of investment based on the model by Romer (1986); (2) growth models with human capital based on the approach of Uzawa (1965) and Lucas (1988); (3) growth models with R&D expenditures and knowledge creation starting with Romer (1990), Grossmann and Helpman (1991), and Aghion and Howitt (1992); and (4) growth models with public infrastructure based on Barro (1990), Futagami, Morita, and Shibata (1993), and Greiner and Semmler (2000).

In the last chapter we will also consider the classic problem of economic growth and inequality. Not all countries grow at the same rate, and, within a country, not everybody gains equally from economic growth. With high and persistent growth rates accompanied by the ascension of some industries and occupations and the decline of others, inequality will increase. Following the seminal work of Schumpeter, as originally suggested by Kaldor (1961), Acemoglu (1998, 2002) and Aghion (2000, 2002) have redirected our attention to this fact.

Having shifted our attention to time series studies of endogenous growth models, Jones (1995b, 1997) contrasts time series data taken from different countries with the predictions of endogenous growth models. The present work takes the same time perspective, but in our empirical evaluation of the time series implications of endogenous growth models we actually estimate the different models with U.S. and European time series data. In contrast to other empirical work, we neither solely estimate the predictions of the model nor match it with the empirical data; rather, we directly estimate the implied parameters of the model. Although the predictions of the new growth theory have been studied indirectly through time series methods such as unit root or cointegration tests, endogenous growth models and their parameters have not been directly estimated by transforming the models into an estimable form. This is no surprise, since the models allow for growth that implies unbounded and nonstationary time series.

Finally, we want to make some remarks on our estimation methods. Estimating endogenous growth models with time series data is not an easy task. First, there are difficulties with data. Many time series data, such as human capital, are not readily available; therefore, we have to use some method (for example, the perpetual inventory method) to construct them through flow data, such as education expenditures.

Second, the moment restrictions of the estimation equations often appear to be nonlinear and simultaneous in the sense that the structural parameters appear in different equations. This requires that our estimation method be able to deal with nonlinear systems simultaneously, with correction for possible autocorrelation in the disturbance terms. In this regard we basically employ two estimation methods. One is the generalized method of moments (GMM) estimation; the other is the nonlinear least square (NLLS) estimation. In the technical appendix we briefly present the GMM method and the NLLS estimation (which are more extensively treated in many advanced econometric text books; see, for instance, Judge et al. 1988 and Hamilton 1994). It should also be noted that both methods must be somewhat modified to correct for possible autocorrelation in the disturbance terms. The modification of both of the methods is described in the technical appendix.

Third, all the estimations need a numerical optimization algorithm. In this study we basically employ two such algorithms. One is the Newton-Raphson algorithm; the other is the simulated annealing algorithm. The Newton-Raphson algorithm can often detect only a local optimum. We apply this algorithm to the NLLS method when only a single equation is to be estimated. When the estimation becomes more complicated, as in the simultaneous nonlinear system where we use the GMM estimation, we will employ the simulated annealing method. This will allow us to escape from local optima and eventually find a global optimum instead. Although this algorithm usually requires a much longer computation time, sometimes two to three days on a personal computer, we believe it is necessary in order to obtain plausible results of the estimations. The technical appendix again provides a detailed description of the procedure of the simulated annealing. A description of the Newton-Raphson algorithm can be found in many econometric textbooks (such as Hamilton 1994).

Since we have formulated and estimated different variants of endogenous growth models, one easily might get the impression that we allow for some model misspecification to occur. This impression might arise if one presumes that there should have been only one true model. However, the assumption that there is only one true model needs some further consideration. Suppose A_t is what we want to explain in the models. If one model says that A_t is determined by X_t while in another model it is determined by Y_t, that is,

$$A_t = f(X_t)$$
$$A_t = g(Y_t),$$

then, it is true that one model must be misspecified if there is no relation between X_t and Y_t. However, if there is a relationship between X_t and Y_t, that is,

$$X_t = y(Y_t)$$

then either model can be true and is not a misspecified model. This is exactly what happens in models of endogenous growth. One could regard A_t as technology, and X_t and Y_t as knowledge capital and human capital. There is no doubt that a relationship between X_t and Y_t exists.

To be more specific, let us look at the problem from an econometric point of view. There are basically two types of misspecifications. One is the argument of missing relevant variables and the other is the inclusion of irrelevant variables. It is well known that missing relevant variables will cause biased estimates and thus fitting (and matching of empirical data) is usually not successful. Adding irrelevant variables will usually cause overfitting, but the standard deviation will be inflated. Therefore, if we look at both the fitting and standard deviation of estimates, we can judge how serious a misspecified problem could be there. We have provided both results (fitting and standard deviation) in our book. This will allow readers to make a judgment on our results. Moreover, we want to note that in some of the models we have allowed for time trends of some parameters that allow us to capture other forces of growth.

Another justification for our procedure is that we intend to combine theoretical and empirical analysis. So, our goal is to analyze basic endogenous growth models theoretically and to evaluate each model using empirical data in order to check whether it should be rejected or not. Constructing a theoretical framework that contains all relevant growth factors would lead to large-scale models that do not represent the classical core models of economic growth and that, in addition, are not analytically solvable any longer. Further, it is doubtful whether such models would permit results that would help us to understand the process of economic growth.

1.4 Further Outlook

The remainder of the book is organized as follows. Chapter 2 discusses time series facts particularly for the U.S. and German economies, the latter being one of the core countries of the European Monetary Union. Among the Euro-area countries, the German economy has the largest population and represents about one-third of total GDP. Thus, it could be considered an engine of growth for the area. We will, therefore, restrict the empirical application of our study primarily to the U.S. and German economies. One could, of course, apply our methodology of constructing time series data and time series estimation to other countries for which time series data of high quality are available. By and large, we focus here on only two countries to exemplify our method.

Chapter 3 presents and discusses the models that explain endogenous growth due to externalities. We present empirical evidence for a variety of countries and study whether externalities are a driving force for growth. Chapter 4 presents the analytical structure of the Uzawa-Lucas model of endogenous growth, in which education and human capital are the driving force, and estimates a slightly modified model with U.S. and German time series data. As it turns out, the introduction of nonlinearities in the effect of educational attainment on economic growth makes the model fit the data. Chapter 5 introduces the Romer (1990) model of endogenous growth, which stresses the role of knowledge accumulation (the role of ideas) and estimates an extended version of the model with time series methods. Here also nonlinearities come into play.

Chapter 6 presents and estimates an endogenous growth model in which public infrastructural investment and public capital contribute to economic growth. In contrast with Barro (1990), we take into account public deficit and debt. This requires an evaluation of the intertemporal budget constraint of the government by studying empirically the sustainability of the debt policy. In chapter 7 we are concerned with endogenous growth, income distribution, and wage inequality, a topic that has not been considered much in the context of modern growth models, but recently has become an important node of economic research. Chapter 8, finally, presents our conclusions.

CHAPTER 2

Growth Models and Time Series Evidence

Studies of economic growth have stressed time series regularities in economic growth, primarily examining the history of advanced countries since the beginning of industrialization. The best summary of these stylized time series facts in growth theory is by Kaldor (1961, pp. 178–179), who lists the following: (1) Continued growth in aggregate production and in the productivity of labor, with no tendency of the growth rate to fall. (2) Continued increase in capital per worker. (3) A constant rate of return to capital that is higher than the long-term rate of interest. (4) A constant capital-output ratio in the long run. (5) A high correlation between the share of profits in income and the share of investment in output, and a constant share of wages and physical capital in national income. (6) Considerable differences in the rate of growth of labor productivity and of total output in different economies.

Barro and Sala-i-Martin (1995, pp. 5–9) present empirical studies that illustrate these facts for different countries. They conclude that all of these facts, with the exception of the third, can be more or less confirmed for developed countries. Barro and Sala-i-Martin argue that the assumption of a stable real rate of return should be replaced by the hypothesis of a slightly declining rate of return as an economy evolves over time. Justification for this position is presented in a study by Young (1995), who shows that the real rates of return in some fast-growing countries, such as South Korea or Singapore, are much higher than those in the United States, for example, but have declined over time.

In addition to these facts, Kuznets (1973) points to other characteristic features of modern economic growth. He mentions a fast rate of structural transformation, implying, for example, the shift from the agricultural to the industrialized sector and then to the service sector, or the increasing importance of technological change in the growth process. He also emphasizes the increased significance of governments for economic growth. This results from the need for laws to regulate economic transactions and from the growing significance of public infrastructure in the growth process. Other characteristics identified by Kuznets are a reduced dependence on natural resources, the rising importance of foreign trade, and an increased role for formal education.

2.1 PERSISTENT PER CAPITA GROWTH

One of the stylized facts mentioned most frequently is a positive growth over time in per capita output with no tendency toward a decline in the growth rate. As we have mentioned, the growth theory dominating the economics literature until the 1980s, the Solow (1956), Cass (1965), and Koopmans (1965) models, predicted convergence to a steady state with no per capita growth. If positive per capita growth is to be observed in the long run, it is the result of exogenous factors, for example, technological progress. Exogenous growth models display positive per capita growth rates only on the transitional path, that is, as long as the economy has not yet reached the long-run steady state. Arguing that economies are still on the transitional path to explain sustained growth may not be a good explanation because on this path the growth rates of output per capita tend to decline as the economy approaches its long-run steady state. This trajectory, however, does not seem to be compatible with time series data. To see this, we consider the growth rates of per capita GDP in the United States and in Germany from 1900 to 1994.

The average growth rates (geometric mean) are 1.8 percent for the United States and 1.9 percent for Germany. Further, there is no tendency toward a decline in growth rates. This is confirmed by the augmented Dickey-Fuller (ADF) test, which clearly rejects the assumption of a unit root.[1] The ADF test statistic is −5.607, while the 1 percent critical value is −3.503, so that the null hypothesis of nonstationarity of the time series can be rejected.

The same seems to hold for Germany. In this case, the ADF test statistic has the value −5.141, while the 1 percent critical value is again given by −3.503. However, if one takes the shorter time period from 1950 to 1982, the results change. In this case, the ADF test statistic is −2.547, while the 10 percent critical value is −2.615, so that the assumption of nonstationarity cannot be rejected. If one extends the time series from 1950 to 1994, the ADF test suggests that this series may again be stationary. Now the ADF test statistic is −3.194, compared to a 5 percent (1 percent) critical value of −2.927 (−3.581), implying that the null hypothesis of nonstationarity can be rejected at the 5 percent significance level but not at the 1 percent level.

The latter observation suggests that the growth rates of low-income countries are higher but decline over time as they become richer. This holds for Germany, where the physical capital stock was largely destroyed

---

[1] The Dickey-Fuller test is a test for the presence of a unit root in a time series that characterizes a nonstationary process.

during World War II and where GDP was small at the beginning of the 1950s compared to the United States. However, this does not demonstrate that such economies converge toward zero per capita growth in the long run. Instead, there may be convergence to a balanced growth path with a constant but strictly positive growth of per capita GDP. This would imply convergence of countries that are out of their long-run steady state toward countries with a higher level of income.[2]

These considerations are not a proof of sustained per capita growth, but they seem to confirm the stylized fact of growth. Exogenous growth theory seems to give us an unsatisfactory description of the time series data. Endogenous growth models, however, allow for sustained per capita growth without resorting to exogenous factors, and the growth rate becomes endogenously determined.

Four approaches to the sources of growth have now been distinguished:[3] (1) Growth models with positive externalities of investment, implying that investment not only raises production possibilities of the investor but also has positive effects for the aggregate economy. This type of model goes back to Romer (1986). (2) Growth models in which individuals spend time on the formation of human capital. A prototype example is the Uzawa-Lucas model (based primarily Uzawa 1965 and Lucas 1988). (3) Models in which economic agents spend resources for the creation of new knowledge. This type is often called an R&D model of economic growth and was initiated by Romer (1990). (4) An approach that goes back to Barro (1990) and Futagami, Morita, and Shibata (1993) in which the government undertakes productive investment that raises the marginal product of capital and stimulates economic growth. As a consequence, there may be persistent economic growth over the long run.[4]

Most of the new models predict lasting effects on growth rates if the level of variables changes. This is true, for example, of the two prototypical models in the second and third groups, namely the Uzawa-Lucas model as formulated by Lucas (1988) and the Romer (1990) model. Next we will briefly discuss those scale effects.

---

[2] In this book we do not intend to address the question of whether low-income countries converge to high-income countries in per capita income levels (often referred to as β convergence) or only convergence in standard deviations can be observed (often called σ convergence). In the latter case, there might be a convergence of the per capita income of countries to a double-peaked distribution, one for poor and one for rich countries. See Durlauf and Quah (1999) and Quah (1996).

[3] For details of the models mentioned here, see chapter 3.

[4] We do not deny the role of other factors such as openness of the economy and trade, financial deepening, cultural factors, the legal system, or political stability. In this book, however, we focus on the four major sources of growth listed here.

2.2 SCALE EFFECTS OF EDUCATION AND KNOWLEDGE

In the Romer (1990) model of endogenous growth, an increase in the amount of resources spent on R&D leads to a higher balanced growth rate, implying that the growth rate of GDP varies positively with level of R&D. In reality, however, the amount spent for research and development has risen during the last decades, but the growth rate of GDP has not. The Uzawa-Lucas model confronts a similar problem. There, an increase in years of education implies a higher growth rate in the stock of human capital, which also raises the growth rate of GDP. An increase in the balanced growth rate can also be observed when the ratio of human to physical capital rises. But these features do not seem to hold for advanced economies in the long run, where years of education and the ratio of human to physical capital have greatly increased in the last decades.

Tables 2.1 and 2.2 illustrate the relation between the level of economic variables and growth rates for some advanced countries.

As table 2.1 shows, in the United States not only has the level of R&D risen, but so has the research intensity measured by R&D/GDP, which has tripled. The growth rate of output per worker, however, has declined, taking five-year averages. A similar pattern holds for other advanced countries such as Germany, Japan, the United Kingdom, and France. In those countries, R&D expenditure both in absolute numbers and as a share of GDP has increased, but the growth rates of output have fallen. Similarly, educational attainment, a proxy for the stock of human capital, has grown in the United States, Germany, and the United Kingdom while output growth rates have fallen. Educational attainment has greatly increased over the last decades.

From the results reported in table 2.1, one would at first sight be tempted to argue that growth effects do not arise from educational efforts or R&D spending. These latter measures, relevant for human capital or R&D-based growth models, increased more than the growth rate. In spite of this, the long-run growth rate does not seem to have been much affected. If anything, it has decreased, as can be seen in table 2.1.

The time trends for specific stocks and level variables can be observed in table 2.2, where we consider three countries more specifically.

Table 2.2 shows the evolution of specific variables that explicitly appear in the two major types of growth models, the Uzawa-Lucas human capital model (Lucas 1988) and the Romer (1990) R&D model, and contrasts their trends with the average growth rate of GDP. Here again, the stock of human capital has increased far more than physical capital, for example. Growth rates, however, have either remained constant or decreased. This holds for the United States, Germany, and the United Kingdom

TABLE 2.1
Time Trends of Growth Rates, R&D, and Educational Attainment

	$g_{Y/L}$ (percent)	R&D/GDP (percent)	E_A (percent)
United States			
1950–1955	3.54	0.6	25 (5)
1990–1995	1.13	1.9	80 (20)
Germany			
1970–1975	2.81	1.9	2.4
1991–1996	2.07	2.4	4.8
Japan			
1970–1975	4.97	1.7	—
1990–1995	1.16	2.8	—
United Kingdom			
1970–1975	2.06	1.5	1.0
1990–1995	1.97	1.7	1.6
France			
1970–1975	3.09	1.4	—
1990–1995	0.96	1.8	—

Source: see appendix to this chapter.

$g_{Y/L}$ = annual average GDP growth rate per employed; R&D/GDP = average R&D expenditure as share of GDP (nondefense); E_A = educational attainment. For the United States, the number without parentheses stands for high school degrees as a percentage of the total population, while the number in parentheses refers to college degrees as a percentage of the total population; for Germany and the United Kingdom, the entry stands for number of students/total labor force.

for the ratio H/K (although for the United Kingdom to a lesser extent). Moreover, it can be seen that in all three countries the number of scientists and engineers engaged in R&D has risen greatly.

For most of the relevant variables, the United States shows higher values than does Germany, yet the German rates of GDP growth were higher on average over the period 1960–1965 although it declined in the 1990s.

Together, tables 2.1 and 2.2 suggest that scale effects indeed seem to be missing. Another way of interpreting the stylized facts is that the level variables may only weakly contribute to output growth. Thus, as we will argue later, increases in level variables, such as the stock of human capital, will not translate into proportionally higher growth rates. Nonlinearities seem to be at work, dampening growth effects of variables. In addition,

TABLE 2.2
Time Trends for Growth Rates and Stocks

	$g_{Y/L}$ (percent)	H/K (percent)	H_A (number)
United States			
1960–1965	3.14	17	518.5 (1965)
1990–1996	1.23	31	979
Germany			
1962–1965	4.70	9	61 (1965)
1991–1996	2.07	21	245.9
United Kingdom			
1960–1965	2.39	22	66.4 (1965)
1990–1996	1.89	26	139.9

Source: for $g_{Y/L}$, see appendix to this chapter; for the computation of H/K, see chapter 4; and for the computation of H_A, see chapter 5.

$g_{Y/L}$ = annual average GDP growth rate per employed; H/K = ratio of average human capital (cumulative public educational spending) to private capital; H_A = average human capital (number of scientists and engineers in thousands) engaged in R&D.

the impact of level variables on growth rates may be weakened by other factors producing lower growth rates. For example, higher tax rates that financed the building up of human capital and knowledge may have had offsetting effects that outweighed the contributions of human and knowledge capital to growth. Such considerations seem to be important to make the models fit the data for advanced countries.

2.3 EXTERNALITIES AND INCREASING RETURNS

Returning to the earlier stage of economic growth—or to the less developed countries—the persistent growth rate of per capita income is here likely to arise from positive externalities and increasing returns, or so it is often posited. In particular, investment in physical capital is associated with positive externalities that have stimulating effects on the marginal product of physical capital. As a consequence, the marginal product of physical capital does not decline when the capital stock increases but stays constant or even rises. This is the basic endogenous growth model from Romer (1986), in which investment in capital is associated with positive externalities. This implies that the marginal product of investment does not decline as the capital stock rises but instead increases. As a

TABLE 2.3
Level of GDP per Capita, 1989 (USA = 100); Annual Compound
Rates of GDP per Capita Growth, 1973–1989; Gross Capital
Stock per Capita, 1989 (USA = 100)

	GDP/Capita 1989	Rates of Growth 1973–1989	Capital Stock 1989
Argentina	22.3	−1.2	19.5
Chile	29.6	1.5	17.4
Mexico	20.4	1.0	21.8
Korea	35.6	6.4	23.7
Taiwan	39.7	6.1	28.1
Germany	75.2	1.9	101.7
Japan	83.9	3.0	83.1
USA	100	1.6	100

Source: Maddison (1994), table 2-2, table 2-6.

consequence, the incentive to invest does not decrease, and sustained per capita growth is likely.

However, the assumption that physical capital persistently shows increasing returns does not seem to be justified by empirical observations. The capital stock of the industrialized countries is much greater than that of less developed countries, but growth rates have not been rising. Further, the assumption of increasing returns to physical capital cannot be confirmed in general for different countries. This is shown in table 2.3, which gives data for GDP per capita, average annual rates of growth of GDP per capita, and per capita gross capital stock for eight countries.

Taking Germany, Japan, and the United States as one group and comparing it with Korea and Taiwan, one sees that the first group has a larger stock of capital but the second clearly shows higher rates of growth. Therefore, increasing returns to capital due to positive externalities of investment cannot explain differences in the growth rates for these two groups. These data are better explained if we suppose an aggregate production function with increasing returns at an earlier stage and then with diminishing returns to capital at a later stage.[5] On the other hand, if we

[5] See Durlauf and Quah (1999) and Skiba (1978), who assumed a convex-concave production function representing the idea of first increasing and then decreasing returns to scale in development.

compare Germany, Japan, and the United States with Argentina, Chile, and Mexico, the second group has a much smaller stock of physical capital but at the same time slightly smaller growth rates than the first group. Therefore, other forces seem to be at work. Diminishing returns to physical capital fail to explain the differences in rates of growth.

However, it must be noted that many empirical studies analyzing the question of whether investment in physical capital is associated with positive externalities conclude that this association exists for real economies, at least for some time periods (see the studies mentioned in chapter 3). Therefore, it seems to be necessary to build a growth model, in particular one pertaining to earlier stages of development, that contains such an idea. This is why we will present a modification of the Romer (1986) endogenous growth model with externalities of investment in the next chapter and test its empirical relevance using time series methods.

2.4 OTHER SOURCES OF GROWTH

Another source of sustained per capita growth is public investment, which may stimulate the incentive to invest. This line of research has been made popular by a study by D. A. Aschauer (1989), who found very strong effects of public capital on total factor productivity for the U.S. economy.[6] Barro (1990) and Futagami, Morita, and Shibata (1993) have shown theoretically that productive public investment can indeed generate endogenous growth if it is integrated in a growth model with optimizing agents. In the Barro model, public investment raises the marginal product of private capital directly; in the Futagami, Morita, and Shibata model, public investment raises the stock of public capital, which, in turn, affects the marginal product of private capital.

An interesting feature of such models is that the growth rate may rise with the income tax rate. More concretely, a hump-shaped function exists for the relationship between the balanced growth rate and the income tax rate. This holds because a higher income tax rate implies greater tax revenue, which is used for productive public spending. If the income tax rate is low, the positive growth effect of more productive public spending dominates the negative growth effect of a higher income tax rate, and economic growth will rise when the income tax rate is increased. If the income tax rate is rising over time and finally exceeds a certain threshold, the relationship may be reversed. In that case, the negative direct growth

---

[6] Erenburg (1993) confirms that outcome by estimating the data in first differences, which circumvents the problem of spurious regression.

effect dominates the positive indirect one resulting from higher productive public investment. Here again, nonlinearities may be at work.

In chapter 6 we will also allow for nonproductive public spending and study the growth effect of public expenditures. However, we relax the assumption of a balanced public budget (as in Barro 1990; and Futagami, Morita, and Shibata 1993), which requires us to also test for the intertemporal budget constraint of the government.

APPENDIX

All data are measured in constant prices with $1990 = 100$. Sources and computations of stocks (H, K) and H_A are discussed in chapters 4 and 5. Data sources of tables 2.1 and 2.2 are

- *Total Employment and GDP:* for Germany, see Sachverständigenrat (1998); for the other countries, see OECD (1998); own computations.
- *R&D:* for the United States, see National Science Foundation (2000), Office for National Statistics (1965–1998); for Germany, see Bundesministerium für Bildung und Forschung (1996; 2000); for the other countries, see OECD (1980–1998a).
- *Educational Attainment:* For the United States, see Jones (1998); National Science Foundation (2000); Office for National Statistics (1965–1998); for Germany, see Statistisches Bundesamt (1977; 1991–1996); for other countries, see OECD (1998).
- *Scientists and Engineers Engaged in R&D:* for the other countries, see OECD (1980–1998a); for Germany, see Institut der Deutschen Wirtschaft (2000); for the United States, see National Science Foundation (1996; 1998; 2000).

CHAPTER 3

Externalities of Investment and Economic Growth

As we have discussed in the preceding chapters, one strand of endogenous growth theory assumes that investment in capital shows positive external effects. This type of growth theory goes back to the development literature of the 1950s and was revived by Romer (1986), who presented an endogenous growth model in which capital shows decreasing returns to scale on the microeconomic level of an individual firm but increasing returns on the macroeconomic level, due to spillovers. Because of increasing returns to capital on the economy-wide level, the model predicts positive sustained per capita growth. However, Romer focused not on pure physical capital but rather on knowledge, as a more general concept of capital. This concept appears to be very important for an earlier stage of development and remains important to a lesser degree in advanced countries that have gone through periods of catch-up.

Applying the concept of positive externalities of investment to physical capital alone makes it more measurable. DeLong and Summers (1991), for example, have demonstrated that investment, particularly in machinery, is associated with strong positive externalities.[1] Further, Levine and Renelt (1992) and Sala-i-Martin (1997) have shown that the investment share is a robust variable in explaining economic growth. This positive and statistically significant effect of investment on the growth rate of countries suggests that investment not only affects the stock of physical capital but also increases intangible capital, for example knowledge, such that the social return to investment is larger than the private return. This result is supported by other studies. For example, Jorgenson, Gollop, and Fraumeni (1987), Wolff (1996), Cooley, Greenwood, and Yorukoglu (1997), and Greenwood, Hercowitz, and Krusell (1997) argue that investment in physical capital has a larger influence on economic growth than is suggested by the factor share. This relationship holds because technological improvements are incorporated in physical capital that are not reflected in the share paid to physical capital. For these reasons, building a theoretical model that relates positive externalities of investment to physical capital seems to be a reasonable approach.

---

[1] See also the paper by Hamilton and Monteagudo (1998), who find that capital is associated with positive external effects by estimating the Solow growth model.

However, assuming constant or increasing returns to capital broadly conceived—that is, including both physical capital and knowledge capital—implies that the balanced growth rate is independent of the aggregate stock of capital (in case of constant returns) or increases with the aggregate stock of capital (in case of increasing returns). Those properties, however, are not confirmed by empirical data, as table 2.3 shows. Further, the Romer (1986) model implies that, in the long run, all economies converge to the same balanced growth rate (cf. Xie 1991). That is, asymptotically the economies all grow at the same rate. For real-world economies, this property could neither be confirmed nor rejected up to now. Some studies argue that rich and poor groups are diverging in the level of income per capita but the growth rates of those two groups are the same (see, e.g., Paap and van Dijk 1998). On the other hand, Quah (1996) asserts that poor countries become poorer and rich countries become richer, implying that these two groups are characterized by different growth rates. Independent of that issue, the existence of so-called convergence clubs is confirmed by empirical data. That is, there are countries with a relatively low level of per capita income and countries with a relatively high level of per capita income. Some economists consider this to be a stylized fact in economic growth (see Durlauf and Quah 1999).

In the next section, we present and analyze a more general version of the growth model with positive externalities of investment by treating physical and knowledge capital as two separate state variables. Then we use calibration techniques combined with empirical estimations to test the model for selected countries.

3.1 THE MODEL

We consider a decentralized economy that consists of a representative household and a representative firm that behaves competitively. Further, there is a positive externality associated with investment that builds up knowledge capital.

The Productive Sector

The productive sector consists of many firms, which can be represented by one firm that produces a homogeneous good $Y_a(t)$ with a Cobb-Douglas production function:

$$Y_a(t) = (A(t)L(t))^\alpha K_a(t)^{1-\alpha}, \tag{3.1}$$

with $Y_a(t) = L(t)Y(t)$ aggregate output, $K_a(t) = L(t)K(t)$ the aggregate stock of physical capital, and $A(t)$ individual stock of knowledge, and

$\alpha \in (0, 1)$ denotes the labor share in the production function. In per capita terms, the production function can be written as

$$Y(t) = A(t)^\alpha K(t)^{1-\alpha}.$$

It should be noted that our specification of the production function implies that knowledge is a nonexcludable but rivalrous public good, just as in the Lucas (1988) model (see chapter 4). This holds because none of the firms can be excluded from the use of the stock of knowledge, but its use is subject to congestion. The latter is modeled by assuming that the per capita stock of knowledge, $A(t) = A_a(t)/L(t)$, affects the productivity of labor input. This assumption also eliminates a scale effect that would be present if $A_a(t)$ replaced $A(t)$ in (3.1).

The firm behaves competitively, yielding the interest rate r and the wage rate w as[2]

$$r = (1 - \alpha)K^{-\alpha}A^\alpha \tag{3.2}$$

$$w = \alpha A^\alpha K^{1-\alpha}. \tag{3.3}$$

The External Effect

The stock of knowledge capital A is assumed to be a by-product of cumulated past gross investment (see Arrow 1962; Levhari 1966; Sheshinski 1967). In contrast to the usual procedure, however, we assume that investment at different dates makes differently weighted contributions to the current stock of knowledge capital (on the use of weighting functions in growth models see, e.g., Ryder and Heal 1973; Wan 1970). Formally, this stock can be expressed as

$$A(t) = \varphi \int_{-\infty}^{t} e^{\delta_A(s-t)} I(s)\,ds, \tag{3.4}$$

with I gross investment per capita and $\delta_A \geq 0$ depreciation rate of per capita knowledge, while $\varphi > 0$ is the contribution of one unit of investment to the formation of knowledge capital, which is assumed to be given exogenously. This becomes clearer by differentiating A with respect to time, leading to

$$\dot{A} = \varphi I - \delta_A A. \tag{3.5}$$

Thus, this formulation implies that the stock of knowledge may be subject to depreciation, which can be justified by adopting a Schumpeterian perspective in which new investment increases the stock of knowledge but, at the same time, makes a fraction of knowledge obsolete. This way of proceeding can be justified by supposing that any new capital good requires

---

[2] In the following we omit the time argument.

new knowledge in order to be operated efficiently. Consequently, a certain fraction of the current stock becomes irrelevant for the production process, although it is still present.

With this assumption we intend to formalize what Abramovitz (1986, 1994) has summarized under the rubric of social capability, which is a necessary condition to achieve economic growth and prosperity. According to this concept, countries must be able to adopt existing technologies and to operate them in order to achieve economic growth. Social capabilities appear to be more important than developing new products or methods of production. That approach seems of particular relevance for less developed countries that intend to catch up with highly developed economies. Indeed a prerequisite for adopting modern technologies and achieving economic growth is that economies possess a sufficiently high social capability. By social capability Abramovitz means technical competence, which determines the ability to adopt modern methods of production, but also such factors as the stability of governments and of the monetary sector and the attitude toward the accumulation of wealth.

However, it must be underlined that our model is only a very modest attempt to put Abramovitz's ideas into a formal framework. This is because φ is given exogenously in our framework, whereas in reality it is expected to be determined also by endogenous variables such as education or other institutional or cultural factors.[3] But our approach is justified as a first approximation in integrating the Abramovitz effect in a formal model.

The Household Sector

The household maximizes the discounted stream of utility resulting from consumption C over an infinite time horizon:

$$\max_{C} \int_0^{\infty} e^{-(\rho-n)t} U(C)dt. \tag{3.6}$$

$\rho > 0$ gives the discount rate and n is the growth rate of labor supply, which is normalized to 1 at $t = 0$, that is, $L(0) = 1$. $U(\cdot)$ stands for the utility function, with $U'(\cdot) > 0$ and $U''(\cdot) < 0$. As for the utility function, we assume a constant elasticity of substitution function, $U(C) = (C^{1-\sigma} - 1)/(1 - \sigma)$. The constant elasticity of substitution of consumption between two points in time is given by $1/\sigma$. For $\sigma = 1$, the utility function is given by the natural logarithm $ln\ C$. Numerous empirical studies have been undertaken to estimate the coefficient σ by looking

---

[3] At the end of this section we present a simple extension of this framework where φ is an endogenous variable that depends on educational efforts.

at consumers' willingness to shift consumption across time in response to changes in interest rates. The estimates of σ vary substantially but lie around or below 1 in most studies (see Blanchard and Fischer 1989, p. 44; Boskin 1978; Hall 1988; and Amano and Wirjanto 1998).

The household's budget constraint in per capita terms is written as

$$C + \dot{K} + (\delta_K + n)K = w + rK, \tag{3.7}$$

with K physical capital and δ_K the depreciation rate. To derive optimality conditions for problem (3.6) subject to (3.7), we first note that a solution to the household's optimization problem exists if the growth rate of K and A, g, is bounded by $g < \rho - n$ (see Greiner and Semmler 1996). The necessary conditions for a maximum of (3.6) subject to (3.7) are derived by formulating the current-value Hamiltonian[4]

$$H(\cdot) = U(C) + \theta(-C - (\delta_K + n)K + w + rK), \tag{3.8}$$

with θ the current value costate variable. The maximum principle gives $U'(C) = \theta$.

The evolution of θ is described by

$$\dot{\theta} = (\rho + \delta_K)\theta - r\theta. \tag{3.9}$$

Furthermore, we need the transversality condition $\lim_{t \to \infty} e^{-(\rho-n)t} \theta(t)K(t) = 0$ to hold, which is automatically fulfilled for $g < \rho - n$.[5] Combining the condition $U'(C) = \theta$ with the equation giving $\dot{\theta}$ yields the growth rate of private consumption as

$$\frac{\dot{C}}{C} = -\frac{\rho + \delta_K}{\sigma} + \frac{r}{\sigma}. \tag{3.10}$$

Equilibrium Conditions

The use of equilibrium conditions can be justified by supposing a theoretical dichotomy between growth and business cycles and by arguing that growth theory is primarily concerned with the long-run behavior of economies. Since components that are fixed in the short run become flexible in the long run, adjustment mechanisms may take effect such that the economy attains an equilibrium.

The household's budget constraint, (3.7), together with (3.2) and (3.3), which give the return to capital and the wage rate, respectively, describe

---

[4] For a brief introduction to optimal control theory, see the technical appendix at the end of the book.

[5] The assumption $g < \rho - n$ is also sufficient for (3.6) to take on a finite value.

the evolution of the physical capital stock. The growth rate of consumption is given by (3.10), and the growth rate of knowledge capital, finally, is described by (3.5) with $I = Y - C$. This leads to the following differential equation system, which completely describes our competitive economy.

$$\frac{\dot{C}}{C} = -\frac{\rho + \delta_K}{\sigma} + \frac{(1-\alpha)K^{-\alpha}A^{\alpha}}{\sigma} \tag{3.11}$$

$$\frac{\dot{K}}{K} = -(\delta_K + n) - \frac{C}{K} + \left(\frac{A}{K}\right)^{\alpha} \tag{3.12}$$

$$\frac{\dot{A}}{A} = -\delta_A + \varphi\left(\frac{I}{A}\right). \tag{3.13}$$

The initial conditions are $K(0) = K_0 > 0$, $A(0) = A_0 > 0$ and $C(0) > 0$ is free to be chosen appropriately by the optimization procedure. Further, the transversality condition $\lim_{t \to \infty} e^{-(\rho-n)t}\theta(t)K(t) = 0$ must be fulfilled, with $\theta = \theta(C)$ determined by the maximum principle.

Looking at this system, we realize that for a constant level of knowledge capital $A(t)$ the growth rates $\dot{C}/C$ and $\dot{K}/K$ become negative for $K \to \infty$, implying that in this case sustained per capita growth is not feasible and our model is equal to the conventional neoclassical Ramsey-type growth model and does not reveal sustained per capita growth. Only if the external effect of investment on the formation of knowledge capital is strong enough, so that the marginal product of physical capital does not necessarily converge to $\rho + \delta_K$ in the long run, is endogenous growth feasible. This is possible only if social capability is sufficiently high that through any unit of investment, knowledge capital can be increased. For $\delta_A = 0$ and $\varphi > 0$ that condition is trivially satisfied, and we observe endogenous growth as long as investment is positive.

A point we should also like to emphasize is that in case of endogenous growth, the balanced growth rate, which is given by (3.11), crucially depends on the marginal product of physical capital, which varies positively with the stock of knowledge capital. Thus, countries with smaller stocks of purely physical capital tend to have higher growth rates than countries with larger stocks. But this is neither a sufficient nor a necessary condition for high growth rates. Instead, the level of knowledge capital plays an important role, too. Therefore, economies with large stocks of knowledge capital may compensate for large stocks of physical capital, and countries with very small stocks of physical capital may have only a relatively small marginal product of physical capital and, thus, little growth if they are endowed with a very small knowledge capital stock. Consequently, the growth rate will be highest in those countries in which the stock of physical capital is small but the stock of knowledge capital relatively large. This combination gives a very high marginal product of physical capital and, as a consequence, high growth rates. Therefore, those countries will show convergence in the long run. Thus, this type of framework explains the high growth rates of Germany and Japan after World War II.

Let us in the following assume that the parameters in our economy are such that sustained per capita growth is possible. This is the more interesting and also more relevant case if one looks at the long-run behavior of market economies. In this case, on a balanced growth path (BGP) all variables grow at the same constant growth rate, implying that the ratios $k = K/A$ and $c = C/A$ are constant over time. Differentiating k and c with respect to time gives $\dot{k}/k = \dot{K}/K - \dot{A}/A$ and $\dot{c}/c = \dot{C}/C - \dot{A}/A$ or explicitly:

$$\frac{\dot{k}}{k} = -(\delta_K + n) - \frac{c}{k} + \delta_A + \varphi c + (1 - \varphi k)k^{-\alpha}, \tag{3.14}$$

$$\frac{\dot{c}}{c} = -\frac{\rho + \delta_K}{\sigma} + \frac{1 - \alpha}{\sigma}k^{-\alpha} + \delta_A + c\varphi - \varphi k^{1-\alpha}. \tag{3.15}$$

A rest point of system (3.14)–(3.15) corresponds to a BGP of (3.11)–(3.13) with $\dot{A}/A = \dot{K}/K = \dot{C}/C = g_c = const.$, and (3.14)–(3.15) completely describe the local dynamics of our model around such a BGP.

The Dynamics

In studying the local dynamics of (3.14)–(3.15) we confine our analysis to interior BGPs only, that is, BGPs with $\bar{k} \neq 0$ and $\bar{c} \neq 0$, so that we can consider system (3.14)–(3.15) in the rates of growth.[6] We do so because $\bar{k} = 0$ is not feasible, since it is raised to a negative power in (3.15). Further, $\bar{c} = 0$ would imply that the level of consumption is zero, which does not make sense from the economic point of view.

Analyzing our two-dimensional system, we can observe either a unique BGP that is a saddle point or two BGPs in which the one giving the higher balanced growth rate is a saddle point, while the BGP yielding the lower growth rate cannot be a saddle point. More precisely, we can derive the following result:

PROPOSITION

(i) *If $\delta_K + n > \delta_A$ the existence of a BGP implies that it is unique and the BGP is stable in the saddle point sense.*

---

[6] The bar $:^-:$ denotes the values for k and c on the BGP.

(ii) *If $\delta_K + n < \delta_A$ the following is true: If $(\rho + \delta_K)/\sigma \leq \delta_K + n$, the existence of a BGP implies that it is unique and that it is a saddle point. If $(\rho + \delta_K)/\sigma > \delta_K + n$, there exist two BGPs in case of sustained per capita growth or a unique BGP that, however, is not generic. The BGP giving the higher growth rate is a saddle point; the BGP yielding the lower growth rate cannot be a saddle point.*

The proof of this result is given in the appendix to this chapter. The proposition tells us that our economy may be both globally and locally indeterminate. Global indeterminacy refers to the balanced growth rate that is obtained in the long run and states that the initial value of consumption, which can be chosen freely by society, crucially determines the BGP to which the economy converges and, thus, the long-run balanced growth rate. Local indeterminacy means that the transitional dynamics of two economies that converge to the same BGP in the long run crucially depend on the choice of initial consumption, $C(0)$. Thus, the transitional growth rates of those economies are determined by $C(0)$ but not the long-run growth rate, which is the same (for a more thorough treatment of these two concepts, see Benhabib and Perli 1994).

A necessary condition for that outcome in our model is $\sigma < (\rho + \delta_K)/(n + \delta_K)$, that is, a relatively high intertemporal elasticity of substitution. Most of the empirical work estimating σ gives values at or above unity (see, e.g., Blanchard and Fischer 1989, p. 44), although some estimates obtain lower values (see, e.g., Boskin 1978; Amano and Wirjanto 1998). Supposing that $\rho > n$ holds, which is certainly realistic for advanced economies, this necessary condition for indeterminacy is in line with empirical observations. Further, that result confirms the outcome in most of the economics literature stating that the representative individual must have a relatively high intertemporal elasticity of substitution for local indeterminacy to occur if labor supply is exogenous (see Benhabib and Perli 1994, p. 114).

Moreover, for $\delta_K + n < \delta_A$ and $\sigma < (\rho + \delta_K)/(n + \delta_K)$, local indeterminacy, around the BGP with the lower growth rate, can be observed if the parameter constellation is such that the trace of the Jacobian matrix is smaller than zero, so that both eigenvalues have negative real parts. If in that situation a certain parameter is varied, two purely imaginary eigenvalues may be observed that generate a Hopf bifurcation, which leads to stable limit cycles. The calculation of the trace of the Jacobian in our model is straightforward but does not give conditions that can be interpreted economically. The phenomenon of indeterminacy as well as the emergence of a Hopf bifurcation leading to stable limit cycles has been demonstrated by Greiner and Semmler (1996) with the help of numerical examples for a special case of that model with $\varphi = \delta_A$.[7] In the next section, we test the empirical relevance of our model.

3.2 TIME SERIES EVIDENCE

In this section we will analyze the empirical relevance of our theoretical model by looking at time series for different countries. To do so, we first note that around a BGP the ratio C/K is described by $D(\ln(C/K)) = \dot{C}/C - \dot{K}/K$, with $D \equiv d/dt$, which only contains observable variables, and the evolution of A is given by (3.5). The equation $D(\ln(C/K))$ is obtained as

$$D(\ln(C/K)) = (\delta_K + n) - \frac{\delta_K + \rho}{\sigma} + \frac{1-\alpha}{\sigma}\left(\frac{A}{K}\right)^\alpha - \frac{I}{K}, \tag{3.16}$$

with $I = Y - C$.

To find whether our model is compatible with real-world economies, we resort to a mixture of calibration and econometrics. The reason is twofold: First, it is not possible to estimate (3.13) because the stock of knowledge A, formed as a by-product of investment, is not observable. Therefore, we first have to construct the series of $A(t)$. We do that by using different plausible values for the parameter φ.[8] Second, in estimating equation (3.16) the constant contains δ_K, n, ρ, and σ; that is, values for those parameters cannot be obtained from our empirical estimation. Therefore, we will take values that are considered realistic in calibration studies and test whether those are compatible with the coefficients obtained by our empirical estimation.

To estimate (3.16) we replace the differential operator by first differences and consider one period to comprise one year. The equation to be estimated by nonlinear least squares (NLLS), then, is

$$D(\ln(C_t/K_t)) = c_1 + \frac{c_2}{\sigma}\left(\frac{A_{at}}{K_t}\right)^{1-c_2} - c_3\frac{I_t}{K_{t-1}}, \tag{3.17}$$

with $c_3 = 1$.

---

[7] Externalities of investment may also generate endogenous cycles in the standard exogenous growth model (see Greiner 1996). There, plausible economic conditions can be identified leading to growth cycles. We will not pursue here the question of whether those cycles are optimal in the sense that they fulfill sufficient conditions for optimality. For the latter, see Beyn, Pampel, and Semmler 2002.

[8] We tried to evaluate the parameters φ and δ_A by estimating a regression with the change in labor productivity as a proxy for $\dot{A}$, which is explained by investment. The results gave approximately the values we then used in constructing the time series for A, but they were not statistically significant.

Although the theory discussed here and made testable may be very relevant for less developed countries, because of a lack of data we select only a few countries where large catch-up effects have been observable. We start with Germany and consider the period after World War II.

Germany

In estimating (3.17) for Germany[9] with data from 1950 to 1994, we use different values for φ in constructing the variable $A(t)$. δ_A is left unchanged throughout and set to $\delta_A = 0.06$.[10] σ is set to 1, which is the value obtained by most of the empirical studies (see Blanchard and Fischer 1989, p. 44). In general, values for σ between 1 and 4 are considered to be compatible with reality, although 4 seems to be very high (cf. Lucas 1990).[11]

As to the magnitude of the external effect of investment, we resort to the study by DeLong and Summers (1991), who found that the external effect of investment is about 30 percent. DeLong and Summers carried out cross-section studies with a large sample of countries. However, it would be expected that externalities of investment heavily depend on country-specific factors such as education. Since there are no time series analyses available that study the magnitude of the external effect associated with physical investment, we resort to the result obtained by DeLong and Summers. Other studies in which the whole aggregate production is associated with externalities, and not only investment, suggest that the externality is in the range of 40–60 percent (see Benhabib and Farmer 1995).

To obtain an initial value for $A(1950)$ we follow Park (1995, p. 590) and set[12]

$$A(0) = \varphi\, I(0)\, \frac{1+g}{g+\delta_A},$$

with g the average growth rate of investment for the period 1950–1994.[13] In addition, we raised $A(1950)$ by values between 20 and 75 percent in order to obtain statistically significant results. In general, it turns out that the increase in $A(1950)$ had to be greater the lower the external effect of investment φ is set. We suppose that this increase is necessary because capital stocks in most of the countries we considered were almost completely destroyed during World War II, so the ratio of knowledge to physical

---

[9] Data for Germany are for West Germany only.

[10] For lower or higher values of δ_A the results did not change importantly.

[11] But there are also empirical studies that find values for σ below unity; see section 3.1.

[12] Note that we use aggregate total variables in our estimation. Consequently, $AL = A_a$.

[13] Coe and Helpman (1995) use the same method to obtain initial values.

TABLE 3.1
Estimation of Equation (3.17) for Germany

	Par.	Est.	Std. Err.	t-Stat.
$\varphi = 0.3$	c_1	−0.106	0.044	−2.417
	c_2	0.405	0.065	6.214
	R^2	0.38		
$\varphi = 0.4$	c_1	−0.08	0.034	−2.516
	c_2	0.327	0.053	6.175
	R^2	0.38		
$\varphi = 0.5$	c_1	−0.073	0.029	−2.549
	c_2	0.272	0.044	6.124
	R^2	0.38		
$\varphi = 0.6$	c_1	−0.08	0.029	−2.729
	c_2	0.255	0.043	5.997
	R^2	0.38		
$\varphi = 0.7$	c_1	−0.268	0.149	−1.8
	c_2	0.474	0.161	2.954
	R^2	0.4		
$\varphi = 0.8$	c_1	−0.294	0.187	−1.571
	c_2	0.478	0.197	2.423
	R^2	0.4		

capital, A/K, was very high at the beginning of the period we consider. However, building $A(1950)$ according to the procedure described above does not take account of that fact, which is only captured if $A(1950)$ is raised by a certain percentage.

The data for consumption and investment are from Statistisches Bundesamt (1974) and Sachverständigenrat (1995) and for private capital from Statistisches Bundesamt (1991, 1995).

Table 3.1 gives the outcome for different values of φ.

The table shows that the capital share $c_2 = 1 - \alpha$ varies between 26 and 48 percent, which are plausible values, depending on the value for φ.[14] The coefficient $c_1 = n - \rho$, which gives the difference between

[14] We should like to point out that the Durbin-Watson and the Breusch-Godfrey tests did not suggest that the residuals are serially correlated. That holds for all our estimations unless stated otherwise. Further, the hypotheses of nonsignificance of the complete regression could be rejected at the 1 percent significance level for all of our regressions unless stated otherwise.

the population growth rate and the discount rate of the household sector, lies between -7.3 and -29.4 percent. Values of the discount rate around 6.5 percent are often considered realistic in calibration exercises (see Benhabib and Farmer 1994; Benhabib and Perli 1994). The labor supply increased in number of persons between the 1950s and the 1990s, but total labor input decreased because of a decline in the number of hours worked per employee. The total amount of labor input in Germany between 1960 and 1994 decreased from 56 million to 45 million hours, an annual decline of about 0.6 percent. Therefore, regarding n as zero or even slightly negative seems to be justified.

Looking at table 3.1 and keeping that value of n in mind, we see that supposing $\varphi = 0.3$, $\varphi = 0.4$, $\varphi = 0.5$, and $\varphi = 0.6$ yields plausible outcomes, whereas higher and lower values for that coefficient do not seem to be compatible with empirical observations because they yield values for $n - \rho$ that are too low. This means that one unit of investment increases the stock of knowledge by 30 to 60 percent. Those values for the external effect of investment seem very high if one compares the results obtained by DeLong and Summers. But it must be underlined that our model considers positive externalities of investment as the only source of economic growth, neglecting others such as intentional investment in the formation of human capital or R&D investment. Consequently, those aspects can be expected to be included in the positive externalities of investment, giving a higher value for φ.

In figure 3.1 we show the actual time series of the first differences of $\ln(C_t/K_t)$, $D(\ln(C_t/K_t))$, compared to the fitted one for $\varphi = 0.5$.

Setting $\varphi = 0.2$ (0.8), the capital share is $1 - \alpha = 0.42$ (0.49) and $n - \rho = -0.08$ (insignificant). For values lower than 0.2 and higher than 0.8 no statistically significant results are obtained or the capital share is not plausible, that is, 0.6 or larger.

We also estimated equation (3.17) assuming $\sigma = 1.5$. The estimated coefficients in that case are less plausible. The estimations yield $1 - \alpha = 0.49$ (0.47) for $\varphi = 0.5$ (0.6). The coefficient $c_1 = (\delta_K + n) - (\rho + \delta_K)/1.5$, however, is no longer statistically significant. For all other values of φ our estimations do not produce statistically significant results.

Thus, the estimates for Germany indicate that our generalized growth model with positive externalities of investment yields plausible estimates for different quantitative external effects of investment.[15]

Another point to be made concerns our assumption of constant returns to scale in the aggregate production function, $Y = A^{\alpha} K^{1-\alpha}$. A more

[15] We also estimated (3.17) without the restriction $c_3 = 1$. c_3 was significant and took on values around 0.9. However, the hypothesis that $c_3 = 1$ could not be rejected.

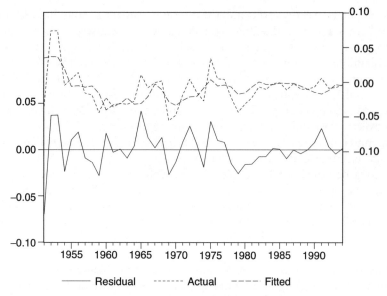

Figure 3.1.   Observed and predicted time series, German economy.

general formulation would be $Y = A^\alpha K^\beta$, with $\alpha, \beta \in (0, 1)$. If $\alpha + \beta < 1$, we have decreasing returns to scale, and sustained per capita growth is not feasible. For $\alpha + \beta > 1$ we have increasing returns, and we can again observe sustained per capita growth. However, it is difficult to completely characterize the dynamics of our model for the latter case. Further, increasing returns to scale would imply that the growth rate of market economies is increasing over time, which seems unrealistic. For these reasons, we assume $\alpha + \beta = 1$. From an empirical point of view, that assumption may seem very restrictive. Therefore, we next estimate equation (3.17) without the assumption of constant returns.

Equation (3.17) then becomes

$$D(\ln(C_t/K_t)) = c_1 + \frac{c_2}{\sigma} \left(\frac{A_{at}^{c_4}}{K_t^{1-c_2}} \right) - c_3 \frac{I_t}{K_{t-1}}, \tag{3.18}$$

with $c_3 = 1$. The results for $\sigma = 1$ and $\varphi = 0.4$ and $\varphi = 0.5$ are shown in table 3.2.[16]

---

[16] We also made the estimation for $\varphi = 0.3$ and $\varphi = 0.6$. For those values of φ, the results are the same from a qualitative point of view, in comparison to the estimation with $\alpha + \beta = 1$.

TABLE 3.2
Estimation of Equation (3.18) for Germany

	Par.	Est.	Std. Err.	t-Stat.
$\varphi = 0.4$	c_1	−0.086	0.037	−2.346
	c_2	0.305	0.269	1.135
	c_4	0.709	0.439	1.613
	R^2	0.38		
$\varphi = 0.5$	c_1	−0.074	0.034	−2.186
	c_2	0.255	0.271	0.94
	c_4	0.757	0.458	1.652
	R^2	0.38		

Table 3.2 demonstrates that the basic results do not change very much. As for $\alpha = c_4$, $\beta = c_2$, we see that $\alpha + \beta$ is slightly larger than 1, but only marginally. However, neither coefficient is statistically significant. We also performed the Wald coefficient test, checking whether the hypothesis $\alpha + \beta = 1$ can be rejected. It turns out that the hypothesis cannot be rejected. Thus, we conclude that the assumption of constant returns in our theoretical model is compatible with empirical data for Germany.

Next we analyze the model for France.

France

In estimating equation (3.17) for France for the period after World War II, we proceed as we did for Germany. δ_A is again set to 0.06 and φ takes on values between 0.3 and 0.6. The inverse of the intertemporal elasticity of substitution, however, is set higher, with $\sigma = 1.5$. The data for France are taken from the Summers and Heston (1991) database for the period 1950–1992.[17]

Estimating (3.17) with the restriction $c_3 = 1$ generates almost the same coefficients; the residuals, however, then are serially correlated and R^2 takes on very low values (around 0.05). But the capital coefficient is nevertheless statistically significant, which may be seen by calculating the Newey-West autocorrelation consistent standard errors. We decided to take the coefficient c_3 into the regression because then the autocorrelation vanishes and the fit is considerably better.

---

[17] Investment in that sample comprises both private and public investment. The capital stock was computed with the perpetual inventory method assuming a depreciation rate of 5 percent.

TABLE 3.3
Estimation of Equation (3.17) for France

	Par.	Est.	Std. Err.	t-Stat.
$\varphi = 0.3$	c_1	−0.095	0.06	−1.595
	c_2	0.398	0.125	3.196
	c_3	0.423	0.115	3.674
	R^2	0.42		
$\varphi = 0.4$	c_1	−0.08	0.045	−1.759
	c_2	0.317	0.097	3.259
	c_3	0.422	0.115	3.666
	R^2	0.42		
$\varphi = 0.5$	c_1	−0.071	0.038	−1.851
	c_2	0.261	0.079	3.283
	c_3	0.421	0.115	3.66
	R^2	0.42		
$\varphi = 0.6$	c_1	−0.065	0.034	−1.907
	c_2	0.22	0.067	3.305
	c_3	0.42	0.115	3.655
	R^2	0.42		

Table 3.3 shows that the capital share $c_2 = 1 - \alpha$ lies between 22 and 40 percent, which are plausible values. The coefficient $c_1 = (\delta_K + n) - (\rho + \delta_K)/1.5$ is relatively high in absolute values. For example, if $c_1 = -0.07$, the subjective discount rate is about 13 percent for $n = 0$, which seems to be high. So $\varphi = 0.5$ or $\varphi = 0.6$ yields the most plausible results, whereas for $\varphi = 0.3$ (0.4) the discount rate is too high.

Setting φ equal to 0.2 and to 0.7 gives a capital share of $1 - \alpha = 0.53$ and 0.19 respectively, which are unrealistically high and low, respectively. Setting φ still lower or higher yields still larger and lower values for the capital coefficient that are no longer plausible.

We also did the estimations with $\sigma = 1$. In this case, the capital share turns out to be lower by 10 to 20 percent. For example, setting $\varphi = 0.2$ (0.3, 0.4) yields $1 - \alpha = 0.34$ (0.25, 0.2). Supposing again $n = 0$, the discount rate implied by those values is $\rho = 8.3$ (6.9, 6.3) percent, which are plausible values.

For France we also estimated (3.18) with $\varphi = 0.5$ and $\varphi = 0.6$. For $\sigma = 1.5$ the results are given in table 3.4.

Both α and β are statistically significant, and the sum is again slightly larger than 1. The hypothesis $\alpha + \beta = 1$, however, cannot be rejected using the Wald coefficient test. Therefore, a theoretical model with constant

TABLE 3.4
Estimation of Equation (3.18) for France

	Par.	Est.	Std. Err.	t-Stat.
$\varphi = 0.5$	c_1	−0.084	0.127	−0.661
	c_2	0.26	0.084	3.092
	c_4	0.758	0.159	4.777
	c_3	0.403	0.201	2.008
	R^2	0.42		
$\varphi = 0.6$	c_1	−0.078	0.117	−0.665
	c_2	0.217	0.071	3.047
	c_4	0.802	0.179	4.488
	c_3	0.402	0.2	2.012
	R^2	0.42		

returns to scale also reflects the growth rate of the ratio C/K for France pretty well.

Next we test our model on the Japanese economy.

Japan

For Japan in the post–World War II period, our results are similar to the ones obtained for Germany and France.[18] Again, we set $\delta_A = 0.06$ and try different values for φ. The inverse of the intertemporal elasticity of substitution is set as for Germany, that is, $\sigma = 1$.

Table 3.5 shows that the capital share falls in the range 0.29 to 0.57.[19] While the capital coefficient can be considered as plausible for all values of φ in table 3.5 except for $\varphi = 0.6$, the coefficient c_1 is reasonable only for $\varphi = 0.4$. In that case, the subjective discount rate is about 11 percent for $n = 0$, which still seems to be relatively high. If we set $\varphi = 0.2$, the capital coefficient is 0.49 and c_1 is still smaller, namely −0.18. For values of φ larger than 0.7, no statistically significant results are obtained.

Performing the above estimations for $\sigma = 1.5$ does not yield interpretable results. Therefore, no statistically significant outcomes can be obtained.

Figure 3.2 shows the actual and fitted time series for $\varphi = 0.4$.

[18] The data for Japan are again from the Summers and Heston database. The variables were computed as for France.

[19] Note that we must again introduce the coefficient c_3 in order to get uncorrelated residuals.

TABLE 3.5
Estimation of Equation (3.17) for Japan

	Par.	Est.	Std. Err.	t-Stat.
$\varphi = 0.3$	c_1	−0.135	0.059	−2.281
	c_2	0.37	0.091	4.071
	c_3	0.474	0.078	6.066
	R^2	0.55		
$\varphi = 0.4$	c_1	−0.114	0.045	−2.543
	c_2	0.292	0.071	4.118
	c_3	0.473	0.078	6.071
	R^2	0.55		
$\varphi = 0.5$	c_1	−0.23	0.122	−1.886
	c_2	0.412	0.148	2.79
	c_3	0.485	0.079	6.134
	R^2	0.55		
$\varphi = 0.6$	c_1	−0.411	50.221	−0.008
	c_2	0.566	48.627	0.012
	c_3	0.413	0.132	3.135
	R^2	0.38		

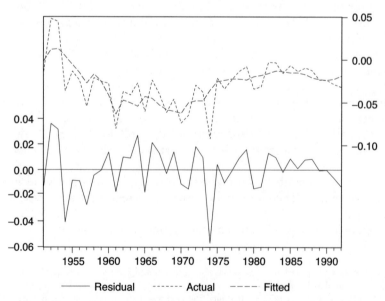

Figure 3.2. Observed and predicted time series, Japanese economy.

TABLE 3.6
Estimation of Equation (3.18) for Japan

		Par.	Est.	Std. Err.	t-Stat.
$\varphi = 0.3$	c_1		−0.125	0.138	−0.905
	c_2		0.364	0.123	2.947
	c_4		0.632	0.093	6.832
	c_3		0.481	0.12	4.01
	R^2		0.55		
$\varphi = 0.4$	c_1		−0.106	0.112	−0.948
	c_2		0.288	0.085	3.397
	c_4		0.707	0.07	10.027
	c_3		0.481	0.119	4.032
	R^2		0.55		

Estimating (3.18) for Japan with $\sigma = 1$ and $\varphi = 0.3$ and $\varphi = 0.4$ gives the results shown in table 3.6.

As for France, both α and β are statistically significant for Japan but the sum is now a slightly smaller one. But again, the hypothesis $\alpha + \beta = 1$ cannot be rejected using the Wald coefficient test.

Great Britain and the United States

For Great Britain and the United States,[20] which were not characterized by postwar catch-up periods, the model with positive externalities does not perform well. In the case of Great Britain, we estimated equation (3.17) for $\delta_A = 0.06$ and with $\varphi = 0.1$, $\varphi = 0.5$, and $\varphi = 1$. As for the initial conditions concerning knowledge formed as a by-product of investment, we proceeded as above. In addition, we multiplied the initial value of $A(t)$, $A(1950)$, by 0.1, 0.5, 1, 1.5, and 1.75 and reestimated (3.17) for each value of $A(1950)$. In all estimations the capital coefficients are either implausible or plausible but not statistically significant, which is seen by calculating the Newey-West autocorrelation consistent (AC) standard errors. The serial correlation was present independent of the choice of σ. We also did the computations using the average growth rate of real investment from 1950 to 1960 in constructing $A(1950)$, instead of the average from 1950 to 1992. The outcome, however, was the same from the qualitative point of view. Table 3.7 gives the result of the estimation

[20] The data for Great Britain and the United States are again from the Summers and Heston database.

TABLE 3.7
Estimation of Equation (3.17) for Great Britain

	Par.	Est.	Std. Err. (Newey-West AC)	t-Stat. (Newey-West AC)
$\varphi = 0.5$	c_1	−0.053	0.110	−0.483
	c_2	0.185	0.181	1.024
	c_3	0.576	0.263	2.193
	R^2	0.18		

for Great Britain with $\varphi = 0.5$ and $\sigma = 1$. The coefficients are reasonable and the value of R^2 is not too bad. However, c_1 and c_2 are not statistically significant and the residuals are autocorrelated, which may indicate that the model is misspecified for Great Britain.

For the United States we also estimated equation (3.17) for $\delta_A = 0.06$ and with $\varphi = 0.1$, $\varphi = 0.5$, and $\varphi = 1$. In those computations, serial correlation of the residuals could be observed, too. We tried to remove the autocorrelation by resorting to different starting values for $A(1950)$, as we did for Great Britain, but did not succeed. Further, the estimated coefficients are implausible, so that the model completely fails in explaining the growth performance of the United States.

3.3 EXTENSIONS OF THE MODEL

Before we conclude this chapter we want to sketch a variant of our growth model in which investment is associated with externalities, which, how-ever, can only be observed if the individual devotes time to education. For this type of model we cannot provide empirical evidence, yet it does enrich the model discussed here.

To integrate education into the theoretical model, we assume that the change in the stock of knowledge, $\dot{A}$, is a function depending on the time spent on education and on investment. In particular, we suppose

$$\dot{A} = \varphi(u)I - \delta_A A. \tag{3.19}$$

As above, $\varphi(u)$ represents the contribution of one unit of investment to the formation of the stock of knowledge capital and is assumed to be a positive function of the time devoted to education, $1 - u \in (0, 1)$ or, equivalently, a negative function of the time used for production, that is, $\varphi'(u) < 0$. The larger the fraction of time devoted to education, the stronger the external effect of investment on the formation of knowledge.

Further, we suppose that $\varphi(u) \to 0$ for $u \to 1$. This assumption states that without education no learning effect takes place and individuals are not capable of building up knowledge as a by-product of investment in new machines. In that case, investment does not show any externalities. This assumption can be justified by requiring that employees and workers undergo a minimum level of education, for example, be able to read and write, in order to be able to increase their skills as a by-product of investment. However, in the industrialized or newly industrializing countries the case $u = 1$ will not be observed for the average individual because governmental regulations prescribe a minimum of education for every child. Thus, education without investment will not generate much growth. In our view, investment and education are complementary in the sense that neither of these activities is capable of increasing the stock of knowledge capital by itself.

But it should be underlined that our assumption concerning $\varphi(\cdot)$ does not necessarily mean that in economies with a higher level of education any unit of investment undertaken increases the stock of knowledge capital to a higher degree. Instead $\varphi(u)$ may differ between countries even if they spend the same amount of time for education. This holds because other factors, such as institutional, cultural, or environmental factors, will also influence the social capability of a country and, thus, its ability to build up knowledge as a by-product of investment.

The household maximizes the discounted stream of utility resulting from consumption $C(t)$ over an infinite time horizon:

$$\max_{C(t),u(t)} \int_0^\infty e^{-\rho t} U(C(t)) dt. \tag{3.20}$$

$\rho > 0$ gives the rate of time preference and $U(\cdot)$ is the utility function. The household's budget constraint is written as

$$C + \dot{K} + \delta_K K = \tilde{w} u + r K. \tag{3.21}$$

$\delta_K \geq 0$ is the depreciation rate of physical capital and r is the return to physical capital. Recall that the labor supply is assumed to be constant and normalized to 1, so that all variables give per capita quantities.

$\tilde{w}$ is the wage rate the household expects to receive for its labor input. The household assumes the wage rate to be a function that positively depends on the time spent on education. This holds because education has a positive impact on the marginal product of labor and, thus, on the household's income. The economic justification for this assumption is that in modern economies, higher wages positively co-vary with education. It is implicitly acknowledged that better-trained workers are more productive over time because they are able to build up knowledge capital, according to $\dot{A} = \varphi(\cdot)I - \delta_A A$. Therefore, we assume that the wage rate that the household expects to receive is a positive function of the time spent on education and of exogenous parameters, or equivalently, a negative function of the time used for production, that is, $\tilde{w} = f(u, \cdot)$, with $f_u(u, \cdot) < 0$. Further, we also assume that $f(u, \cdot)$ is such that there exists an interior maximum for $\tilde{w}u$, the wage income of the household.

In equilibrium, however, the household is paid the marginal product of labor; that is, $\tilde{w} = w$ holds, with w given by (3.3). Now, what would happen if the household expected to get the equilibrium wage rate, that is, if it sets w from (3.3) in its budget constraint? It is immediately clear that the household would not undergo any education at all; that is, it would set $u = 1$ so that its wage income $w(\cdot)u$ is maximized, because it could not expect any remuneration for education. That result holds because in the competitive economy the positive external effect of investment, that is, the formation of knowledge capital according to (3.4), is not taken into account. But then we would have the conventional Ramsey-type growth model with zero per capita growth in the long run. The same outcome would be obtained if the household took w as given in solving its optimization problem. In that case, the household would set $u = 1$; that is, it would spend no time on education.

However, the household's expectation that the wage rate positively varies with the time spent on education indeed makes it better off compared to the situation in which the household takes the wage rate as given. This holds because then the household spends time on education, which brings about positive external effects of investment, which may lead to sustained per capita growth. So education is a merit good for society because it is the prerequisite for positive externalities of investment in the competitive economy.

An alternative specification one could imagine is that u is given exogenously. In that case, the wage rate w and u are parameters that the household takes as given in solving the optimization problem. The economic reason behind that assumption might be that the government fixes how much basic education the population has to have. It is that sort of education which contributes to the productivity of an economy. For example, it is often argued that the increase in basic education in the fast-growing economies of Southeast Asia has been a major reason for their high per capita growth rates.

Solving the optimization problem of the household gives the same optimality conditions as in section 3.1. In addition, we have

$$0 = f_u(u, \cdot)u + f(u, \cdot),$$ (3.22)

implicitly defining $u^\star$, the optimal value of u. The second-order condition guaranteeing that $u^\star$ yields a maximum is fulfilled if $f_{uu}(u^\star, \cdot) < 2(f_u(u^\star, \cdot))^2 / f(u^\star, \cdot)$ holds. That inequality holds if $f(u, \cdot)$ is linear in u, exponential or isoelastic with an absolute elasticity larger than 1.[21] The production function now is

$$Y = (uAL)^\alpha K^{1-\alpha} \equiv (uA)^\alpha K^{1-\alpha}. \tag{3.23}$$

α denotes the labor share in the production function, and labor L is constant over time and normalized to 1. K and A denote the stock of physical and knowledge capital respectively, where A increases the labor productivity and is taken as given by the firm in solving its optimization problem. u is the time devoted to production and is determined by the household. The wage rate and the return to capital are again equal to their marginal products respectively.

Solving this model yields the balanced growth rate g as

$$g = -\frac{\rho + \delta_K}{\sigma} + \frac{(1-\alpha)(u^\star)^\alpha K^{-\alpha} A^\alpha}{\sigma} \tag{3.24}$$

Analyzing this model demonstrates that economies spending more time on education are not necessarily characterized by a higher balanced growth rate. This holds because more time spent on education has two opposite effects: On the one hand, more education implies that any investment has a stronger positive external effect, generating a larger stock of knowledge, which increases the marginal product of investment and, thus, the balanced growth rate. On the other hand, more time spent on education implies that the household spends less time on work. This, however, shows a negative direct effect on the marginal product of private capital, as can immediately be seen from $r = (1 - \alpha)(u^\star)^\alpha K^{-\alpha} A^\alpha$. Thus, we see that countries that spend more time on education are not necessarily characterized by a higher balanced growth rate.

3.4 Conclusions

This chapter has presented a simple generalization of the Romer (1986) model of endogenous growth. Investment in physical capital shows positive externalities that increase the stock of knowledge capital, but investment in physical capital does not increase knowledge and physical capital one for one, so these two stocks cannot be summarized in one state variable.

---

[21] For example, the function $f(u, \cdot) = (1 - u)^{0.5} + a$ yields $u^\star = 0.93$ $(0.91, 0.86, 0.81, 0.74, 0.67)$ for $a = 1.5$ $(1.2, 0.8, 0.5, 0.2, 0)$.

It was demonstrated that our growth model with externalities of investment may generate endogenous growth in earlier stages of development or in catch-up periods of advanced countries. A prerequisite from the economic point of view consists in a sufficiently strong external effect of investment that positively affects the marginal product of private capital. We have found that such economies may be characterized by two balanced growth paths, depending on the intertemporal elasticity of substitution of consumption and on exogenous parameters.

Our model aims to explain a phenomenon that earlier models of a convex-concave production function have tried to explain (see Skiba 1978, for example). In those earlier versions of growth models it was presumed that countries with small capital stocks enjoy increasing returns to scale production and countries with large capital stocks exhibit decreasing returns to scale. In these models there would then be multiple equilibria and a threshold separating domains of attraction. Because the marginal product of capital in the increasing returns (i.e., convex) region depends on the amount of capital, a take-off of a country is predicted to occur only if the country's capital stock moves above a certain threshold.

Our approach, however, combines the property of diminishing returns to physical capital of the Ramsey-type model with endogenous growth and underlines the importance of the interrelation between knowledge and physical capital for economic growth. The model demonstrates that countries with small stocks of physical capital but relatively large stocks of knowledge capital have a very large marginal product of physical capital and, consequently, high growth rates. This pattern can be observed in Japan and Germany after World War II, where almost the whole stock of physical capital was destroyed while the stock of knowledge capital, embodied in people, was still present[22] and in countries such as Korea and Taiwan up to the 1990s. But a small stock of physical capital is not a sufficient condition for high growth rates. For that reason, economic aid in the form of capital goods to developing countries that have not built up a sufficiently large stock of knowledge capital is likely to fail if it is not accompanied by efforts to improve skills. On the other hand, countries with large capital stocks can overcome diminishing returns to physical capital by large external effects of investment on the knowledge capital stock.

As to the empirical verification of our model, we would like to point out that the goal of this chapter is not to find the exact magnitude of the external effect of investment. Instead, we test whether our endogenous

---

[22] See Shell 1967, pp. 78–79, for this example.

growth model with positive externalities of investment is compatible with time series data.

With respect to Germany, France, and Japan, the estimation results show that our endogenous growth model fits the time series in these countries so that it can be used to describe the growth process of those countries for the period after World War II. The assumption of constant returns to scale in the aggregate production function also seems to be compatible with empirical data for those countries. That holds because in all of our estimations the Wald coefficient test did not allow us to reject the hypothesis of constant returns.

We would also like to emphasize that the growth process differs in different countries. For this reason we believe time series analyses are preferable to cross-section studies, in which different countries are summarized in one sample. For example, we saw that for France, $\sigma = 1$ and $\sigma = 1.5$ yield reasonable outcomes, whereas for Japan, only $\sigma = 1$ gives plausible results. In addition, the poor performance of our model for Great Britain and its rejection using U.S. data confirm our view. One possible explanation of why the model does not explain economic evolution in these two countries is that the capital stock in Great Britain and the United States was not destroyed after World War II, in contrast to that in Germany, France, and Japan. Because the model with positive externalities from learning by investing seems of particular relevance for countries at a stage of development with a smaller initial stock of physical capital, economic evolution in the former three countries is better reflected in our model than the evolution in Great Britain and the United States.

However, we must be aware that our model is a highly stylized one that contains only one source of economic growth, namely positive externalities of investment, which seem to be important for certain stages of growth. All other feasible sources, such as buildup of human capital and knowledge capital, that may give rise to per capita growth are not considered here. This may be one reason why the model cannot be expected to yield high values for R^2. Further, we must recognize that actual time series are influenced by business cycles, which are not captured by the growth model. This is clearly seen if one compares the actual time series with the fitted time series in figures 3.1 and 3.2. Although the fitted time series reflects the general evolution of the growth rate of C/K pretty well, it does not follow the peaks and troughs of the actual series.

We did not address the question of what role human capital and the buildup of knowledge play in the process of economic growth. This is, of course, a shortcoming because those variables are generally considered important factors in economic growth. Nevertheless, R&D expenditures, for example, that build up knowledge and move the country close to the technology frontier of advanced countries, may play an implicit role in the empirical estimation since technical progress may be embodied in new capital goods (see Hamilton and Monteagudo 1998). But building up of knowledge and human capital are not yet considered in our theoretical framework. Therefore, in chapters 4 and 5 we will present variants of the Uzawa-Lucas and Romer growth models, in which education and knowledge play an important role in explaining economic growth.

APPENDIX

The proof of the proposition in section 3.1 proceeds as follows. First, we prove part (i). To do so, we compute $\bar{c}$ on the BGP from setting the right-hand side of (3.14) $= 0$, giving

$$\bar{c} = \bar{k}^{1-\alpha} - \frac{(\delta_K + n - \delta_A)\bar{k}}{1 - \varphi\bar{k}}. \tag{3.25}$$

From that expression it is seen that for $\delta_K + n > \delta_A$, $1 - \varphi\bar{k} > 0$ must hold so that $\bar{c} < \bar{k}^{1-\alpha}$. Next, we insert $\bar{c}$ in $\dot{c}/c$, yielding

$$f(k, \cdot) := -\frac{\rho + \delta_K}{\sigma} + \delta_A + \frac{1 - \alpha}{\sigma}k^{-\alpha} + (\delta_A - \delta_K - n)\frac{\varphi k}{1 - \varphi k}. \tag{3.26}$$

A point for which $f(k, \cdot) = 0$ holds gives a BGP. $f(k, \cdot)$ has the following properties: $\lim_{k \to 0} f(k, \cdot) = +\infty$ and $\lim_{k \nearrow \varphi^{-1}} f(k, \cdot) = -\infty$, where $\nearrow$ means that k approaches φ^{-1} from below, and $f(k, \cdot)$ is continuous for $k \in (0, \varphi^{-1})$. Differentiating $f(k, \cdot)$ with respect to k gives

$$\frac{\partial f(k, \cdot)}{\partial k} = \frac{\varphi(\delta_A - \delta_K - n)}{(1 - k\varphi)^2} - \frac{\alpha(1 - \alpha)}{\sigma}k^{-\alpha-1}. \tag{3.27}$$

Since $\delta_K + n > \delta_A$, it is immediately seen that the derivative is negative, so uniqueness of a BGP is proved for $\delta_K + n > \delta_A$.

To prove saddle point stability we linearize system (3.14)–(3.15) around the rest point $(\bar{k}, \bar{c})$ and compute the determinant of the Jacobian matrix. The Jacobian evaluated at the rest point (that is, on the BGP) is given by

$$J = \begin{bmatrix} \bar{c}/\bar{k}^2 - \alpha\bar{k}^{-\alpha-1} - \bar{k}^{-\alpha}(1 - \alpha)\varphi & \varphi - 1/\bar{k} \\ ((1 - \alpha)(-\alpha)\bar{k}^{-\alpha-1}/\sigma) - \varphi(1 - \alpha)\bar{k}^{-\alpha} & \varphi \end{bmatrix}. \tag{3.28}$$

Next, we show $\det J < 0$, which is necessary and sufficient for saddle point stability. The determinant is calculated as

$$\det J = (1 - \bar{k}\varphi)\bar{k}^{-1}\left(\frac{\varphi(\delta_A - \delta_K - n)}{(1 - \bar{k}\varphi)^2} - \frac{\alpha(1 - \alpha)}{\sigma}\bar{k}^{-\alpha-1}\right). \tag{3.29}$$

The derivative of $f(k, \cdot)$ with respect to k is given by

$$\frac{\partial f(k, \cdot)}{\partial k} = \frac{\varphi(\delta_A - \delta_K - n)}{(1 - k\varphi)^2} - \frac{\alpha(1 - \alpha)}{\sigma} k^{-\alpha - 1}. \tag{3.30}$$

This shows that sign $\det J = \text{sign} \left(\partial f(k, \cdot)/\partial k \right)(1 - \varphi \bar{k})$. For $\delta_K + n > \delta_A$, $1 - \varphi \bar{k} > 0$ holds and we have $0 > \partial f(k, \cdot)/\partial k$. Consequently, $\det J < 0$ and part (i) is proved.

To prove part (ii), we first state that a k that solves $f(k, \cdot) = 0$ also solves $f(k, \cdot)k^\alpha(1 - \varphi k) \equiv f_1(k, \cdot) = 0$, with $k^\alpha(1 - \varphi k) \neq 0$, and vice versa. Therefore, we can analyze the function $f_1(k, \cdot)$ instead of $f(k, \cdot)$.

Multiplying $f(k, \cdot)$ with $k^\alpha(1 - \varphi k) \neq 0$ leads to

$$f_1(k, \cdot) = \left(\frac{1 - \alpha}{\sigma} \right)(1 - \varphi k) + k^\alpha \left(\delta_A - \frac{\rho + \delta_K}{\sigma} \right)$$
$$+ k^{1+\alpha} \varphi \left(-\delta_K - n + \frac{\rho + \delta_K}{\sigma} \right). \tag{3.31}$$

A point at which $f_1(k, \cdot) = 0$ also gives a rest point for $f(k, \cdot)$ and, therefore, a BGP for our model. Note that $f_1(k, \cdot)$ is continuous for all $k \in (0, \infty)$.

For $k \to 0$ we have $f_1(k, \cdot) \to (1 - \alpha)/\sigma > 0$. Differentiating $f_1(k, \cdot)$ with respect to k gives

$$\frac{\partial f_1(k, \cdot)}{\partial k} = -\left(\frac{1 - \alpha}{\sigma} \right)\varphi + \alpha k^{\alpha - 1}\left(\delta_A - \frac{\rho + \delta_K}{\sigma} \right)$$
$$+ (\alpha + 1)k^\alpha \varphi \left(-\delta_K - n + \frac{\rho + \delta_K}{\sigma} \right). \tag{3.32}$$

First, we consider the case $(\delta_K + \rho)/\sigma \leq \delta_K + n$. $(\delta_K + \rho)/\sigma \leq \delta_K + n$ and $\delta_A \leq (\delta_K + \rho)/\sigma$ implies $\lim_{k \to \infty} f_1(k, \cdot) = -\infty$ and $\partial f_1(k, \cdot)/\partial k < 0$ for all $k > 0$ so that for this case uniqueness is immediately apparent.

If $(\delta_K + \rho)/\sigma \leq \delta_K + n$ but $\delta_A > (\delta_K + \rho)/\sigma$, uniqueness is shown as follows: Because of $f_1(k, \cdot) > 0$ for $k \to 0$ the existence of a BGP implies that $\partial f_1(k, \cdot)/\partial k < 0$ must hold at least locally. Since $\partial^2 f_1(k, \cdot)/\partial k^2 < 0$ holds for all $k > 0$ in that case, $\partial f_1(k, \cdot)/\partial k > 0$ is not feasible once $\partial f_1(k, \cdot)/\partial k$ has become negative and, consequently, there is no second BGP.

If $(\delta_K + \rho)/\sigma > \delta_K + n$ and $\delta_A \leq (\delta_K + \rho)/\sigma$, the existence of two BGPs in case of sustained per capita growth is proved as follows: At the first BGP the curve $f_1(k, \cdot)$ must cross the horizontal axis from above; that is, $\partial f_1(k, \cdot)/\partial k < 0$ must hold at this point. For the second BGP the curve $f_1(k, \cdot)$ must cross the horizontal axis from below; that is, at this point $\partial f_1(k, \cdot)/\partial k > 0$ must hold. Since $\lim_{k \to \infty}(\partial f_1(k, \cdot)/\partial k) = \lim_{k \to \infty} f_1(k, \cdot) = \infty$ and $\partial^2 f_1(k, \cdot)/\partial k^2 > 0$ holds for all $k > 0$, there exists a finite k such that $f_1(k, \cdot) = 0$ holds and a second BGP exists. For a third BGP to exist, $\partial f_1(k, \cdot)/\partial k < 0$ would have to hold at this point. But that is not possible because of $\partial^2 f_1(k, \cdot)/\partial k^2 > 0$, implying that no inflection point exists.

If $(\delta_K + \rho)/\sigma > \delta_K + n$ but $\delta_A > (\delta_K + \rho)/\sigma$, the existence of two BGPs in case of sustained per capita growth is shown as follows: In this case we have $\lim_{k \to 0}(\partial f_1(k, \cdot)/\partial k) = \infty$ and $\lim_{k \to \infty}(\partial f_1(k, \cdot)/\partial k) = \lim_{k \to \infty} f_1(k, \cdot) = \infty$. That means that if there exists a BGP, $f_1(k, \cdot)$ must first intersect the horizontal axis from above and then from below (because of $\lim_{k \to \infty}(\partial f_1(k, \cdot)/\partial k) = \lim_{k \to \infty} f_1(k, \cdot) = \infty$). That implies that there must exist an inflection point (because of $\lim_{k \to 0}(\partial f_1(k, \cdot)/\partial k) = \infty$). It is easily seen that there is a unique inflection point of $f_1(k, \cdot)$ given by $k_w = (1 - \alpha)(\delta_A - (\rho + \delta_K)/\sigma)/(\varphi(1 + \alpha)(-\delta_K - n + (\rho + \delta_K)/\sigma)) > 0$. If there existed a third BGP, a second inflection point would have to exist. But that possibility is not given. Further, if $(\delta_K + \rho)/\sigma > \delta_K + n$ and $\delta_A > (\leq) (\delta_K + \rho)/\sigma$, the case $f_1(k, \cdot) = 0$ and $\partial f_1(k, \cdot)/\partial k = 0$ cannot be excluded a priori. However, this has measure zero. Therefore, we exclude that case.

To show saddle point stability of the BGP if it is unique in case (ii), we first recall that $\text{sign} \det J = \text{sign} (\partial f(k, \cdot)/\partial k)(1 - \varphi \bar{k})$ holds. Further, in case of a unique BGP in (ii) we have $\delta_A > \delta_K + n$, $\delta_K + n - (\rho + \delta_K)/\sigma \geq 0$ and $\bar{k} \in (\varphi^{-1}, \infty)$ (necessary for $\bar{c} < \bar{k}^{1-\alpha}$). That gives[23]

$$\lim_{k \searrow \varphi^{-1}} f(k, \cdot) = -\infty \quad \text{and} \quad \lim_{k \to \infty} f(k, \cdot) = \delta_K + n - (\rho + \delta_K)/\sigma \geq 0,$$

(3.33)

$$\lim_{k \searrow \varphi^{-1}} \frac{\partial f(k, \cdot)}{\partial k} = +\infty \quad \text{and} \quad \lim_{k \to \infty} \frac{\partial f(k, \cdot)}{\partial k} = 0.$$

(3.34)

Since the BGP is unique, these properties demonstrate that $f(k, \cdot)$ intersects the horizontal axis from below; that is, $\partial f(k, \cdot)/\partial k > 0$ holds at the intersection point, and this point is in the range $k \in (\varphi^{-1}, \infty)$. Consequently, $\det J < 0$ and the rest point is again saddle point stable.

If $\delta_K + n - (\rho + \delta_K)/\sigma = 0$, $f(k, \cdot)$ must intersect the horizontal axis from below and then converge to 0. Since there may exist an inflection point for $f(k, \cdot)$ for $\delta_A - \delta_K - n > 0$ and $k > \varphi^{-1}$ this possibility is given.

The existence of two BGPs implies $\delta_A - \delta_K - n > 0$, $\delta_K + n - (\rho + \delta_K)/\sigma < 0$ and $\bar{k} \in (\varphi^{-1}, \infty)$. Moreover, we know that $\text{sign} \det J = \text{sign} (\partial f(k, \cdot)/\partial k)(1 - \varphi \bar{k})$.

---

[23] $\searrow$ means that k approaches φ^{-1} from above.

For $\delta_A - \delta_K - n > 0$, now $f(k, \cdot)$ has the following properties:

$$\lim_{k \searrow \varphi^{-1}} f(k, \cdot) = -\infty \quad \text{and} \quad \lim_{k \to \infty} f(k, \cdot) = \delta_K + n - (\rho + \delta_K)/\sigma < 0,$$

$$(3.35)$$

$$\lim_{k \searrow \varphi^{-1}} \frac{\partial f(k, \cdot)}{\partial k} = +\infty \quad \text{and} \quad \lim_{k \to \infty} \frac{\partial f(k, \cdot)}{\partial k} = 0. \qquad (3.36)$$

Since the values for k on the BGPs are from (φ^{-1}, ∞), we have $1 - \varphi \bar{k} < 0$, and $f(k, \cdot)$ first intersects the horizontal axis from below and then from above. That is, $\partial f(k, \cdot)/\partial k > 0$ holds at the first $\bar{k}$ (lower $\bar{k}$) and $\partial f(k, \cdot)/\partial k < 0$ at the second $\bar{k}$ (larger $\bar{k}$). This shows that $\det J < 0$ for the BGP with the lower value of $\bar{k}$, which yields the higher growth rate, and $\det J > 0$ for the BGP with the higher value of $\bar{k}$, which yields the lower growth rate. Thus, the proof is completed.

CHAPTER 4

Education and Economic Growth

4.1 Introduction

We now introduce education and human capital into a growth model more formally. We concentrate on the model introduced by Uzawa (1965) and Lucas (1988), known as the Uzawa-Lucas model. It resembles Solow's (1956) neoclassical model of growth, but total output depends on both physical and human capital. Moreover, the saving rate is not exogenous, as in Solow's model, but endogenously determined by the preference and technology parameters.[1] In particular, it is assumed that a representative household maximizes the discounted stream of utility arising from consumption. The Lucas model (1988), which has recently become the prototype growth model with human capital, considers a closed economy with competitive markets, identical rational agents, and constant returns to scale technology; at time t there exist $L(t)$ persons who are involved in production.

As for empirical evidence of the model in cross-country studies, Barro and Sala-i-Martin (1995, chapter 12) present regression results for the growth rate of real per capita GDP. They do not presume a certain economic model by which growth rates are explained but simply undertake regressions with the growth rate of real per capita GDP as the dependent variable that is explained by various exogenous variables. They also consider cross-country studies with eighty-seven countries included for the time period 1965–1975 and ninety-seven countries for the period 1975–1985. With respect to education, the outcome is that the average years of secondary and higher schooling for both males and females, observed at the start of each decade (that is, in 1965 and 1975), are significantly correlated with the average growth rates of per capita GDP over these two periods. Primary education, however, is not significantly correlated with economic growth.

Like Barro and Sala-i-Martin's, most cross-country studies demonstrate that schooling and human capital have positive effects on the growth rates of countries. Yet the variable for schooling, for example, is not necessarily

---

[1] For a detailed comparison of the Solow model and the two-sector Uzawa-Lucas model, see Flaschel, Franke, and Semmler (1997), chapter 5.

robust in empirical cross-country studies (see, e.g., Sala-i-Martin 1997). In such studies, a variable is said to be robust if the sign of the coefficient of this variable remains the same and is statistically significant in 95 percent of the regressions that are done, independent of the other exogenous variables that are included. Indeed, only the investment share and the openness of the economy turn out to be robust variables. On the other hand, in Levine and Renelt (1992) the secondary school enrollment rate is not fragile but is a robust variable. These authors also study the question of which coefficients do not change sign and always have a statistically significant impact. Further, as remarked in chapter 1, results from cross-country studies may change if one looks at the time series evidence of growth models. Although schooling and education may have a scale effect on economic growth[2] for countries with less development, such scale effects may not hold for later stages of growth, as Krüger and Lindahl (2001) have shown.[3] There seem to be nonlinearities at work, since educational efforts in advanced countries show less than proportional effects on growth rates.

In the next section, we present in detail the Uzawa-Lucas endogenous growth model with human capital, estimate that model using time series data for the United States and Germany, and give considerable attention to the problem of scale effects.

4.2 THE MODEL

Let us start by describing the basic Uzawa-Lucas model. The preferences over consumption streams in the Uzawa-Lucas model are described as follows:

$$\int_0^\infty L(t) \frac{c(t)^{1-\sigma} - 1}{1 - \sigma} e^{-\rho t} dt \tag{4.1}$$

with ρ the discount rate, $1/\sigma > 0$ the intertemporal elasticity of substitution of consumption between two points in time and $c = C/L$ consumption per capita.[4] This formulation implies that social welfare equals individual welfare times the number of individuals or households in the economy.

---

[2] In this context, scale effect means that an increase in the time spent on education increases the balanced growth rate of the economy.

[3] Uzawa (1965) also seems to assume that his model is relevant only for earlier stages of growth.

[4] In the Uzawa-Lucas model as presented by Lucas (1988), the labor supply is assumed to be constant.

The productive sector consists of two sectors. One produces the physical good using labor, physical capital, and human capital as input factors. This good can be consumed or invested in the creation of physical capital goods. The second sector produces human capital, using as an input factor only human capital.

Human capital is defined as the general skill level embodied in workers. Important in this context are two aspects, namely, how human capital influences current production and how the current time allocation affects the accumulation of human capital. With regard to these aspects, the fraction $u(t)$ is introduced as the nonleisure time that a worker with skill level h devotes to current production, and the fraction $1-u(t)$ denotes the time devoted to human capital accumulation. The average level of skill h_a is defined as

$$h_a = \frac{\int_0^\infty hL(h)dh}{\int_0^\infty L(h)dh}. \tag{4.2}$$

In Lucas (1988) this generates an external effect in the production function of the physical good. That is, the productivity of all factors of production positively depends on the average skill level of workers in the economy. The economic motivation for this externality associated with human capital is that a higher general level of human capital has a stimulating effect on overall productivity.

The resource constraint is given by

$$L(t)c(t) + \dot{K}(t) = AK(t)^{1-\alpha}[u(t)h(t)L(t)]^\alpha h_a^\zeta, \tag{4.3}$$

where the right-hand side denotes aggregate production $Y(t)$, with $Y(t) = AK(t)^{1-\alpha}[u(t)h(t)L(t)]^\alpha h_a^\zeta$. A is the constant level of technology, $(1-\alpha) \in (0,1)$ is the share of capital, and $\zeta \geq 0$ is the externality parameter. It should be noted that (4.3) implies that human capital is a nonexcludable but rivalrous public good, that is, a public good that is subject to congestion because the total stock of human capital per worker, Lh/L, increases the efficiency of the labor input L. This is obvious because human capital is embodied in workers, so the use of skills in one activity precludes their use in another activity.

Now the fraction of nonleisure time devoted to human capital accumulation must be combined with the rate of change in the skill level. Lucas (1988, pp. 18–19) uses the Uzawa-Rosen linear formulation:

$$\dot{h}(t) = h(t)\kappa(1 - u(t)), \tag{4.4}$$

where κ is the maximum growth rate of human capital. If no effort is dedicated to human capital accumulation, $u(t) = 1$, then $\dot{h}(t) = 0$. If all effort is dedicated to human capital accumulation, $u(t) = 0$, then $h(t)$ grows at the rate κ.

To summarize, the model is given by the solution of the following optimization problem:

$$\max_{c,u} \int_0^\infty L(t)\frac{c(t)^{1-\sigma} - 1}{1-\sigma}e^{-\rho t}dt \tag{4.5}$$

subject to

$$\dot{K}(t) = AK(t)^{1-\alpha}(u(t)h(t)L(t))^\alpha h_a^\zeta - L(t)c(t) \tag{4.6}$$

$$\dot{h}(t) = h(t)\kappa(1 - u(t)) \tag{4.7}$$

$$K(0) \geq 0, \quad h(0) \geq 0.$$

To solve this problem, the current-value Hamiltonian and the first-order conditions derived from it have to be computed. In a first simplified estimation of the model we neglect the externality (so that $\zeta = 0$) and the second control variable u; that is, we assume that u is not chosen optimally but given exogenously. We call this version the Uzawa-Lucas I model.

The optimization problem then is to solve equation (4.5), where c is the only control variable, subject to (4.6), with (4.7) given exogenously. The current-value Hamiltonian for this optimization problem is defined as

$$H(K, h, \theta_1, c, u) = \frac{L}{1-\sigma}(c^{1-\sigma} - 1) + \theta_1(AK^{1-\alpha}(uLh)^\alpha - Lc) \tag{4.8}$$

The first-order conditions are

$$\frac{\partial H}{\partial c} = 0 \Leftrightarrow c^{-\sigma} = \theta_1 \tag{4.9}$$

$$-\rho\theta_1 + \frac{\partial H}{\partial K} = -\dot{\theta}_1 \Leftrightarrow \dot{\theta}_1 = \rho\theta_1 - \theta_1(1-\alpha)AK^{-\alpha}(uLh)^\alpha \tag{4.10}$$

and the transversality condition

$$\lim_{t \to 0} e^{-\rho t}\theta_1(t)K(t) = 0. \tag{4.11}$$

To obtain an estimable system we have to rewrite the equations in growth rates using $y = h/K$ and $z = c/h$.

$$y = \frac{h}{K} \Leftrightarrow \frac{\dot{y}}{y} = \frac{\dot{h}}{h} - \frac{\dot{K}}{K} \tag{4.12}$$

$$z = \frac{c}{h} \Leftrightarrow \frac{\dot{z}}{z} = \frac{\dot{c}}{c} - \frac{\dot{h}}{h} \tag{4.13}$$

Now we express θ_1 in terms of its corresponding control variable c. Differentiating (4.9) with respect to time we get

$$-\sigma \frac{\dot{c}}{c} = \frac{\dot{\theta}_1}{\theta_1} \tag{4.14}$$

We can transform (4.10) into

$$\frac{\dot{\theta}_1}{\theta_1} = \rho - (1-\alpha)AK^{-\alpha}h^{\alpha}(uL)^{\alpha} \tag{4.15}$$

and substitute it in 4.14

$$\frac{\dot{c}}{c} = \frac{-\rho + (1-\alpha)A\left(\frac{1}{y}\right)^{-\alpha}(uL)^{\alpha}}{\sigma} \tag{4.16}$$

We rewrite the resource constraint (4.3) and the Uzawa-Rosen formulation (4.4) as follows:[5]

$$\frac{\dot{K}}{K} = A\left(\frac{1}{y}\right)^{-\alpha}(uL)^{\alpha} - Lzy \tag{4.17}$$

$$\frac{\dot{h}}{h} = \kappa(1-u) \tag{4.18}$$

Finally, we substitute (4.17) and (4.18) into (4.12), and (4.16) and (4.18) into (4.13). This yields the following system:

$$\frac{\dot{y}}{y} = \kappa(1-u) - A\left(\frac{1}{Y}\right)^{-\alpha}(uL)^{\alpha} + Lzy \tag{4.19}$$

$$\frac{\dot{z}}{z} = \frac{-\rho + (1-\alpha)A\left(\frac{1}{y}\right)^{-\alpha}(uL)^{\alpha}}{\sigma} - \kappa(1-u) \tag{4.20}$$

where $y = h/K$ and $z = c/h$.

It is easily seen that there exists a unique balanced growth path (BGP) for this model that is obtained by setting $\dot{y} = \dot{z} = 0$ and solving these two equations with respect to y and z. This gives

$$y = \left(\frac{\rho + \sigma\kappa(1-u)}{(1-\alpha)A(uL)^{\alpha}}\right)^{1/\alpha}$$

$$z = \frac{A(u)^{\alpha}(\rho + \sigma\kappa(1-u))/((1-\alpha)A(u)^{\alpha}) - \kappa(1-u)}{(\rho + \sigma\kappa(1-u))/((1-\alpha)A(u)^{\alpha})}$$

---

[5] Note that if A rose over time as in Romer (1990), the growth rates of C and K would increase without bounds.

The determinant of the Jacobian of (4.19)–(4.20) is negative, implying that the Uzawa-Lucas I model has a saddle point property. From an economic point of view, these results show that the simplified Uzawa-Lucas model is both locally and globally determinate.[6]

If we allow for the externality ($\zeta > 0$) and the second control variable u, we get the Uzawa-Lucas II model. For this model the current-value Hamiltonian can be written as

$$H(K, h, \theta_1, \theta_2, c, u) = \frac{L}{1 - \sigma}(c^{1-\sigma} - 1) + \theta_1(AK^{1-\alpha}(uLh)^\alpha h_a^\zeta - Lc)$$
$$+ \theta_2(\kappa h(1 - u)) \qquad (4.21)$$

The first-order conditions now are

$$\frac{\partial H}{\partial c} = 0 \Leftrightarrow c^{-\sigma} = \theta_1 \qquad (4.22)$$

$$\frac{\partial H}{\partial u} = 0 \Leftrightarrow \theta_2 \kappa h = \alpha u^{\alpha-1}\theta_1 AK^{(1-\alpha)}(Lh)^\alpha h_a^\zeta \qquad (4.23)$$

$$-\rho\theta_1 + \frac{\partial H}{\partial K} = -\dot{\theta}_1 \Leftrightarrow \dot{\theta}_1 = \rho\theta_1 - \theta_1(1 - \alpha)AK^{-\alpha}(uLh)^\alpha h_a^\zeta \qquad (4.24)$$

$$-\rho\theta_2 + \frac{\partial H}{\partial h} = -\dot{\theta}_2 \Leftrightarrow \dot{\theta}_2 = \rho\theta_2 - \theta_1\alpha AK^{1-\alpha}(uL)^\alpha h^{\alpha-1}h_a^\zeta - \theta_2\kappa(1 - u)$$
$$(4.25)$$

plus two transversality conditions:

$$\lim_{t \to 0} e^{-\rho t}\theta_1(t)K(t) = 0 \qquad (4.26)$$

$$\lim_{t \to 0} e^{-\rho t}\theta_2(t)h(t) = 0 \qquad (4.27)$$

We follow Benhabib and Perli (1994) to get the four-dimensional system in k, h, c, and u, which completely describes the economy, where $k = K/L$ and $c = C/L$.[7] $\dot{k}/k$ is obtained in a similar way as $\dot{K}/K$, and $\dot{c}/c$ is obtained as in the Uzawa-Lucas I model. To obtain $\dot{u}/u$, we solve the equation $\partial H/\partial u = 0$ with respect to θ_2, where we substitute for θ_1 from $\partial H/\partial c = 0$, take the logarithm, and differentiate it with respect to time. Further, we use the fact that in equilibrium $h_\alpha = h$ holds. We solve the resulting expression with respect to $\dot{\theta}_2/\theta_2$ and set it equal to (4.25) divided by θ_2, where we again use $\partial H/\partial u = 0$ to substitute for θ_1/θ_2. This, finally,

---

[6] For an explanation of these terms see chapter 3.
[7] For the derivation of those equations, see Benhabib and Perli (1994), pp. 117–119.

gives an equation for $\dot{u}/u$. The complete system of differential equations, then, is obtained as

$$\frac{\dot{k}}{k} = Ak^{-\alpha}h^{\alpha+\zeta}u^{\alpha} - \frac{c}{k} \tag{4.28}$$

$$\frac{\dot{h}}{h} = \kappa(1-u) \tag{4.29}$$

$$\frac{\dot{c}}{c} = \frac{A(1-\alpha)}{\sigma}k^{-\alpha}h^{\alpha+\zeta}u^{\alpha} - \frac{\rho}{\sigma} \tag{4.30}$$

$$\frac{\dot{u}}{u} = \frac{\kappa(1-\alpha-\zeta)}{1-\alpha}u + \frac{\kappa(\alpha+\zeta)}{1-\alpha} - \frac{c}{k} \tag{4.31}$$

The dynamic behavior of the Uzawa-Lucas II system has been studied intensively by Benhabib and Perli (1994). Therefore, we will only sketch the procedure. A BGP for the Uzawa-Lucas II model is defined as a set of functions of time $\{k(t), h(t), u(t), c(t)\}$ that solves the optimization problem of the household and where $k(t)$, $h(t)$, and $c(t)$ grow at a constant rate while $u(t)$ is constant. To analyze the model around a BGP, the following two variables are defined:

$$x \equiv kh^{-(\alpha+\zeta)/\alpha}, \quad q \equiv c/k$$

Differentiating x and q with respect to time and using the differential equation $\dot{u}$ gives an autonomous system of differential equations in x, q, and u, with a rest point of this system corresponding to a BGP of the Uzawa-Lucas II model. Benhabib and Perli (1994) give sufficient conditions for this model to be characterized by local indeterminacy for reasonable parameter values. From an economic point of view, local indeterminacy occurs if the subjective discount rate of the household is larger than κ, the parameter determining how strongly education affects the growth rate of human capital. In addition, the external effect of human capital in the production function of aggregate output must be greater than the share of capital, and the intertemporal elasticity of substitution of consumption must be sufficiently high. In addition, Benhabib and Perli (1994) demonstrate that both local and global indeterminacy may occur for reasonable parameter values if the labor supply is an endogenous variable.

In the following we will extend these two models to eliminate scale effects. As pointed out in chapter 2, some endogenous growth models contain scale effects implying that increases in the level of economic variables lead to a rise in the growth rate of GDP. A similar observation also holds for the Uzawa-Lucas model. In that model, if the time spent on education rises, the growth rate of human capital rises, too, and, thus, the balanced growth rate. Yet empirical evidence for advanced countries does not seem to support that effect.

Although those direct scale effects may hold for earlier stages of growth, those effects do not seem to hold for recent time series data in the United States and Germany.[8] In both countries the time spent on education rises, whereas the growth rate of human capital slightly declines over time. Therefore, estimating the equation $\dot{h}/h = \kappa(1 - u)$ yields a negative κ, which does not make sense because it would imply a negative marginal product of education in the process of generating human capital. This shows that the original Uzawa-Lucas model is not compatible with U.S. and German time series data. To take account of this fact, we modify our two versions of the Uzawa-Lucas model.

To eliminate the scale effects present in the Uzawa-Lucas model, we modify the equation describing the evolution of the stock of human capital. There are several ways to do this. We will consider two variants. First, we suppose that the equation $\dot{h}/h$ is given by

$$\frac{\dot{h}(t)}{h(t)} = h(t)^{p_1-1}\kappa(1 - u(t))^{p_2} - \delta_h, \tag{4.32}$$

with $p_1, p_2 \in (0, 1)$. This formulation implies that the higher the level of human capital, the more difficult it is to generate additional human capital. The same holds for the time spent on education. The more time already spent on education, the smaller the increase in the change of human capital as a result of more education. That is, we assume decreasing returns. Further, we also allow for depreciation of human capital.

Second, we consider a version in which the exogenous variable κ is a function depending on time. Thus, we also want to recognize that other variables, subsidies from the government for example, that are not explicitly taken into account may play a role in the process of generating human capital. In this case, the function $\dot{h}(t)/h(t)$ is written as

$$\frac{\dot{h}(t)}{h(t)} = h(t)^{p_1-1}\kappa(t)(1 - u(t))^{p_2} - \delta_h. \tag{4.33}$$

As in the original Solow growth model, we postulate here that there are additional exogenous factors affecting the economy. However, in contrast to Solow, these exogenous factors are not posited to influence the aggregate production function for final output but instead the

---

[8] As for the measurement of these variables, see section 4.4.

growth rate of human capital. We propose this as an alternative formulation of the Uzawa-Lucas I and II models because there are likely
to be, as cross-country studies have revealed, other forces affecting the
growth rate of effective human capital and, thus, the growth rate of the
economy.

Moreover, to be more realistic, we will also allow for depreciation of
physical capital with $\delta_K \in (0, 1)$ denoting the depreciation rate. But, of
course, this has nothing to do with the scale effects mentioned earlier.
Further, we take into account that the labor input is not constant but
may vary over time, which seems to be realistic. The growth rate of the
labor supply is denoted by n.

The Uzawa-Lucas I and the Uzawa-Lucas II models, which we call
the modified models, then, are obtained in analogy to the procedure
applied previously. We will undertake theoretical considerations for the
models with equation (4.32). The modified Uzawa-Lucas models with
equation (4.33) will be briefly discussed later. In particular, the modified Uzawa-Lucas I model can then be described by the following four
equations:

$$\frac{\dot{K}}{K} = A \left(\frac{1}{y}\right)^{-\alpha} (uL)^\alpha - Lzy - \delta_K \tag{4.34}$$

$$\frac{\dot{c}}{c} = \frac{-(\rho + \delta_K) + (1 - \alpha)A \left(\frac{1}{Y}\right)^{-\alpha} (uL)^\alpha}{\sigma} \tag{4.35}$$

$$\frac{\dot{h}}{h} = h^{p_1-1}\kappa(1 - u)^{p_2} - \delta_h \tag{4.36}$$

$$\frac{\dot{L}}{L} = n. \tag{4.37}$$

To derive the equations of the modified Uzawa-Lucas II model, we
proceed as in deriving equations (4.28)–(4.31). The only difference
now is that $\dot{h}/h$ is given by (4.32), which makes the derivation a
bit more tedious. Doing so, the modified Uzawa-Lucas II model is
given by:

$$\frac{\dot{k}}{k} = Ak^{-\alpha}h^{\alpha+\zeta}u^\alpha - \frac{c}{k} - n - \delta_K \tag{4.38}$$

$$\frac{\dot{h}}{h} = h^{p_1-1}\kappa(1 - u)^{p_2} - \delta_h \tag{4.39}$$

$$\frac{\dot{c}}{c} = \frac{A(1 - \alpha)}{\sigma}k^{-\alpha}h^{\alpha+\zeta}u^\alpha - \frac{\rho + \delta_K}{\sigma} \tag{4.40}$$

$$\frac{\dot{u}}{u} = \frac{\delta_K \alpha - \delta_h}{1 + (1 - \alpha) - p_2} + \frac{h^{p_1-1}\kappa(1-u)^{p_2-1}p_2 u}{1 + (1 - \alpha) - p_2} + \frac{\alpha n}{1 + (1 - \alpha) - p_2}$$

$$+ \frac{p_1 h^{p_1-1}\kappa(1-u)^{p_2}}{1 + (1 - \alpha) - p_2} + \frac{\alpha + \zeta - p_1}{1 + (1 - \alpha) - p_2}\left(h^{p_1-1}\kappa(1-u)^{p_2} - \delta_h\right)$$

$$- \frac{1 - \alpha}{1 + (1 - \alpha) - p_2}\left(\frac{c}{k}\right) \tag{4.41}$$

$$\frac{\dot{L}}{L} = n \tag{4.42}$$

Subsequently, we will estimate the modified systems Uzawa-Lucas I and Uzawa-Lucas II.

However, before we do so, we want to briefly address the question of what the BGP looks like in our modified systems. In this case, we define a BGP as a path on which the output-to-capital ratio, Y/K, is constant and all variables grow at constant but not necessarily equal growth rates, with the exception of u and $1 - u$, which are constant on a BGP. A constant output-to-capital ratio implies $\dot{Y}/Y = \dot{K}/K$ and, with $\dot{K} + \delta_K K = Y - cL$, a constant consumption-to-capital ratio, $C/K \equiv cL/K$. Thus, we can state that on a BGP the following equalities hold:

$$\frac{\dot{Y}}{Y} = \frac{\dot{K}}{K} = \frac{\dot{C}}{C} = \frac{\dot{c}}{c} + n.$$

Further, the requirement that the growth rates are constant implies that the time derivatives of the growth rates equal zero, that is, $d/dt\,(\dot{h}/h) = d/dt\,(\dot{K}/K) = 0$. Differentiating $\dot{h}/h$ with respect to time and setting the left-hand side equal to 0 gives

$$\frac{\dot{h}}{h} = \frac{p_2}{1 - p_1}\frac{d/dt\,(1 - u)}{1 - u} \equiv \frac{p_2}{1 - p_1}n_{1-u},$$

where we have defined $d/dt\,(1 - u)/(1 - u) \equiv n_{1-u}$. Doing the same for $\dot{K}/K$ yields

$$\frac{\dot{K}}{K} = \frac{p_2}{1 - p_1}n_{1-u} + n_u + n,$$

with $\dot{u}/u \equiv n_u$. Recalling that $n_{1-u} = n_u = 0$ holds on a BGP,[9] we can state that for the modified Uzawa-Lucas models a BGP is given by

$$\frac{\dot{Y}}{Y} - n = \frac{\dot{K}}{K} - n = \frac{\dot{c}}{c} = 0 = \frac{\dot{h}}{h} = n_{1-u} = n_u.$$

[9] For the Uzawa-Lucas II model with an endogenous u, it can be shown that $\dot{u}/u = constant$ implies $\dot{u} = 0$.

This shows that the growth rate of aggregate variables equals the growth rate of the labor supply, n, in the long run. Thus, following such a modification as proposed above implies that the modified Uzawa-Lucas system would not generate sustained per capita growth in the long run.[10] Consequently, the modified models would not be endogenous growth models any longer. Here, then, aggregate variables would grow at the same rate as the labor input, implying that per capita quantities remain constant. The reason for this outcome is that in the long run the time spent on the formation of human capital is constant, that is, $d/dt\,(1 - u) = 0$ holds, implying that the growth of human capital ceases, that is, $\dot{h} \rightarrow 0$. A constant amount of time spent on education cannot generate a positive growth rate of human capital in the long run, given the concavity of $\dot{h}$ in h. This concavity assumption implies that a higher level of human capital requires an increase in the time spent on education in order for the change of human capital to be positive. Only along the transition path, that is, as long as the time spent on the formation of human capital is not constant, is positive per capita growth predicted. As Jones (2002) has shown, such a model can display per capita growth rates only if the economy is out of steady state and the time spent on education grows at a positive rate.

If the equation describing the growth rate of human capital is given by (4.33), the function $\kappa(t)$ is crucial in determining whether the modified Uzawa-Lucas models can generate sustained per capita growth. For $p_1 < 1$, a rising stock of human capital reduces the growth rate of human capital, that is, lowers the left-hand side in (4.33). Since the time spent on education is constant in the long run, the exogenously given function $\kappa(t)$ must rise over time in order to compensate for the negative effect of a rising stock of human capital on the growth rate of human capital. Before we turn to the empirical estimation of our model variants, we want to briefly discuss proxies for human capital.

4.3 PROXIES FOR HUMAN CAPITAL IN EMPIRICAL STUDIES

Although most empirical cross-country studies show that human capital plays an important role in economic growth, at least in earlier stages, the measurement of human capital is not the same across different studies.

Generally, human capital comprises a person's stock of knowledge and abilities, the increase of which increases the productivity of the person. The stock of knowledge and the abilities of a person may be acquired by schooling, but they may also be acquired outside the formal education

---

[10] It should be noted that this holds independent of whether p_2 is smaller or equal to 1, provided that $p_1 < 1$.

system. For example, abilities may be increased by on-the-job training. Therefore, in a broad definition the measurement of human capital should cover formal and informal education, on-the-job-training, physical and mental fitness, nutrition, and social services affecting quality of work. Yet factors such as physical and mental health are not easy to measure. Instead, proxies for human capital are often constructed, which include variables such as enrollment rates or average years of schooling. Further, if one intends to test the Uzawa-Lucas model outlined above, only that type of human capital should be taken into account because in this model human capital is merely the result of time dedicated to the formation of knowledge or abilities. Other forms of human capital formation are not taken into account.

Nevertheless, there is no generally accepted way of correctly constructing the stock of human capital. One way of defining human capital per capita, h, is the following:[11]

$$h_t = \int_0^\infty \theta_t(s)\eta_t(s)ds$$

where $\eta_t(s)$ is the share of population, while s years of schooling and $\theta_t(s)$ are efficiency parameters. These efficiency parameters denote the mapping from a person's years of schooling s to his or her human capital. Mulligan and Sala-i-Martin (1993a) use the wage-schooling relationship in order to identify $\theta_t(s)$ up to a constant:

$$\frac{w_t(s)}{w_t(0)} = \frac{\theta_t(s)}{\theta_t(0)}.$$

In their study on the United States, they assume that $\theta_t(s)$ does not vary across states, so the efficiency parameters can be identified from the slope of the wage-schooling relationship of any particular state.

Barro and Lee (1993) and Psacharopoulos and Arriagada (1986) replace $\theta_t(s)$ with years of schooling s. They take the number of years of schooling as a proxy for human capital:

$$h_t = \int_0^\infty s\eta_t(s)ds.$$

But using years of schooling as a definition of human capital may be problematic. It is subject to errors in cross-country analysis because the number of days and hours of schooling per year can vary substantially

---

[11] The coefficients in this section are independent of those in other sections; they are not involved in any estimations.

across countries. Different educational systems are another reason why years of schooling may not be a good approximation for the stock of human capital. Another problem of measuring human capital in this way is that the true value of s is not known for those who completed only part of each schooling level. Dropouts and repeaters are not accounted for.[12]

Because of this argument, Nehru, Swanson, and Dubey (1995) define the stock of human capital H_{gt} as the sum of person-school years:

$$H_{gt} = \sum_g \sum_t s_{gt}$$

where s_{gt} is the addition to the stock of human capital as a result of one year of education in grade g at year t. s_{gt} is measured as the enrollment rate in grade g at time t without dropouts and repeaters.

It should also be mentioned that the data collection for different countries poses some problems because data sets are often not available or are incomplete. Another difficulty is that reports on schooling data tend to become more accurate with economic development. It is easier to find data sets for industrialized countries than for developing countries. A weakness of all of the above-mentioned constructions of human capital is that they do not measure the quality of education, and this makes intertemporal as well as cross-country comparisons difficult to interpret.

As for the quality of schooling, several measures are conceivable:[13] private school attendance, teacher salaries, expenditures per pupil, or teachers per pupil. In general, all of these variables positively affect the quality of education and, thus, the formation of human capital. For example, in private schools the standards may be higher than in public schools, which has a positive effect on education. A similar argument holds for the salaries of teachers. Poorly paid teachers lack motivation, which may have negative repercussions for instruction at schools and, as a result, for human capital formation. Therefore, human capital could plausibly be approximated using expenditures for education.

All these measures have in common that they are so-called input-based indexes that approximate human capital by looking at the input in a person's abilities. Besides these input-based measures there are also output-based proxies for human capital.

One attempt to construct an index was made by Hanushek and Kimko (2000), who approximate human capital by the results of internationally comparable mathematics and science test scores and by measures of

---

[12] The update of educational attainment in Barro and Lee (2000) takes into account repeaters. The data, however, are available only for five-year intervals.

[13] See Mulligan and Sala-i-Martin (1993a); Nehru, Swanson, and Dubey (1995).

average years of schooling. The tests were taken at different points in time, and each test had a different number of countries participating. The tests were designed in such a way that they allow comparisons between different countries. But the tests changed over time, so they were not comparable across time.

Another way of measuring human capital by an output-based index is to compute labor income as a function of years of schooling.[14] Labor income l_t is defined as the sum of the earnings of all residents:

$$l_t = \int_0^\infty w_t(s)u_t(s)\eta_t(s)ds,$$

where the participation rate $u_t(s)$ is the ratio of employed persons with s years of schooling to total population with s years of schooling. w_t is again the wage rate depending on years of education, and η, as earlier, the share of population with s years of schooling.

To summarize, there are basically two measurement approaches: On the one hand, human capital can be approximated by input-based measures relying on educational data such as enrollment rates and years of schooling or expenditures for education; on the other hand, human capital can be approximated through output-based measures such as wages or tests.[15]

4.4 MEASURING THE VARIABLES

To estimate the Uzawa-Lucas model, we need data for the capital stocks h and K as well as data for aggregate consumption and labor input, C, L. Further, the model needs an approximation for the time spent to build up human capital, $(1 - u)$.

The human capital stock and the physical capital stock are computed according to the perpetual inventory method with a constant depreciation rate, following the procedure introduced in chapter 3. For the physical capital stock we use investment data, and to approximate human capital we use total government and private educational expenditures instead of enrollment rates or schooling years (for details see the appendix to this chapter). The advantage of our approach is that we do not need to deal with differences of educational systems and we do not need to convert years of schooling into capital. Further, the data are available for all countries.

[14] See also Jorgenson, Gollop, and Fraumeni (1987).

[15] Strictly speaking, the indexes by Mulligan and Sala-i-Martin (1993a) and Jorgenson, Gollop, and Fraumeni (1987) are both input- and output-based, combining both approaches.

TABLE 4.1
Data Sets

Variables	United States	Germany
C	private consumption	
K	accumulated gross fixed capital formation	
h	accumulated educational expenditures per capita	
1 − u	weighted shares of university degrees per employee	
L	total employees	

In constructing the series for $(1 - u)$, we had to make a compromise. Though we know that the time devoted to human capital accumulation includes many years of schooling, training on the job, and so forth, we use only earned university degrees as a fraction of total employment. The reason for this decision is that university degrees are comparable from country to country, whereas less advanced degrees are very different. Further, by using university degrees we get persons who spent time on education instead of going to work. Taking university degrees instead of students implies that we are getting at effective education; that is, we neglect those who do not complete their studies. Setting university degrees in relation to employees gives a ratio that can serve as a proxy for the share of time spent on education. Therefore, we define $(1 - u)$ as follows:

$$1 - u = \frac{\text{university degrees}}{\text{employees}} \cdot s$$

with $s = 6$ as approximate time at university.[16]

Table 4.1 presents a survey of how we construct the data sets.

The data for consumption, investment, and total employees for the United States and Germany are from OECD (1998, 1999). The data for consumption, investment, and labor were available quarterly. The data for educational expenditure and university degrees were available only annually. In this case, quarterly data were constructed by linear interpolation. The data for educational expenditure and university degrees are from National Science Foundation (2000) and Office for National Statistics (1965–1998) for the United States, and from Statistisches Bundesamt (1977, 1991–1996) for Germany. All data are real data.

[16] University degrees include diplomas and doctoral degrees.

TABLE 4.2
Estimation of the Uzawa-Lucas I Model

	United States	Germany
Parameters for Matching $(K_t - K_{t-1})/K_{t-1}$		
α	0.5583 (0.1312)	0.5698 (0.2433)
A	0.0591 (0.0056)	0.0550 (0.0031)
ρ_k	0.9799 (0.0166)	0.9878 (0.0125)
DW statistics	0.3420	0.4173
Parameters for Matching $(C_t - C_{t-1})/C_{t-1}$		
ρ	0.0210 (0.0087)	0.0105 (0.0018)
σ	1.0905 (1.0502)	0.4538 (0.2249)
ρ_c	0.8253 (0.0477)	0.6632 (0.0744)
DW statistics	1.7990	2.1488
Parameters for Matching $(h_t - h_{t-1})/h_{t-1}$		
κ	0.0432 (0.0432)	0.0757 (0.0547)
p_1	0.2945 (0.4490)	−0.0619 (0.6058)
p_2	0.1908 (0.4181)	0.0610 (0.1584)
ρ_h	0.8988 (0.0371)	0.9576 (0.0173)
DW statistics	1.2626	0.9295

4.5 ESTIMATION OF THE MODEL FOR THE UNITED STATES AND GERMANY

We estimate equations (4.34) to (4.36) and (4.38) to (4.41) using quarterly data for the modified Uzawa-Lucas I and II versions. Further, we replace (4.32) with equation (4.33) and reestimate the modified Uzawa-Lucas I model. (For discussion of the estimation strategy, see the appendix to this chapter.) For the United States we examine the period from 1962.1 to 1996.4 and for Germany the period from 1962.1 to 1991.4.[17] The parameters to be estimated then are $(\alpha, A, \rho, \sigma, \kappa, p_1, p_2, \delta_h)$. Tables 4.2 and 4.3 present the obtained estimation results (standard errors in parentheses), and figures 4.1 and 4.2 provide the match of predicted and observed time series for the growth rates of K, C, and h.

It should be noted that all the estimations are corrected for the first-order autocorrelation disturbance term, with the parameters given by ρ_K, ρ_C, and ρ_h. (For details, see the appendix to this chapter.)

[17] Data are for West Germany only.

TABLE 4.3
Estimation of the Uzawa-Lucas I Model with a Time-Varying κ

Parameters for Matching $(h_t - h_{t-1})/h_{t-1}$	United States	Germany
κ_0	6.8797 (1.9341)	0.1008 (0.0372)
p_1	0.1115 (0.0204)	0.3282 (0.1830)
p_2	0.9895 (0.2150)	0.1272 (0.0775)
p_h	0.9938 (0.0006)	0.9272 (0.0344)
DW statistics	1.7711	1.2564

Most parameters are statistically significant except those appearing in the equation describing the evolution of human capital, $(h_t - h_{t-1})/h_{t-1}$. The Durbin-Watson (DW) statistics for matching $(K_t - K_{t-1})/K_{t-1}$ suggest that the residuals are serially correlated. This is due to the fact that the growth rate of the capital stock is quite smooth, which makes the estimated residuals autocorrelated even if the data series are closely matched by the estimation (see panel A in figures 4.1 and 4.2). As concerns the parameters of the production function for human capital, we see that the parameters are not statistically significant. Further, p_2 is very low, especially for Germany. This results from the fact that the time series of $1 - u$ and $\dot{h}/h$ are inversely related. κ is also very small but positive. As mentioned earlier, setting p_1 and p_2 equal to 1, as in the original version of the Uzawa-Lucas model, would imply a negative κ, which would not make sense economically. Thus, the Uzawa-Lucas model is compatible with U.S. and German time series only after eliminating the direct scale effects. In our variants this was done by introducing the parameters p_1 and p_2. Next we shall consider the estimation with a time-varying κ to get better results in matching $(h_t - h_{t-1})/h_{t-1}$.

For the time-varying κ, denoted as κ_t, we assume the following function for the United States:

$$\kappa_t = \frac{\kappa_0}{v_t^{p_2}} \tag{4.43}$$

where

$$v_t = \begin{cases} 1 & t \leq 60 \\ 1 + 0.1(t - 60) & \text{otherwise} \end{cases} \tag{4.44}$$

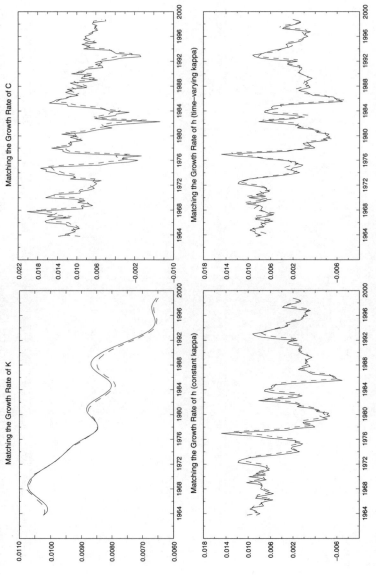

Figure 4.1. Observed (solid line) and predicted (dashed line) series, Uzawa-Lucas I model, U.S. economy.

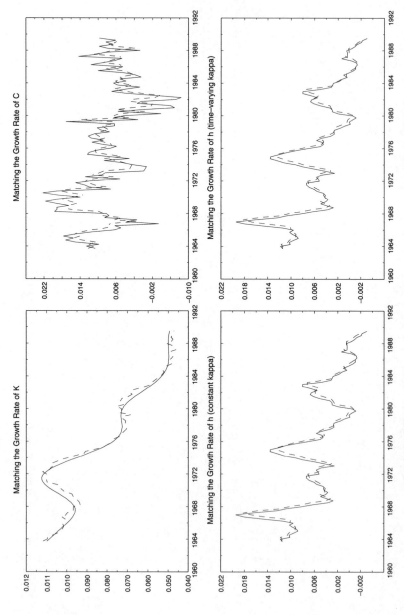

Figure 4.2. Observed (solid line) and predicted (dashed line) series, Uzawa-Lucas I model, German economy.

For Germany we use

$$v_t = \begin{cases} 1 & t \le 80 \\ 1 + 0.1(t - 80) & \text{otherwise} \end{cases} \qquad (4.45)$$

The function v_t does not have the same functional form over the whole period under consideration because we find that after 60 periods, approximately 1976, there is a significant change in trend with regard to $1 - u$ according to our observation for the U.S. economy. This seems to indicate a structural change at that time with regard to u. A similar structural change also occurred in the German economy, in this case after 80 periods, approximately 1983. Therefore, instead of (4.44), we use (4.45) for Germany.

Given this time-varying κ, the estimated parameters for matching $(h_t - h_{t-1})/h_{t-1}$ are as reported in table 4.3. The corresponding graphs are shown in panel C of figures 4.1 and 4.2.

One realizes that the estimation of the human capital equation becomes better when the parameter κ is time dependent. Now, with the exception of p_1 for Germany, all coefficients are statistically significant, and the Durbin-Watson statistics indicate that there is no significant serial correlation in the residuals for the United States and the correlation becomes smaller for Germany. Overall, the estimations of the Uzawa-Lucas I model are reasonable, although we neglect the external effect of human capital and the endogeneity of the second control variable, u. The capital shares in the United States and Germany are significant and about 44 percent, which is a reasonable value. The same holds for the rates of time preference, which are about 8 percent for the United States when considered for one year and 4 percent for Germany. The estimated coefficient for the inverse of the intertemporal elasticity of substitution of consumption for the United States is reasonable, whereas the value for Germany seems a bit low, implying that the intertemporal elasticity of substitution is very high.[18] Next, we will estimate the Uzawa-Lucas II model.

The difference between the Uzawa-Lucas I and the Uzawa-Lucas II models is the presence of the external effect of human capital, ζ in (4.6), and equation (4.41), which gives the growth rate of the time spent on education. It is this latter additional equation that makes this extended version significantly more complicated. The estimation of the Uzawa-Lucas II model yields the results as expressed in table 4.4. (The estimation procedure, again, is provided in the appendix to this chapter.)

---

[18] Note that an equation such as (4.35) or (4.40), the continuous time form of the Euler equation, from which we obtain the estimation of the two preference parameters, has been frequently estimated in the finance literature. Yet the results have always been ambiguous (Campbell, Lo, and MacKinley 1997, chapter 8).

TABLE 4.4
Estimation of the Uzawa-Lucas II Model

	United States	Germany
Parameters for Matching $(k_t - k_{t-1})/k_{t-1}$		
α	0.4560 (0.1289)	0.5192 (0.3569)
A	0.0637 (0.0062)	0.0539 (0.0010)
ζ	−0.0066 (0.0681)	0.0081 (0.2850)
ρ_k	0.7123 (0.0582)	0.8518 (0.0516)
DW statistics	1.9411	1.9164
Parameters for Matching $(c_t - c_{t-1})/c_{t-1}$		
ρ	0.0337 (0.0042)	0.0134 (0.0008)
σ	1.5465 (1.1702)	0.4032 (0.1029)
ρ_c	0.7385 (0.0566)	0.5265 (0.0839)
DW statistics	1.8494	2.0273
Parameters for Matching $(h_t - h_{t-1})/h_{t-1}$ *and* $(u_t - u_{t-1})/u_{t-1}$		
κ	0.0738 (0.0030)	0.0608 (0.0070)
p_1	0.3295 (0.0729)	0.4300 (0.1060)
p_2	0.1341 (0.0119)	0.0155 (0.0032)
ρ_h	0.9517 (0.4975)	0.9936 (0.0655)
ρ_u	0.9369 (0.0175)	0.9712 (0.0037)
DW from matching $(h_t - h_{t-1})/h_{t-1}$	1.2858	0.9199
DW from matching $(u_t - u_{t-1})/u_{t-1}$	0.1696	0.2811

Note that ρ_K, ρ_c, ρ_u, and ρ_h are again the coefficients in the AR(1) process of the disturbance terms in the corresponding estimated equation. The parameter values α, ρ, and σ of the second estimation are very similar to the results of the Uzawa-Lucas I model. So the capital share, the rate of time preference, and the inverse of the intertemporal elasticity of substitution (for Germany) still take values that are generally considered plausible. For the U.S. economy, however, the capital share $1-\alpha$ becomes large. As for the externality effect of human capital, ζ, this parameter is close to zero and not statistically significant either for the United States or for Germany. Thus, this model does not allow us to conclude that human capital is associated with positive externalities.

Figures 4.3 and 4.4 present the match of predicted series and observed series for the U.S. and Germany economies, respectively.

In summary, although we have obtained reasonable parameter values, the preference or technology parameters are of course sensitive to the model specification and sensitive to the empirical measurement of the variables involved. Moreover, there might be variables missing, such as

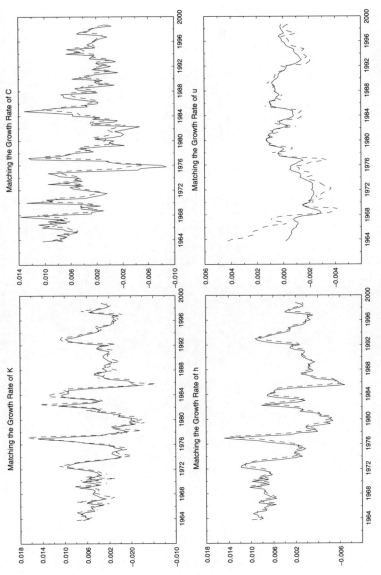

Figure 4.3. Observed (solid line) and predicted (dashed line) series, Uzawa-Lucas II model, U.S. economy.

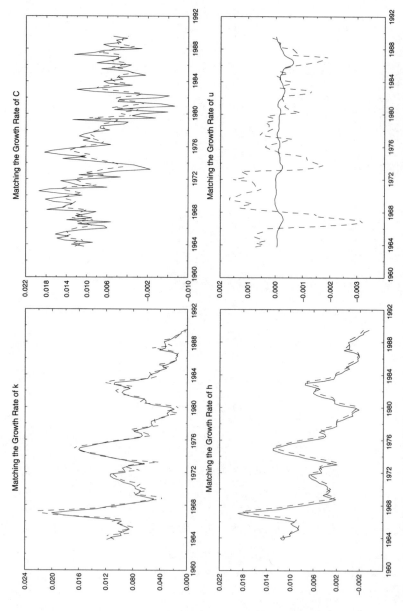

Figure 4.4. Observed (solid line) and predicted (dashed line) series, Uzawa-Lucas II model, German economy.

R&D spending, public investment in infrastructure, openness of the economy, efficiency of the financial sector, political stability, and so on. As we have seen in the cross-country studies, there are numerous variables posited to affect economic growth. The impact of some of those variables on economic growth, which may change over time, is captured by our assumption that κ depends on time, which in fact gave better estimation results.

4.6 CONCLUSION

This chapter has presented an empirical estimation of the Uzawa-Lucas model. The advantage of this model, compared to the model in chapter 3, is that it explicitly takes into account that the education and formation of human capital needs resources (time) in order to be effective, whereas in chapter 3 knowledge was a simple by-product of physical capital formation. Although the prior model is relevant for certain stages of growth, it fails to shed light on the process of generating knowledge or human capital that fosters economic growth.

Looking at the time series of the growth rate of human capital and at the time series of education showed that these two series are inversely related; that is, the growth rate of human capital slightly declines while education rises. To take account of this phenomenon we have modified the production function for human capital. In a first step we posited that the growth rate of human capital negatively depends on the level of human capital, which can be justified by referring to satiation, and that there are decreasing returns to education at a later stage of economic growth. The estimation of the so-modified Uzawa-Lucas model demonstrates that it is compatible with the time series of the U.S. and German economies. After the introduction of those nonlinearities, most of the structural parameters take values that are generally accepted as plausible in the economics literature.

In a second step, the major modification of the original Uzawa-Lucas model was the assumption of an exogenous time trend that is negatively correlated with the growth rate of human capital. This can be justified by variables affecting the growth rate of human capital but which are not explicitly accounted for in our model. The estimation of this modified Uzawa-Lucas model produced statistically significant coefficients for the production function of human capital with the parameters of the other equations left unchanged. This version, then, would imply that the effect of spending time on education on the growth rate of human capital is also affected by other forces and that their impact has changed over time.

We also point out that the modified models fit the time series of both the United States and Germany. However, the estimations demonstrate that the coefficients obtained are different in the two countries. The modification of the Uzawa-Lucas model, however, also has consequences for the analytical model. In the case of an exogenously given time trend, the form of this function is of crucial importance for whether long-run per capita growth can be observed or not. If this function is constant in the long run, the emergence of positive per capita growth depends on the other parameters of the function in the model.

From a theoretical point of view, the first modification without an exogenous time trend is more appealing because in this case the outcome does not depend on exogenous factors. But our modification has important consequences. It implies that the model does not generate endogenous growth at the steady state any longer but becomes an exogenous growth model with the long-run per capita growth rate equal to zero, unless exogenous variables have a stimulating growth effect. Consequently, positive per capita growth can only be observed along the transition path to the long-run steady state, which may of course take a long time to be reached. It may be correct that the economies can be viewed as still on the transition path if one resorts to the Uzawa-Lucas model in order to describe these economies. This may hold true because the education effort on those countries is rising over the time period we are considering. However, this also implies that per capita growth may cease if the economies reach a point where the time spent on education reaches a constant value.

Therefore, our first modification implies that in the long run, economies reach a situation without positive per capita growth, at least if one employs the modified Uzawa-Lucas model and if one does not rely on exogenous factors to eliminate the scale effects. But, recalling chapter 2, this is in contrast to the stylized fact of sustained growth in advanced countries. It can be concluded that the Uzawa-Lucas model may be a good approximation for economies over a certain time period during which education increases, and that there are linear effects of educational effort on growth, or that the economies are on the transition path to the long-run steady state. Although it is in general true that the time spent on education cannot grow without an upper bound, advanced economies, such as the United States and Germany, may still be far away from such a bound.

On the other hand, as stressed above, the Uzawa-Lucas versions I and II are still somewhat incomplete. This fact is well captured by the significant parameters of our function representing the exogenous time trend. In fact, it would be too ambitious a research project to expect the complex problem of economic growth to be reduced to a small-scale model with two state variables only. As we discussed in chapter 1, other forces of economic growth may be relevant too. These will be studied in the next two chapters.

APPENDIX: ESTIMATION PROCEDURE OF THE UZAWA-LUCAS MODEL

1. Data Construction and Preliminary Estimation

To estimate the model, we first have to construct the data series K and H, where H is our measure for human capital, $H = hL$. We compute these data series from the expenditure flows by using the perpetual inventory method. Specifically,

$$K(t+1) = (1 - \delta_K)K(t) + I(t)$$
$$H(t+1) = (1 - \delta_H)H(t) + E(t)^{\mu_H}$$

where I is aggregate investment in physical capital and $E(t)$ is education expenditure. It should be noted that we have raised $E(t)$ to the power of μ_h. This is more general than setting the power equal to 1. Clearly, to construct these data series, we need to specify the parameters δ_K, δ_H, and μ_H. We set these parameters equal to the following values:

United States	Germany
$\delta_K = 0.01$	$\delta_K = 0.01$
$\delta_H = 0.024$	$\delta_H = 0.02$
$\mu_H = 0.63$	$\mu_H = 0.16$

Setting δ_K to 0.01 (recall that we use quarterly data) has been done frequently in the real business cycle literature.[19] The other parameters, δ_H and μ_H, are chosen based on our preliminary estimation to match the growth rates of K and c, whose moment restrictions are expressed as

$$\frac{K_t - K_{t-1}}{K_{t-1}} = A \left(\frac{1}{y_{t-1}} \right)^{-\alpha} (u_{t-1}L_{t-1})^\alpha - L_{t-1}x_{t-1}y_{t-1} - \delta_K + w_{k,t}$$

$$(4.46)$$

$$\frac{c_t - c_{t-1}}{c_{t-1}} = -\frac{\rho + \delta_K}{\sigma} + \frac{(1 - \alpha)}{\sigma} A \left(\frac{1}{y_{t-1}} \right)^{-\alpha} (u_{t-1}L_{t-1})^\alpha + w_{c,t}$$

$$(4.47)$$

[19] A quarterly depreciation rate of physical capital between 0.01 and 0.025 is generally considered plausible.

We assume that $w_{k,t}$ and $w_{c,t}$ follow the $AR(1)$ processes:

$$w_{k,t} = \rho_k w_{k,t-1} + \varepsilon_{k,t} \tag{4.48}$$

$$w_{c,t} = \rho_c w_{c,t-1} + \varepsilon_{c,t} \tag{4.49}$$

where $\varepsilon_{k,t}$ and $\varepsilon_{c,t}$ are both assumed to be *i.i.d.* For this preliminary estimation, we prespecify α, ρ, and σ at 0.6, 0.01, and 2, respectively, which we believe to be reasonable. A is an additional parameter to be estimated along with the parameters δ_H and μ_H. The estimation method is the generalized method of moments (GMM) with the correction for autocorrelation disturbance, and the optimization algorithm used is simulated annealing (see the technical appendix at the end of the book). Since this preliminary estimation is only for constructing the data series h, we do not report the standard deviations.

2. Estimating the Uzawa-Lucas I Model

Given the constructed data K and H, along with the observations of L, c, and u, we are now able to estimate the parameters α, A, ρ, σ, κ, p_1, p_2, and δ_H as defined in the Uzawa-Lucas I model. We estimate these parameters by matching equations (4.46), (4.47), and

$$\frac{h_t - h_{t-1}}{h_{t-1}} = \kappa(1 - u_{t-1})^{p_2} h_{t-1}^{p_1-1} - \delta_H + w_{h,t} \tag{4.50}$$

$$\frac{h_t - h_{t-1}}{h_{t-1}} = \kappa(t)(1 - u_{t-1})^{p_2} h_{t-1}^{p_1-1} - \delta_H + w_{h\kappa,t} \tag{4.51}$$

respectively.

It should be noted that α and A appear in both (4.46) and (4.47), while ρ and σ appear only in (4.47), and κ, p_1, p_2, and δ_h only in (4.50) and (4.51), respectively. Therefore, our estimation strategy is as follows. We first estimate α and A by matching both (4.46) and (4.47) simultaneously. The estimation method is again GMM. In this estimation, we set ρ and σ again equal to 0.01 and 2, respectively. Given the estimated parameters α and A, we then estimate ρ and σ by matching (4.47) only. Since this is a single equation estimation, we now use the method of nonlinear least square estimation (NLLS). The rest of the parameters are estimated by matching (4.50) and (4.51), respectively. Again we use the NLLS method, resorting to the Newton-Raphson algorithm as optimization algorithm. The estimation results are reported in section 4.5.

3. The Uzawa-Lucas II Model

The data were constructed as for the modified Uzawa-Lucas I model. In addition to the parameters that appear in the modified Uzawa-Lucas I model, we now have the parameter ζ that needs to be estimated. We estimate these parameters by matching the following equations:

$$\frac{k_t - k_{t-1}}{k_{t-1}} = A\left(\frac{h_{t-1}u_{t-1}}{k_{t-1}}\right)^\alpha h_{t-3}^\zeta - \frac{c_{t-1}}{k_{t-1}} - n - \delta_K + w_{k,t} \tag{4.52}$$

$$\frac{c_t - c_{t-1}}{c_{t-1}} = -\frac{\rho + \delta_K}{\sigma} + \left(\frac{1-\alpha}{\sigma}\right) A\left(\frac{h_{t-1}u_{t-1}}{k_{t-1}}\right)^\alpha h_{t-3}^\zeta + w_{c,t} \tag{4.53}$$

$$\frac{h_t - h_{t-1}}{h_{t-1}} = \kappa(1 - u_{t-1})^{p_2} h_{t-1}^{p_1-1} - \delta_H + w_{h,t} \tag{4.54}$$

$$\frac{u_t - u_{t-1}}{u_{t-1}} = \frac{\delta_K \alpha - \delta_h}{1 + (1 - \alpha) - p_2} + \frac{h_{t-1}^{p_1-1}\kappa(1 - u_{t-1})^{p_2-1}p_2 u_{t-1}}{1 + (1 - \alpha) - p_2}$$

$$+ \frac{\alpha n}{1 + (1 - \alpha) - p_2} + \frac{p_1 h_{t-1}^{p_1-1}\kappa(1 - u_{t-1})^{p_2}}{1 + (1 - \alpha) - p_2}$$

$$+ \frac{\alpha + \zeta - p_1}{1 + (1 - \alpha) - p_2}\left(h_{t-1}^{p_1-1}\kappa(1 - u_{t-1})^{p_2} - \delta_h\right)$$

$$- \frac{1-\alpha}{1 + (1 - \alpha) - p_2}\left(\frac{c_{t-1}}{k_{t-1}}\right) + w_{u,t} \tag{4.55}$$

Again, we assume that $w_{k,t}$, $w_{c,t}$, $w_{h,t}$, and $w_{u,t}$ follow an AR(1) processes:

$$w_{k,t} = \rho_k w_{k,t-1} + \varepsilon_{k,t} \tag{4.56}$$

$$w_{c,t} = \rho_c w_{c,t-1} + \varepsilon_{c,t} \tag{4.57}$$

$$w_{h,t} = \rho_h w_{h,t-1} + \varepsilon_{h,t} \tag{4.58}$$

$$w_{u,t} = \rho_u w_{u,t-1} + \varepsilon_{u,t} \tag{4.59}$$

where $\varepsilon_{i,t}$, $i = k, c, h, u$ are assumed to be *i.i.d.*

Note that we assume the external effect on the economy to be delayed by three periods. We make this assumption because spillovers or the diffusion of human capital need time to become effective. The estimation strategy is quite similar to the estimation of Uzawa-Lucas model I. Specifically, we first estimate α, ζ, and A by matching $(k_t - k_{t-1})/k_{t-1}$ and $(c_t - c_{t-1})/c_{t-1}$ simultaneously, where n is set to its sample mean. The method is again GMM with a correction of the autocorrelation disturbance. Given α, ζ, and A as estimated, we then estimate ρ and σ by matching $(c_t - c_{t-1})/c_{t-1}$ only. Since this estimation is based on a single equation, we use the NLLS method with the correction for the first-order autocorrelation disturbance. The parameters κ, p_1, and p_2 are estimated by matching $(h_t - h_{t-1})/h_{t-1}$ and $(u_t - u_{t-1})/u_{t-1}$ simultaneously. For this estimation, we use the method of GMM again with the correction of the autocorrelation disturbance. For the GMM estimation, we use simulated annealing as an optimization algorithm, whereas for a single equation NLLS estimation, we use the Newton-Raphson algorithm.

CHAPTER 5

Knowledge Accumulation and Economic Growth

5.1 INTRODUCTION

While the Uzawa-Lucas model stresses the importance of the creation of human capital in promoting economic growth, Romer (1990), Grossmann and Helpman (1991), and Aghion and Howitt (1992) have developed an R&D model in which the accumulation of knowledge (stock of design or ideas) is the most important source of economic growth.

The difference between human capital, as in the Uzawa-Lucas model, and the stock of knowledge, as in the Romer (1990) model, is that human capital represents skills embodied in a person, whereas the stock of knowledge is a good that may not be embodied in a person. Use of human capital, therefore, is rivalrous in the sense that it is not available for several activities at the same time. Knowledge, however, is a nonrivalrous good that can be used for several different purposes simultaneously. This is true because knowledge is stored in books, journals, software, and so on, and is available to any individual in an economy. Although patents regulate the economic use of innovations, they cannot prevent the diffusion of new knowledge. Further, knowledge is only in part an excludable good, since knowledge, as a stock of ideas, is accessible to others. In addition, employees changing their jobs contribute to the diffusion of knowledge over time. So individuals or firms who do not finance new knowledge nevertheless benefit from it, although not necessarily immediately after an invention or discovery is made. There are positive spillovers of knowledge and there exists the free-rider problem.

The existence of international spillovers of R&D that generates new knowledge has been confirmed in an empirical study by Coe and Helpman (1995). They use a panel of twentytwo countries over the period 1971 to 1990 and analyze the impact of cumulated R&D on the total factor productivity of a country. They find that foreign R&D shows positive effects on domestic productivity that are greater the more open the economy is. In addition, returns to R&D are very high in domestic output and they generate international spillovers.

We already have seen that the original Lucas (1988) model implies that changes in the level of a variable will show strong and lasting effects on the growth rate. A similar feature can be found in the Romer model

(1990), which takes labor input and human capital as fixed; the growth rate monotonically increases with human capital employed in the production of knowledge. This phenomenon, which is also characteristic of the models created by Grossmann and Helpman (1991) and Aghion and Howitt (1998), has been criticized as unreasonable from a theoretical point of view and has been empirically contested by Jones (1995a, 1995b, 1997).

Like the model with human capital treated in the previous chapter, the R&D model of growth is modified in the present chapter by changing the production function of knowledge capital (designs) and by estimating the model with U.S. and German time series data. Here, too, in order to match the model with the data of advanced countries we have to introduce nonlinearities. In contrast to other empirical work, we neither solely estimate the predictions of the model nor calibrate it using empirical data. Rather, we try to directly estimate the implied parameters of the model by applying econometric techniques to the nonlinear variant. To our knowledge, this has not previously been undertaken for the R&D model.

5.2 Stylized Facts on R&D and Economic Growth

As with the original Romer (1990) growth model, writing the production function for the stock of knowledge (or designs)

$$\dot{A} = \mu H_A A$$

predicts that the growth rate, $\dot{A}/A$, will depend linearly on the human capital stock (highly qualified labor) in the research sector, H_A. $\mu > 0$ is a constant parameter. This equation shows that an increase in the human capital employed in the research sector causes the growth rate of knowledge to rise proportionally. This in turn has a positive effect on the growth rate of output.

Further, assuming a constant labor supply, the balanced growth rate (in the competitive economy) is obtained as

$$g^{\star} = \frac{\theta \mu H - \rho}{\theta + \sigma},$$

where H is the total stock of human capital in the economy, θ is a constant parameter that is completely determined by the coefficients in the production function of the final goods production, and ρ is the subjective discount rate.

The balanced growth rate is predicted to rise with the total stock of human capital, H, and predicted to fall with ρ.[1] Although the scale effects of H on g^* have been used extensively in trade theory (see Rivera-Batiz and Romer 1991), those direct scale effects do not appear reasonable.

Looking at actual economies, those scale effects are indeed questionable. Table 2.1 shows that in the United States, for example, the fraction of the labor force engaged in R&D increased significantly from 1950 to 1995. If we resort to the Romer (1990) model as an explanation for the growth process in market economies, this trend implies an increase in the growth rate, too, which is not what happened. One way to reconcile the Romer model with that fact is to assume that the positive impact of level variables on the growth rate is weakened by other factors, for example, higher tax rates, that lead to less economic growth.

It is also feasible that the technological opportunities have decreased over time because the most obvious ideas are discovered first, such that it becomes more and more difficult to innovate. This possibility is presented in a formal model by Segerstrom (1998). Another way of interpreting the stylized fact is that there have been regime shifts in the growth path, perhaps due to a regime change of the structural parameters (preference and technology parameters), for example. Parameter changes may have caused the growth rate to decrease, while H or H_A may have positively affected the growth rate.

5.3 THE R&D MODEL

In this section, we first derive the equations of the modified Romer (1990) model that we will use to get an estimable endogenous growth model.

To do so, we consider the competitive economy of the Romer (1990) model (see Benhabib, Perli, and Xie 1994). This economy is composed of three sectors. First, a research sector produces new knowledge (or designs), A, with human capital, H, and knowledge as input factors. This sector behaves competitively. The stock of knowledge, A, is a nonrivalrous good, implying that it can be used simultaneously in several economic activities. Knowledge is independent of any product or person, unlike human capital. So it can be copied and used in several activities at the same time.

Second, the intermediate sector uses knowledge produced by the research sector as an input factor and produces intermediate goods, x,

---

[1] For details of the steady-state properties and transitional dynamics of the competitive economy of the R&D model of growth, see Benhabib, Perli, and Xie (1994). The dynamics of the social optimum have been analyzed in Asada, Semmler, and Novak (1998).

which are used as input factors by, third, the final-good sector. The firms of the intermediate sector cannot be perfect competitors but must have some market power since they use the nonrivalrous factor knowledge as input. The final-good sector employs these intermediate goods together with labor, L, and human capital, H, as input factors and produces the final good that can be consumed or invested.

The production function for final output is given by

$$Y = (H - H_A)^\alpha L^\beta \int_0^A x(i)^{1-\alpha-\beta} di,$$

where $H_Y = H - H_A$ is highly qualified labor (human capital) employed in the production of the final good and L is unqualified labor. H is total human capital in the economy, and H_A denotes human capital employed in the research sector. $(1 - \alpha) \in (0, 1)$ denotes the capital share. This production function implies that the marginal product of each capital good, $x(i)$, is the same, such that each capital good is employed in the same amount. This property is called the symmetry of the capital goods. Since each capital good is employed in the same amount in this model, the total stock of physical capital can be written as $K = \eta A x$, with η the amount of forgone consumption necessary to produce one unit of the intermediate good. The aggregate production function then is given by

$$Y = \eta^{\alpha+\beta-1} A^{\alpha+\beta} (H - H_A)^\alpha L^\beta K^{1-\alpha-\beta} \equiv \bar\eta A^{\alpha+\beta} (H - H_A)^\alpha L^\beta K^{1-\alpha-\beta},$$

$$(5.1)$$

with $\bar\eta = \eta^{\alpha+\beta-1}$.

The firms in the final good sector behave competitively. The solution to their optimization problem gives the inverse demand function for the intermediate good $x(i)$, with i standing for firm i, as

$$p(i) = (1 - \alpha - \beta)(H - H_A)^\alpha L^\beta x(i)^{-\alpha-\beta}. \qquad (5.2)$$

In order to produce $x(i)$, the intermediate firm first must purchase knowledge or a design that constitutes a fixed cost investment for it. The intermediate firm takes the function $p(i)$ as given in solving its optimization problem. The latter is given by

$$\max_{x(i)} \left((1 - \alpha - \beta)(H - H_A)^\alpha L^\beta x(i)^{1-\alpha-\beta} - r\eta x(i) \right), \qquad (5.3)$$

with r denoting the interest rate, which is composed of the net interest rate and the depreciation rate. That is, we assume that capital is subject to depreciation that raises the cost of the intermediate sector. The cost of the intermediate sector is the cost on the ηx units of final output that are needed to produce x durables. The solution to this problem yields the interest rate as

$$r = \bar{\eta}(1 - \alpha - \beta)^2 (H - H_A)^\alpha A^{\alpha+\beta} L^\beta K^{-\alpha-\beta}. \tag{5.4}$$

It should be noted that $p(i) = (\eta/(1 - \alpha - \beta))r$ holds, demonstrating that the price the firm of the intermediate sector sets is just a markup over the marginal cost r. Thus, the profit of the intermediate firm can be written as

$$\pi = p(i)x - r\eta x = \eta(\alpha + \beta)rx/(1 - \alpha - \beta). \tag{5.5}$$

The firms in the research sector behave competitively. Since knowledge is a nonrivalrous good, each firm has access to the entire stock in the economy. The production of firm i is supposed to be given by $g_A(i) = \mu H_A(i)^\gamma A^\phi - \delta_A A$, with $H_A(i)$ the amount of human capital used in the production process by firm i and $\delta_A \in (0, 1)$, the depreciation rate of knowledge. This function differs from the one used by Romer (1990).[2] The motivation for this change will be discussed later. The differential equation describing the evolution of the stock of knowledge A is obtained by aggregation across firms, giving

$$\frac{\dot{A}}{A} = \mu H_A^\gamma A^{\phi-1} - \delta_A, \tag{5.6}$$

with $\gamma, \phi \in (0, 1)$.

The price of knowledge at time t, $P_A(t)$, is equal to the present value of the stream of profits of each intermediate firm. This holds because the research sector behaves competitively. This leads to a differential equation describing $P_A(t)$ over time, which is

$$\dot{P}_A = rP_A - \pi. \tag{5.7}$$

The rental rate of human capital in the final-good sector and in the research sector must be equal. Since both sectors behave competitively, this implies

$$P_A = \bar{\eta}\alpha A^{\alpha+\beta-\phi}(H - H_A)^{\alpha-1} L^\beta K^{1-\alpha-\beta} H_A^{1-\gamma}/(\mu\gamma). \tag{5.8}$$

Taking logarithms and differentiating with respect to time yields an expression for $\dot{P}_A/P_A$, which is given by

$$\frac{\dot{P}_A}{P_A} = (1 - \alpha - \beta)\frac{\dot{K}}{K} + (\alpha + \beta - \phi)\frac{\dot{A}}{A} + (\alpha - 1)\frac{\dot{H} - \dot{H}_A}{H - H_A} + (1 - \gamma)\frac{\dot{H}_A}{H_A} + \beta\frac{\dot{L}}{L}. \tag{5.9}$$

---

[2] This function was introduced by Jones (1995a). The difference between his model and ours is that we explicitly distinguish between skilled labor, H, and unskilled labor, L.

On the other hand, combining (5.7) and (5.8) and using the expression for π as well as $x = K/(\eta A)$ yields

$$\frac{\dot{P}_A}{P_A} = r - \frac{\mu\gamma(1 - \alpha - \beta)(H - H_A)A^{\phi-1}H_A^{\gamma-1}}{\alpha}. \tag{5.10}$$

Setting those two expressions equal and solving for $\dot{H}_A$ leads to

$$\dot{H}_A = ((1 - \alpha)H_A + (1 - \gamma)(H - H_A))^{-1}\left(H_A(H - H_A)\left(\frac{C}{K}(1 - \alpha - \beta)\right.\right.$$

$$+ \delta_K(1 - \alpha - \beta) - (\mu H_A^\gamma A^{\phi-1} - \delta_A)(\alpha + \beta - \phi) - \beta n$$

$$\left.- \bar{\eta}K^{-\alpha-\beta}A^{\alpha+\beta}(H - H_A)^\alpha L^\beta(1 - \alpha - \beta)(\alpha + \beta)\right) + (1 - \alpha)n_H H H_A$$

$$- \frac{\alpha + \beta}{\alpha}(1 - \alpha - \beta)\mu\gamma A^{\phi-1}(H - H_A)^2 H_A^\gamma\Big), \tag{5.11}$$

with $\delta_K \in (0, 1)$ the depreciation rate of physical capital. The capital accumulation equation is

$$\dot{K} = Y - C - \delta_K K = \bar{\eta}A^{\alpha+\beta}(H - H_A)^\alpha L^\beta K^{1-\alpha-\beta} - C - \delta_K K, \tag{5.12}$$

where C is aggregate consumption.

n_H and n denote the growth rate of the total stock of human capital H and the growth rate of labor supply L, respectively; that is,

$$\dot{H} = H n_H \tag{5.13}$$

$$\dot{L} = L n \tag{5.14}$$

Table 5.1 gives a survey of the productive sector in the Romer model.

TABLE 5.1
Survey of the Productive Sector in the Romer Model

R&D Sector	Intermediate-Goods Sector	Final-Goods Sector
$\dot{A} = \mu H_A^\gamma A^\phi - \delta_A A$	produces $x(i)$ using Y, buys a design (fixed cost)	$Y = (H - H_A)^\alpha L^\beta \int_0^A x(i)^{1-\alpha-\beta} di$
competitive	monopolistic	competitive

The model is completed by describing the household sector, which is represented by a household that maximizes the discounted stream of utilities over an infinite time horizon subject to its budget constraint. Formally, the utility functional of the household is written as

$$\int_0^\infty \frac{C^{1-\sigma} - 1}{1 - \sigma} e^{-\rho t} dt, \tag{5.15}$$

with C consumption, ρ the subjective discount rate, and σ the inverse of the intertemporal elasticity of substitution of consumption between two points in time. The budget constraint of the household is given by

$$\dot{K} = rK + w_L L + w_H H - C - \delta_K K, \tag{5.16}$$

with w_L and w_H the wage rate for labor and for human capital, respectively. Maximizing (5.15) subject to the budget constraint (5.16) gives the growth rate of aggregate consumption as

$$\frac{\dot{C}}{C} = \frac{r(t) - \rho}{\sigma} = \frac{\bar{\eta}}{\sigma} (1 - \alpha - \beta)^2 (H - H_A)^\alpha A^{\alpha+\beta} L^\beta K^{-\alpha-\beta} - \frac{\rho + \delta_K}{\sigma}. \tag{5.17}$$

Our system, containing only observable variables, is given by equations (5.6), (5.11), (5.12), (5.13), (5.14), and (5.17). It should be noted that the major innovation in this model over the original in Romer (1990) is the production function for the production of knowledge. The presence of $\phi \in (0, 1)$ in equation (5.6) is intended to capture the fact that the higher the stock of knowledge, the more difficult it becomes to create new knowledge. That is, it captures the effect of satiation. The presence of $\gamma \in (0, 1)$ captures some congestion effects of new researchers or research institutions leading to decreasing returns. If, taking other things as constant, the number of researchers or research institutes doubles, the number of new designs may not double. Some research institutes may duplicate the results of others, and their marginal contribution may be less than the average contribution to the creation of knowledge.

As discussed earlier, this modification is necessary in order to make Romer's (1990) model compatible with time series evidence. Just like the Uzawa-Lucas model presented in chapter 4, the Romer model contains scale effects. This has already been mentioned in chapter 2. There the predicted scale effect was compared with the data for the United States and Germany,[3] and we concluded that, in order to estimate the production function of knowledge, the original Romer model (1990) has to be modified.

---

[3] For the construction of the data, see the next section.

Before we estimate our model, we will define a BGP for our generalized Romer model. As in chapter 4, a BGP is defined as a path on which the output-to-capital ratio, Y/K, is constant and all variables grow at constant but possibly different growth rates. The assumption of a constant output-to-capital ratio implies a constant consumption-to-capital ratio. Thus, we can state that on a BGP we have

$$\frac{\dot{Y}}{Y} = \frac{\dot{K}}{K} = \frac{\dot{C}}{C}.$$

Further, constant growth rates imply $d/dt \, (\dot{A}/A) = 0$ and $d/dt \, (\dot{K}/K) = 0$. Differentiating $\dot{A}/A$ and $\dot{K}/K$ with respect to time and setting the left-hand side equal to zero yields

$$\frac{\dot{A}}{A} = \frac{\gamma}{1 - \phi} \frac{\dot{H}_A}{H_A}$$

and

$$\frac{\dot{K}}{K} = n + \frac{\gamma}{1 - \phi} \frac{\dot{H}_A}{H_A} + \frac{\dot{H}_Y}{H_Y}.$$

Moreover, setting (5.9) equal to (5.10) demonstrates that H_A and H_Y grow at the same rate on a BGP. Further, the growth rate of H_A and H_Y must be equal to the growth rate of H, n_H. Thus, the BGP for the modified Romer model is given by

$$\frac{\dot{Y}}{Y} - n - n_H = \frac{\dot{K}}{K} - n - n_H = \frac{\dot{C}}{C} - n - n_H = \left(\frac{\gamma}{1 - \phi}\right) n_H. \qquad (5.18)$$

This result shows that, in the modified Romer model, the long-run growth rates of aggregate variables are larger than the growth rates of labor and human capital. Thus, the modified Romer model generates positive per capita growth[4] in the long run, in contrast to the modified Uzawa-Lucas growth models. However, the balanced growth rate is completely determined by the parameters of the knowledge production function, γ and ϕ, and by the growth rate of labor, n, and of human capital, n_H. It can also be seen that the growth rate of aggregate variables just equals the growth rate of labor in the long run if the growth rate of human capital equals zero. This follows immediately from (5.18). On the other hand, the government may raise the balanced growth rate only if it can raise the growth rate of human capital or if it has an influence on the parameters in the production function of knowledge. Models where long-run per capita growth depends on the growth rate of labor input are called semi-endogenous growth models.

---

[4] This holds because the per capita growth rate of output is given by $\dot{Y}/Y - n(L/(L+H)) - n_H(H/(L+H)) > \dot{Y}/Y - n - n_H$.

The modification of the production function for knowledge capital as undertaken in equation (5.6) was necessary in order to eliminate scale effects present in the original Romer model. However, additional modifications of the knowledge production function are feasible as well. In the case of the Romer model, it is also advisable to proceed as we did for the Uzawa-Lucas model and assume an exogenous time trend. The major modification of the original function, then, is to assume that μ explicitly depends on time. The function then can be written as

$$\frac{\dot{A}}{A} = \mu(t)H_A^\gamma A^{\phi-1} - \delta_A. \tag{5.19}$$

From an economic point of view, this can again be justified by economic variables that affect the growth rate of knowledge but are not explicitly considered in the production function for knowledge, such as physical capital or public subsidies.

With this equation the Romer model may again yield positive per capita growth even if the growth rate of human capital equals zero. This can be seen as follows. Assume that the growth rates of labor and human capital are zero and $\mu(t)$ grows in a way such that $\mu(t)/A^{1-\phi}$ is constant. Then the right-hand side in (5.19) is constant and positive for $\mu(t)/A^{1-\phi} > 0$ and can lead to sustained per capita growth in the long run. Overall, the emergence of positive per capita growth depends on the values of the parameters in the model, and a situation with no sustained per capita growth is feasible as well.

5.4 DESCRIPTION OF THE DATA

We can now describe the data used to estimate the parameters of the modified Romer model.

The time series data are quarterly data for both the United States and Germany. For the United States, we use data from 1962.1 to 1996.4; for Germany, the data are from 1962.1 to 1991.4.[5] The data for consumption and physical capital are the same as in chapter 4; in particular, physical capital was again constructed using the perpetual inventory method (cf. chapter 4).

As for the stock of human capital H, we use the same concept as in chapter 4. That is, we construct this variable from educational spending using the perpetual inventory method.[6] For the stock of skilled labor employed in research, H_A, and the knowledge capital, or the stock of

---

[5] Again, data are for West Germany only.

[6] A detailed description of the data construction is given in the appendix to this chapter.

designs, A, we also compute those stocks from expenditure flows by using the perpetual inventory method. As a proxy for the stock of skilled labor, H_A, employed in the production of knowledge capital (designs), we take cumulated expenditures for scientists and engineers, whereby the stock H_A is computed the same way as was done for H. The stock of knowledge is computed from total expenditure for R&D.

The data for salaries in the R&D sector and total expenditures for R&D are from National Science Foundation (2000) and Office for National Statistics (1965–1998) for the United States and from Statistisches Bundesamt (1991–1995) for Germany. The number of researchers was obtained from OECD (1998a) for both the United States and Germany. These quarterly data were again computed from annual data using linear interpolation. The sources of all other data are as in chapter 4. All data are again real data.

Jones (1997) uses different measures for H_y and H_A: H_y is measured by hL_y and H_A by hL_A. He assumes that human capital, h, is exponentially growing, L_y being the labor force in final production and L_A the labor force employed in knowledge production. However, because we have used cumulated educational expenditure as a proxy for human capital, H, the fraction of human capital used in the R&D sector, H_A, should also be constructed using a monetary variable. Further, using total salaries in the R&D sector as a proxy has the advantage that the labor input receives a certain weight that is equal to the wages paid to the employees in this sector. Since the wage reflects the productivity of labor, an increase in the wage implies that labor input becomes more productive, which has a positive effect on output. This is captured by taking the wage rate as a weight on labor input. For these reasons, we decided to take total cumulated salaries in R&D as a proxy for human capital employed in this sector.

5.5 ESTIMATION RESULTS

The modified Romer model is completely described by the equations (5.6), (5.11), (5.12), (5.13), (5.14), and (5.17). In estimating this model, it turned that we had to make some compromises in order to get results. First, trying to estimate the model including equation (5.11) did not produce plausible results. The reason is that it is not possible to find parameters γ and ϕ that match the time series (5.6) and (5.11) simultaneously. Therefore, we took H_A to be an exogenous variable. Second, a similar problem was encountered when we tried to estimate (5.17). Given the growth rate of consumption, with little variance, it was not feasible to match it with the right-hand side of equation (5.17). Therefore, we slightly changed the aggregate production function, taking

$Y = \bar{\eta}(A(H - H_A)L)^\alpha K^{1-\alpha}$ instead. This reduces the set of parameters to be estimated by one. We estimate a system of equations that is very close to the Romer model but not identical to it. With these modifications, the system we estimate is given by the equations[7]

$$\frac{\dot{K}}{K} = \bar{\eta}K^{-\alpha}(A(H - H_A)L)^\alpha - \frac{C}{K} - \delta_K \qquad (5.20)$$

$$\frac{\dot{C}}{C} = \frac{\bar{\eta}}{\sigma}(1 - \alpha)^2(A(H - H_A)L)^\alpha K^{-\alpha} - \frac{\rho + \delta_K}{\sigma} \qquad (5.21)$$

$$\frac{\dot{A}}{A} = \mu H_A^\gamma A^{\phi-1} - \delta_A, \qquad (5.22)$$

with the growth rate of H_A taken from empirical observations, as was done for the Lucas I model, where the educational effort, u, was taken from empirical observations. The empirical estimation is undertaken for the parameter set

$$\psi = (\alpha, \bar{\eta}, \rho, \sigma, \mu, \gamma, \phi, \delta_A)$$

There are no unobservable costate variables involved. The growth rates n and n_H are predetermined parameters obtained from empirical observations, and δ_K is also a predetermined parameter that takes the value used in constructing the time series of physical capital (see chapter 4).

The results of our estimations for the United States and Germany are shown in table 5.2. Standard errors are given in parentheses.

As in chapter 4, the parameters ρ_K, ρ_C, and ρ_a are again the coefficients in the AR(1) process that we assume for the disturbance terms in the corresponding estimated equations. Comparing the two countries, we can say that most of the parameters fall in a reasonable range. In particular, the capital shares, $(1 - \alpha)$, which are 44 percent in the United States and 38 percent in Germany, take reasonable values in both countries and are similar to the values obtained for the Uzawa-Lucas models in chapter 4. The (annual) subjective discount rates are about 3 percent, and the value of the intertemporal elasticity of substitution of consumption, $1/\sigma$, in every estimation also falls in a reasonable interval.

As for the parameters of the knowledge production function (5.6), we observe that the parameter for the elasticity of knowledge production with respect to human capital, γ, is 35 percent in the United States. For Germany we get an elasticity of 0.1 percent, which is extremely small. However, this value is not statistically significant because of the standard error, which is almost 70 times higher than the estimated parameter. For the United States, the parameter ϕ is also not statistically significant. For

---

[7] In estimating this system, we replaced the differential operator by first differences and added a stochastic error term. See the appendix to this chapter.

TABLE 5.2
Estimation of the Modified Romer Model

	U.S. Economy	German Economy
Parameters for Matching $(K_t - K_{t-1})/K_{t-1}$		
α	0.5564 (0.1114)	0.6171 (0.1360)
η	0.1179 (0.0065)	1.6094 (0.9742)
ρ_k	0.9686 (0.0039)	0.9904 (0.0002)
DW statistics	0.2992	0.4839
Parameters for Matching $(C_t - C_{t-1})/C_{t-1}$		
ρ	0.0034 (0.0036)	0.0071 (0.0065)
σ	0.5358 (0.4404)	0.6953 (0.7506)
ρ_c	0.8234 (0.0480)	0.7494 (0.0668)
DW statistics	1.7798	2.1585
Parameters for Matching $(A_t - A_{t-1})/A_{t-1}$		
μ	6.8065 (2.8171)	1.5806 (0.3598)
γ	0.3506 (0.049)	0.0010 (0.0681)
ϕ	9.43e-005 (0.0044)	0.4936 (0.0323)
ρ_a	0.9785 (0.0110)	0.9675 (0.0133)
DW statistics	0.0754	0.0396

Germany, ϕ is about 50 percent, implying that an increase in knowledge of 1 percent reduces the growth rate of the (gross) stock of knowledge by 50 percent. It should also be noted that the Durbin-Watson (DW) value suggests strong serial correlation of the residuals in the equation describing the growth rate of knowledge.

Besides our assumption of satiation, captured by the coefficient ϕ, and decreasing returns to human capital in this sector, captured by the parameter γ, the growth rate of knowledge may additionally depend on an exogenous time trend. This can be taken into account by postulating that the coefficient μ is a function depending on time, for example, as mentioned earlier. For our model we use (5.19). This equation is given by

$$\frac{\dot{A}}{A} = \mu(t) H_A^\gamma A^{\phi-1} - \delta_A. \tag{5.23}$$

As for $\mu(t)$, we again assume a function such as

$$\mu(t) = \frac{\mu_0}{\theta(t)} \tag{5.24}$$

where $\theta(t)$ follows

$$\theta(t) = \beta\theta(t-1) + v \tag{5.25}$$

with the initial condition $\theta(0) = 1$.

Estimating the Romer model with (5.19) instead of equation (5.22) shows that the parameters in equations (5.20) and (5.21) do not change. As in the modified Uzawa-Lucas model, this is due to the fact that the parameters in the production function for knowledge appear only in that equation and not in the other two. The estimation results for the parameters of equation (5.19) are shown in table 5.3.

Table 5.3 shows that now all of the estimated coefficients have smaller standard deviations. This also holds for the elasticity of the growth rate of knowledge with respect to human capital in this sector, which is about 48 percent for the United States and 10 percent for Germany. As in the modified-Uzawa Lucas model, the function $\mu(t)$ negatively depends on time. This implies that there is a negative time trend tending to reduce the growth rate of knowledge. This allows us again, as in the Uzawa-Lucas model, the interpretation that the significant (negative) correlation of the time trend with $\dot{A}/A$ indicates other forces to be relevant for the accumulation of knowledge and, thus, for the final output. The low Durbin-Watson statistics are again likely to be caused by too smooth data that have been used for the estimation.

In figures 5.1 and 5.2 we show the observed and the predicted time series for the growth rates of physical capital K, of consumption C, and of knowledge A for the U.S. and German economies, respectively. The predicted time series were obtained by using the parameter values given in table 5.2 and in table 5.3.

TABLE 5.3
Estimation of Equation (5.19)

Parameters for Matching $(A_t - A_{t-1})/A_{t-1}$ with time-varying μ	U.S. Economy	German Economy
μ_0	0.01 (0.0027)	0.0101 (0.0012)
β	0.8917 (0.0303)	0.9001 (0.1206)
v	0.0451 (0.0028)	0.0357 (0.0124)
γ	0.4697 (0.0344)	0.0434 (0.0360)
ϕ	0.4617 (0.0287)	0.9099 (0.0124)
ρ_a	0.9782 (0.0016)	0.9836 (0.0057)
DW statistics	0.3446	0.4797

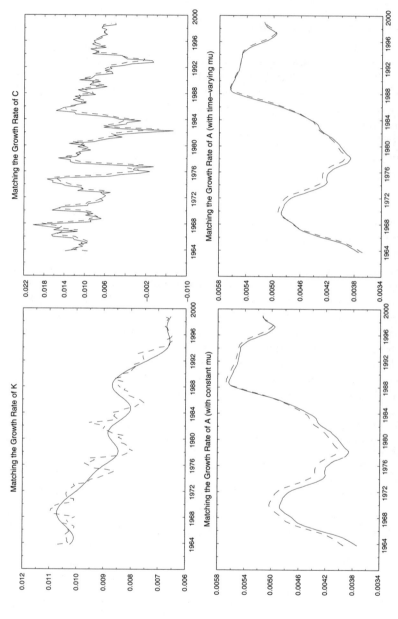

Figure 5.1. Observed (solid line) and predicted (dashed line) series, U.S. economy.

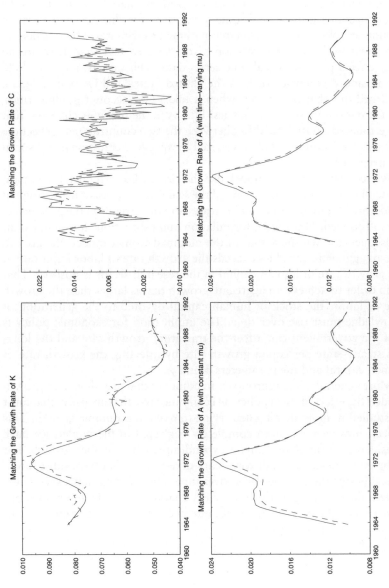

Figure 5.2. Observed (solid line) and predicted (dashed line) series, German economy.

5.6 CONCLUSION

In this chapter we have transformed and estimated the R&D model of endogenous growth with time series data for the U.S. and German economies. We obtain reasonable parameter estimates. Our results are consistent with the interpretation of the stylized fact that there are no scale effects present in real time series data. This at least seems to hold for advanced countries such as the United States and Germany. Again, it turned out that the model, when it takes into account nonlinearities, fits the data in these two countries. But, as in the previous chapters, that the estimated coefficients differ between the two countries may reflect the fact that each country is characterized by specific institutional and social environments.

We see that the Romer model, like the Uzawa-Lucas model, is compatible with time series evidence only if the scale effects present in the original model are eliminated and nonlinearities and time trends in the parameters are introduced. Our model formulation and estimations have important consequences. We show that in the modified Romer model, the growth rate of aggregate variables exceeds the growth rate of labor input only if the growth rate of human capital in the research sector is positive. That is, in order to achieve an aggregate growth that is larger than the growth rate of labor, the stock of human capital devoted to the generation of knowledge must rise over time. The implication for economic policy is that the government can affect the transitory growth rate and the long-run steady-state per capita growth rate by affecting the growth rate of human capital and the parameters ϕ and γ.

More generally, it is appropriate to point out that in endogenous growth models the effect of fiscal policy on economic growth is an aspect that must be studied in more detail when trying to explain economic growth. This aspect, however, has been completely neglected in the models we have considered so far. Government expenditures may enhance growth, but if the government raises distortionary taxes (taxes that have substitution effects beside the income effect) over time, this measure may exert a negative influence on growth. In the next chapter we study an endogenous growth model that explicitly takes into account the effect of government activity on economic growth.

APPENDIX

1. Data Construction and Preliminary Estimation

To estimate the model, we first construct the data series K, H, H_A, and A. We compute these stocks from expenditure flows by using the perpetual inventory method. Specifically we have,

$$K_t = (1 - \delta_k)K_{t-1} + I_{t-1} \tag{5.26}$$

$$H_t = (1 - \delta_H)H_{t-1} + E_{t-1}^{\mu_H} \tag{5.27}$$

$$H_{A,t} = (1 - \delta_{H_A})H_{A,t-1} + S_{t-1}^{\mu_{H_A}} \tag{5.28}$$

$$A_t = (1 - \delta_A)A_{t-1} + R_{t-1}^{\mu_A} \tag{5.29}$$

where I is investment in physical capital, E is education expenditures, S is total salary in R&D, and R is the total expenditure in R&D. All data are quarterly. Apparently, to construct these data we need to specify the parameters δ_K, δ_H, δ_{H_A}, δ_A, μ_H, μ_{H_A}, and μ_A. For both the U.S. and the German economies, we set these parameters equal to the values in table 5.4.

δ_K is set to 0.01, as in chapter 4. The other parameters are chosen based on our preliminary estimation to match the growth rates of K and C,

TABLE 5.4
Parameter Values

	U.S. Economy	German Economy
δ_K	0.01	0.01
δ_H	0.0022	0.0420
δ_{H_A}	0.0022	0.0420
δ_A	0.0013	0.0221
μ_H	0.4466	0.1128
μ_{H_A}	0.4466	0.1128
μ_A	0.8602	0.9380

whose moment restrictions are given by

$$\frac{K_t - K_{t-1}}{K_{t-1}} = \bar{\eta} \left(\frac{A_{t-1}L_{t-1}(H_{t-1} - H_{A,t-1})}{K_{t-1}} \right)^\alpha - \frac{C_{t-1}}{K_{t-1}} - \delta_K + u_{k,t} \quad (5.30)$$

$$\frac{C_t - C_{t-1}}{C_{t-1}} = -\frac{\rho + \delta_k}{\sigma} + \frac{(1-\alpha)^2 \bar{\eta}}{\sigma} \left(\frac{A_{t-1}L_{t-1}(H_{t-1} - H_{A,t-1})}{K_{t-1}} \right)^\alpha + u_{c,t}$$

$$(5.31)$$

where $u_{k,t}$ and $u_{c,t}$ are assumed to follow the $AR(1)$ process:

$$u_{k,t} = \rho_k u_{k,t-1} + \varepsilon_{k,t} \qquad (5.32)$$

$$u_{c,t} = \rho_c u_{c,t-1} + \varepsilon_{c,t} \qquad (5.33)$$

with $\varepsilon_{k,t}$ and $\varepsilon_{c,t}$ *i.i.d.* For this preliminary estimation, we use the GMM method (with the correction for autocorrelation for the two disturbances $u_{k,t}$ and $u_{c,t}$).[8] The optimization algorithm used is simulated annealing. The parameters α, ρ, and σ in this preliminary estimation are prespecified at 0.6, 0.01, and 2, respectively. $\bar{\eta}$ is an additional parameter to be estimated since we do not have any information regarding its magnitude. δ_{H_A} and μ_{H_A} are assumed to equal δ_H and μ_H, respectively. This will allow us to avoid the possible negative $H - H_A$ for each observation when searching the parameter space via simulated annealing. Since this preliminary estimation is only for constructing the data series A, H, and H_A, we do not report the standard deviations.

2. Estimating the Romer Model

Given the constructed data K, H, A, and H_A, along with the observation C and L, we are now able to estimate the parameters $(1 - \alpha)$, $\bar{\eta}$, ρ, σ, δ, γ, ϕ, and δ_A. We estimate these parameters by matching the equations (5.30), (5.31), and

$$\frac{\dot{A}}{A} = \mu H_A^\gamma A^{\phi-1} - \delta_A \qquad (5.34)$$

Given the constructed data K, H, A, and H_A, along with the observation C, we are now able to estimate the structural parameters α, $\bar{\eta}$, ρ, σ, μ, and γ (δ_K and δ_A are assumed to be given by the preliminary estimation). We estimate these parameters by matching the equations (5.30), (5.31), and

$$\frac{A_t - A_{t-1}}{A_{t-1}} = \mu H_{A,t-1}^\gamma A_{t-1}^{\phi-1} - \delta_A + u_{a,t} \qquad (5.35)$$

---

[8] See the technical appendix at the end of this book.

where the AR(1) process for $u_{a,t}$ takes the form

$$u_{a,t} = \rho_a u_{a,t-1} + \varepsilon_{a,t} \qquad\qquad (5.36)$$

with $\varepsilon_{a,t}$ *i.i.d.*

Note that α and $\bar{\eta}$ appear in both (5.30) and (5.31), while ρ and σ appear only in (5.31). The parameters μ and γ appear only in (5.35). Therefore, our estimation strategy is as follows. We first estimate α and $\bar{\eta}$ by matching $(K_t - K_{t-1})/K_{t-1}$ and $(C_t - C_{t-1})/C_{t-1}$ simultaneously. For this estimation, we use the generalized method of moments with the correction of the autocorrelation disturbance terms. It is conducted by the simulated annealing algorithm. Given the estimated α and $\bar{\eta}$, we then estimate ρ and σ by matching $(C_t - C_{t-1})/C_{t-1}$. The parameters μ and γ are estimated by matching $(A_t - A_{t-1})/A_{t-1}$. Since these are all single-equation estimations, we use the method of nonlinear least square. All these estimations need an optimization algorithm. Here we use the Newton-Raphson algorithm. The estimation procedure in the equation for $\dot{A}/A$ was the same. The results are shown in tables 5.2 and 5.3.

CHAPTER 6

Endogenous Growth with Public Infrastructure

In the last type of growth model to be studied here, sustained per capita growth results from productive public investment. This structure can also generate a positive per capita growth rate (see Barro 1990; Barro and Sala-i-Martin 1992; and Glomm and Ravikumar 1994).

In the present chapter we study the contribution of public infrastructure to economic growth, along the line of work by Barro (1990), Barro and Sala-i-Martin (1992), and Turnovsky (1995, chapter 13). But instead of considering the flow of public services, we will refer to the stock of public capital when studying growth effects (see Futagami, Morita, and Shibata 1993). In contrast to prior researchers, we also admit capital market borrowing by the government. This has been disregarded in previous work when the effect of public spending (public consumption and infrastructure investment) was analyzed. In our model there will be one decision variable, private consumption, and three state variables, private and public capital stock and public debt. We will study both the composition effect of (possibly deficit-financed) public expenditure on growth and the effect of the level of public deficit (debt) on growth. Doing so, one of course has to check whether the debt remains sustainable.

Numerous empirical studies have tested whether public investment or public capital has a stimulating effect on the performance of economies (for a survey see Sturm, Kuper, and de Haan 1998). That line of research was made popular with the work by Aschauer (1989), who found strong effects of public capital on economic growth.[1]

Since the tax rate and the components of public expenditure are not choice variables, we need to define budgetary regimes (rules) that define the tax rates and the spending and borrowing behavior of the government.[2] In order to undertake a comparative static analysis of expenditure effects, we define a variety of fiscal regimes and the associated rules for borrowing and spending by the government. In strict fiscal

---

[1] Models with government expenditure have also been discussed in the context of real business cycle models. See Baxter and King (1993) for a model with a balanced budget, and Chari, Christiano, and Kehoe (1994) for a model with a public deficit.

[2] This has been implicitly or explicitly undertaken in a variety of macroeconomic studies on public debt; see, for example, Domar (1957); Blinder and Solow (1973); Barro (1979); see also the survey by van Ewijk (1991).

regimes, public sector borrowing is used for public investment. In less strict regimes, it can be used for debt service and public investment. In all of our regimes, capital market borrowing by the government does not necessarily entail a declining growth rate of the economy, but the growth effects will be different according to which fiscal rule is adopted. We also show that the results of our model are relevant to the optimal tax literature. The growth-maximizing income tax rate will not be zero.

A further problem to be studied in the context of our model is out-of-steady-state dynamics. As it turns out, the dynamics of endogenous growth models are not easily analyzed. It is usually shown that a standard endogenous growth model may be characterized by saddle path stability. The saddle path stability of the balanced growth path (BGP) for models closely related to the Lucas (1988) version has been proved by Caballe and Santos (1993) and Mulligan and Sala-i-Martin (1993b) for the case of the competitive economy, and by Asada, Semmler, and Novak (1998) for the planning version of the Romer (1990) model. Some literature has studied the dynamic properties of extensions of the Lucas (1988) and Romer (1990) models. See, for example, Benhabib and Perli (1994) for the Lucas version, and Benhabib, Perli, and Xie (1994) for the Romer model. The dynamics of endogenous growth models with externalities are studied in Boldrin and Rustichini (1994) and in chapter 3 of this book. As it turns out, externalities easily can generate multiple equilibria and indeterminacy and also possibly persistent fluctuations.[3]

The major endeavor in this chapter is to test the proposed model and find whether it is compatible with time series data for the United States and Germany. The estimation of the subsequent model is more cumbersome than the models of the previous chapters. We will use generalized method of moments (GMM) estimation here.[4] In this version, the econometric model to be estimated is nonlinear in parameters and may exhibit multiple optima. To circumvent this problem, the simulated annealing global optimization algorithm is employed.

As in the previous chapters, after substituting the consumption growth variable for the unobservable costate variable, we obtain the decision variable in feedback form. This gives us a dynamic system in three variables that, however, may exhibit multiple steady states and thus global and possibly also local indeterminacy. Assuming certain fiscal regimes for the United States and Germany, which are explored by studying stylized

---

[3] For an extensive treatment of the indeterminacy in endogenous growth models, see Benhabib and Perli (1994); Benhabib, Perli, and Xie (1994).

[4] The maximum likelihood method has been employed by Altug (1989), Chow (1993), and Semmler and Gong (1996a). The GMM has been used by Christiano and Eichenbaum (1992) and Semmler and Gong (1996b).

facts, we can estimate the structural parameters for the U.S. and German economies using time series data from 1952 to 1990. In the GMM estimation we employ Newey and West (1987) weighting matrices. As we will see, the estimated parameters for the two economies fall into a reasonable range. On the basis of our results the contribution of public capital to economic growth of the U.S. and German economies in the postwar period can be interpreted.

If growth enhanced by public infrastructure is feasible, public debt should be sustainable. This amounts to evaluating whether the intertemporal budget constraint of the government can hold, given certain preference and technology parameters. This can be examined by testing whether the nonexplosiveness condition (or transversality condition) will hold for our growth model. In addition, we resort to a test that has been employed to check for bubbles in stock markets and exchange rates. We will undertake such a test for U.S. and German time series data.

6.1 THE GROWTH MODEL AND STEADY-STATE RESULTS

We consider a closed economy that is composed of three sectors: the household sector, a representative firm, and the government.[5] The household sector is assumed to optimize, whereas the government sector follows certain budgetary rules that are given by the budgetary regimes.

The household is supposed to maximize the discounted stream of utilities arising from consumption subject to its per capita budget constraint, that is,

$$\max_{C(t)} \int_0^\infty e^{-(\rho-n)t} L_0 u(C(t)) dt, \tag{6.1}$$

subject to

$$C(t) + \dot{K}(t) + (\delta_K + n)K(t) + \dot{B}(t) + nB(t)$$
$$= (w(t) + r_1(t)K(t) + r_2(t)B(t))(1 - \tau) + T_p(t).$$

where $C(t)$ is per capita consumption at time t. The assets accumulated by the household are physical capital $K(t)$, which depreciates at the rate δ_K, and government bonds or public debt $B(t)$. $T_p(t)$ is the lump-sum transfer payment to the household that the household takes as given in solving its optimization problem. The term τ is the income tax rate and $w(t)$, $r_1(t)$, and $r_2(t)$ denote the wage rate, the return to physical capital,

---

[5] A more detailed analytical treatment of the subsequent model, without population growth and depreciation, is given in Greiner and Semmler (2000).

and the return to government bonds, respectively. The no-arbitrage condition requires the after-tax equalization of the two rates of returns (see the appendix to this chapter). Moreover, ρ is the constant rate of time preference. The labor supply, which equals L_0 at $t = 0$, is assumed to grow at the constant rate n.

For the utility function, we use the same function as in the previous chapters,

$$U(C(t)) = (C(t)^{1-\sigma} - 1)/(1 - \sigma) \tag{6.2}$$

with $1/\sigma$ denoting again the elasticity of substitution between consumption at two points in time, which is assumed to be constant.

The productive sector is assumed to be represented by a firm that behaves competitively, exhibiting a per capita production function of the form[6]

$$f(K, G) = K^\beta (\bar{G}/L)^\alpha, \tag{6.3}$$

where $\bar{G}$ is the aggregate stock of public capital that is subject to congestion. As for congestion, we assume that the per capita stock of public capital $G = \bar{G}/L$ affects per capita output. That specification implies that an increase in the labor input leads to a decline in the contribution of public capital to total output.[7] β, and α, $\beta, \alpha \in (0, 1)$, denote the share of private and public per capita capital in the production function, respectively. Since K denotes per capita capital, the wage rate and the return to private capital are determined as $w = (1 - \beta)K^\beta G^\alpha$ and $r_1 = \beta K^{\beta-1} G^\alpha$.

The budget constraint of the government in per capita terms is given by

$$\dot{B} = r_2 B + C_p + T_p + I_p - T - nB, \tag{6.4}$$

where $r_2 B$ is the debt service, C_p stands for public consumption, T_p for transfers, I_p for public investment, and T for tax revenue, given by $T = \tau(w + r_1 K + r_2 B)$.

As for the sustainability of public debt, we posit that the government is not allowed to play a Ponzi game. We thus state that the usual transversality condition

$$\lim_{t \to \infty} B(t)e^{-\int_0^t (r_2(s)-n)ds} = 0 \tag{6.5}$$

must hold.

With respect to the aforementioned budgetary regimes, we define the behavior of the government in terms of ratios. This allows us to study the growth effects when we assume alternative fiscal rules.

---

[6] In the following we will suppress the time argument t if no ambiguity arises.

[7] Note that this assumption eliminates a scale effect otherwise present.

Budgetary Regimes

In the economics literature, budgetary regimes are in general formulated in terms of the instruments (expenditure and tax rates) (see, e.g., Blinder and Solow 1973), or in terms of some target variables such as the budget deficit (see, e.g., Domar 1957) or the size of the government debt. The essential point about such a regime is that it imposes a constraint on the budgetary policy of a government. Therefore, governments may have full scope within a certain regime, but they cannot change it. This holds because in reality budgetary regimes are defined for longer periods and are legitimized beyond the direct political process. If a government intends to alter a regime, this needs thorough preparation where ideology and institutional factors play an important role. Therefore, a budgetary regime acts as a constraint on the decisions a government can take.

Van Ewijk and van de Klundert (1993, pp. 123–124) present three budgetary regimes from the existing literature and analyze their impact on the dynamics and growth of an economy.[8] They consider the following regimes, which are named according to the authors who have introduced them. In terms of our model, they are written as follows:

(1) Blinder and Solow $\quad X - T \qquad = const.,$
(2) Domar $\qquad\qquad X - T + iB \quad = const.,$
(3) Barro $\qquad\qquad X - T + iB \quad = gB,$

with $X \equiv C_P + T_P + I_p$ and g denoting the growth rate.

The first regime was introduced by Blinder and Solow (1973) in their analysis of a short-term Keynesian model. In this case, total government spending without interest payments is constant, meaning that the budget deficit of the government varies with the interest payments for public debt. The second was originally examined by Domar (1957). It states that governments must reduce their spending over time if public debt is growing because the sum of total expenditures must stay constant. The last regime, finally, states that the government adopts a target directly for the size of public debt as a ratio to the capital stock or to the productive capacity. This regime is not strictly advocated by Barro (1979), but is nevertheless named after him because it was the starting point of his tax-smoothing rule.

These three regimes, however, are not suitable for our endogenous growth model either because they imply that some variables that grow without bound in our setting are constant (regimes 1 and 2) or because they are automatically fulfilled for the balanced growth path to which

---

[8] More regimes can be found in van Ewijk (1991), pp. 101–102.

we will limit our analysis. Therefore, we define four alternative regimes within which the impact of fiscal policy is investigated.

We suppose that public consumption and transfer payments to the household constitute a certain part of tax revenue, that is, $C_p = \varphi_2 T$ and $T_p = \varphi_1 T$, $\varphi_1, \varphi_2 < 1$. Moreover, we define per capita government expenditure for public (gross) investment as $I_p = \varphi_3(1 - \varphi_0)T$, with $\varphi_3 \geq 0$. The fraction φ_0 depends on the budgetary regime under consideration. The per capita public capital stock then evolves according to

$$\dot{G} = \varphi_3(1 - \varphi_0)T - (\delta_G + n)G, \tag{6.6}$$

with δ_G the depreciation rate of public capital.

In particular, we consider four alternative rules that define the government spending and borrowing rules. There are, roughly speaking, two types of regimes. In regimes of type A the government is posited to use the borrowed funds from the capital market for the deficit, mostly for infrastructure investment, and, perhaps to a small extent, for debt service. In regimes of type B the borrowed funds are allowed to be used for debt services and, to a smaller extent, for infrastructure investment.

More specifically, in regime A1 we first posit that government expenditures for public consumption, transfers, and interest payment must be smaller than tax revenue, $C_p + T_p + r_2 B = \varphi_0 T$, with $\varphi_0 < 1$.[9] A slight modification of this regime, regime A2, is obtained when allowing that only a certain part of the interest payment on public debt must be financed out of tax revenue and the remaining part may be paid by issuing new bonds. In this case, the budgetary regime is described by $C_p + T_p + \varphi_4 r_2 B = \varphi_0 T$, with $\varphi_4 \in (0, 1)$.

For the second type of regimes, regime B, we assume that public consumption plus transfers to individuals must not exceed tax revenue, but the government may borrow in order to finance interest payments and public investment, $C_p + T_p = \varphi_0 T$, $\varphi_0 < 1$. Within this regime, we further distinguish between the situation where the sum of public consumption plus transfer payments plus public investment (i.e., the primary deficit) is smaller than tax revenue, referred to as regime B1, and the situation where this sum exceeds tax revenue, regime B2. Table 6.1 gives a summary of the regimes.

Solving the optimization problem of the household,[10] taking into account the marginal productivity rules and the budgetary regimes, the

---

[9] This regime, for example, can be found in the German constitution and is binding on the government.

[10] A sketch of the derivation is contained in the appendix to this chapter.

TABLE 6.1
Budgetary Regimes

	Target	Deficit due to
A1	$C_p + T_p + r_2 B < T$	public investment
A2	$C_p + T_p + \varphi_4 r_2 B < T$	public investment $+ (1 - \varphi_4) r_2 B$
B1	$C_p + T_p + I_p < T$	interest payment on national debt
B2	$C_p + T_p + I_p > T, \; C_p + T_p < T$	$C_p + T_p + I_p +$ interest payment

dynamics of our economy are completely described by the following system of differential equations.

$$\frac{\dot{K}}{K} = -\frac{C}{K} - (\delta_K + n) + K^{\beta-1} G^\alpha - \tau (\varphi_2 + \varphi_3(1 - \varphi_0))$$

$$\times \left(K^{\beta-1} G^\alpha + \frac{B}{K} \left(\beta K^{\beta-1} G^\alpha - \frac{\delta_K}{1-\tau} \right) \right) \tag{6.7}$$

$$\frac{\dot{B}}{B} = (\varphi_0 - 1)(1 - \varphi_3)\tau \left(\beta K^{\beta-1} G^\alpha - \frac{\delta_K}{1-\tau} + \frac{K^\beta G^\alpha}{B} \right)$$

$$- n + (1 - \varphi_4) \left(\beta K^{\beta-1} G^\alpha - \frac{\delta_K}{1-\tau} \right) \tag{6.8}$$

$$\frac{\dot{C}}{C} = -\frac{\rho + \delta_K}{\sigma} + \frac{(1 - \tau)\beta K^{\beta-1} G^\alpha}{\sigma} \tag{6.9}$$

$$\frac{\dot{G}}{G} = \varphi_3(1 - \varphi_0)\tau \left(G^{\alpha-1} K^\beta + \beta K^{\beta-1} G^\alpha \frac{B}{G} - \frac{B}{G} \frac{\delta_K}{1-\tau} \right) - \delta_G - n \tag{6.10}$$

The different budgetary regimes can be modeled by appropriate choices of the parameters φ_4 and φ_3. Setting $\varphi_3 > 1$ and $\varphi_4 = 1$, we get regime A1. In that case, all of the nonproductive expenditure must be financed by tax revenue and the government may run a deficit in order to finance public investment. If $\varphi_3 > 1$ and $\varphi_4 \in (0, 1)$, we have regime A2. Now only $\varphi_4 r_2 B$ is paid from tax revenue, and the rest, $(1 - \varphi_4) r_2 B$, is financed by issuing new debt. In the extreme, that is, for $\varphi_4 = 0$, and $\varphi_3 > 1$, we get regime B2. Now all of the interest payment on public debt is paid by issuing additional debt and the sum $C_p + T_p + I_p$ exceeds tax revenue (for $\varphi_3 > 1$). Regime B1, finally, is obtained when we set $\varphi_3 < 1$ and $\varphi_4 = 0$. In that case, the sum $C_p + T_p + I_p$ is lower than tax revenue and the interest payment on public debt is paid by issuing additional debt. It should also be noted that equation (6.7), giving the economy-wide resource constraint, is independent of the budgetary regime under consideration.

A comparative static analysis of the balanced growth path with $\beta = 1 - \alpha$ and $\delta_K = \delta_G = n = 0$ is undertaken in Greiner and Semmler (2000) for the analytical model. A general result that holds for all of the regimes is that the increase in public consumption and transfers will reduce the growth rate of the economy (see table 6.2, column 1). The negative (positive) sign stands for a decrease (increase) in the growth rate. For the more general case $\delta_K \neq 0$, $\delta_G \neq 0$, and $n \neq 0$, however, the model turned out to be too complicated to derive results for the analytical model. Nevertheless, with the help of numerical examples we could show that the analytical results also hold for the general model. In column 2 of table 6.2, we give the results.

As table 6.2 shows, the growth effects of public investment expenditure and deficit spending crucially depend on the budgetary regime under consideration. In fact, the growth effects of a deficit-financed increase in public investment in each of our four regimes depend on two opposing forces. On the one hand, a deficit-financed increase in public investment spurs economic growth. On the other hand, a higher government debt implies a negative growth effect that acts through two channels: first, an increase in public debt increases interest payments that must be financed by tax revenue and consequently reduces the resources available for public investment. Here, we may speak of internal crowding out (as in van Ewijk and van de Klundert 1993, p. 123). But that effect only holds for regimes A1 and A2. Second, the introduction of the budgetary regimes implies that the interest payments on public debt appear in the economy-wide resource constraint (1) and lead to an external crowding out of private investment. That effect holds for regimes of both type A and type B. Under certain parameter constellations, we also could observe that even a less strict budgetary regime, where more of the additional

TABLE 6.2
Effects of Fiscal Policy on the Balanced Growth Rate

Regime	Analytical Model		Simulation	
	Rise in C_p, T_p	Rise in $\dot{G}$	Rise in C_p, T_p	Rise in $\dot{G}$
A1	−	+/−	−	−
A2 ($\varphi_4 = 0.9$)	−	+/−	−	−
A2 ($\varphi_4 = 0.8$)	−	+/−	no BGP with $b \geq 0$	
B1	−	+/−	−	+
B2	−	+	no BGP with $b \geq 0$	

Parameters: $\alpha = 0.25$, $\sigma = 2$, $\rho = 0.1$, $\varphi_1 = 0.3$, $\varphi_2 = 0.35$, $\delta_K = 0.2$, $\delta_G = 0.05$, $n = 0.02$, $\varphi_3 = 1.5$ (Regime A1, A2), $\varphi_3 = 0.35$ (Regime B1, B2).

interest payments may be financed by raising public debt, may show positive growth effects of deficit-financed investment in public capital. That effect could be observed, for example, for regime B2 analytically and for B1 numerically.

The analytical results of our study are represented in table 6.2 under the heading "Analytical Model," where the ambiguous growth effects of deficit-financed public investment are shown. However, simulation studies (represented by "Simulation" in table 6.2) demonstrate that for reasonable parameter constellations, a less strict budgetary regime is accompanied by a higher debt-capital ratio, entailing a higher debt service that may offset the positive direct effect of a less strict budgetary regime. For example, comparing regimes A1 and A2, we found that regime A2 is accompanied by a higher ratio B/K such that in the latter regime a positive growth effect of a deficit-financed increase in public investment did not increase the balanced growth rate, although in regime A2 only φ_4 of the interest payments on outstanding debt must be financed by tax revenue.

As for the growth rate across regimes, our simulations showed that the magnitude of the ratio B/K is most decisive and that this ratio is higher in less strict budgetary regimes. So comparing regimes A1 and B1, we found that regime A1 gives slightly higher growth rates than regime B1 for roughly the same share of public investment to GDP. The reason is that in the latter, the ratio B/K takes on higher values. Further, regime A1 yields a higher growth rate than regime A2 when we take for A2 $\varphi_4 = 0.9$.[11]

In regime B2, the least restrictive budgetary regime, where the sum of government expenditure without payments on outstanding debt exceeds tax revenue, it turned out that for certain parameter values of the utility function (that is, for $\sigma \geq (1 - \tau)$), no sustained per capita growth is feasible. In this case, the government must be a creditor if it wants to achieve sustained per capita growth. However, that result only holds for the special case of no depreciation and a zero growth rate of the population. For the more general case that condition did not hold, but our numerical examples also demonstrated that sustained per capita growth is not feasible for reasonable parameter values unless the government is a creditor. That problem also appeared for regime A2 if φ_4 is lower than a certain threshold level that depends on the other parameter values of the model.

Our simulations also showed that the growth-maximizing income tax is higher in regime B1 than in A1 or A2. In table 6.3 we give a survey of

[11] For $\varphi_4 \leq 0.8$ sustained per capita growth was no longer feasible in regime A2 for a positive government debt.

TABLE 6.3
Growth-Maximizing Income Tax Rate,
τ_{max}, Maximum Growth Rate, g_{max}, and
the Ratio B/K on the BGP

Regime	τ_{max}	g_{max}	B/K
A1	0.23	0.056	0.14
A2 ($\varphi_4 = 0.9$)	0.20	0.044	0.17
B1	0.26	0.053	0.17

the growth-maximizing income tax rate, the maximum growth rate, and
the ratio B/K. The parameters are as in the example given in table 6.2.[12]

The growth-maximizing income tax rate in endogenous growth models
with public investment or public capital is equal to the share of public investment or public capital in the aggregate production function, if
the government runs a balanced budget (cf. Barro 1990 and Futagami,
Morita, and Shibata 1993). In our model variants with public deficit and
public debt, simulations show that the growth-maximizing income tax
rate is smaller than this share, except for regime B1, where public investment is financed by tax revenue. The economic motivation for this result
is that with public borrowing the government has an additional source
for financing public investment, so the tax rate that maximizes the balanced growth rate is smaller. This holds because the income tax rate has
a negative effect on the marginal product of private capital and, thus,
on the incentive to invest. Further, our simulations also suggest that the
growth-maximizing income tax is lower in regime A2 than in regime A1.
This is true independent of whether public capital is subject to congestion
when congestion is modeled as a pure level effect, as in our approach.

Since regime B2 appears to be rather unrealistic, we will disregard this
case. The dynamics will be studied for the remaining three regimes and
the estimation of the model will be undertaken for two regimes: regime
A1, which roughly represents the German case, and regime A2, which by
and large stands for the United States.

6.2 THE DYNAMICS OF THE MODEL

The dynamic behavior of our economy can be analyzed after defining the
ratios $c = C/K$, $b = B/K$, and $x = G/K$. Differentiating c, b, and x with

---

[12] Interpreting one time period as two years, the annual growth rate is about 2.8 percent
and the annual discount rate is 5 percent.

respect to time, we get a new dynamic system that completely describes our model around a BGP. The dynamic system is given by

$$
\frac{\dot{c}}{c} = -\frac{\rho + \delta_K}{\sigma} + \frac{(1-\tau)\beta G^\alpha}{\sigma K^{1-\beta}} + \frac{C}{K} + (\delta_K + n) - \frac{G^\alpha}{K^{1-\beta}}
$$
$$
+ \tau\left(\varphi_2 + \varphi_3(1-\varphi_0)\right) \cdot \left(\frac{G^\alpha}{K^{1-\beta}} + \frac{B}{K}\left(\beta\frac{G^\alpha}{K^{1-\beta}} - \frac{\delta_K}{1-\tau}\right)\right) \tag{6.11}
$$

$$
\frac{\dot{b}}{b} = (\varphi_0 - 1)(1 - \varphi_3)\tau\left(\beta\frac{G^\alpha}{K^{1-\beta}} - \frac{\delta_K}{1-\tau} + \frac{K^\beta G^\alpha}{B}\right)
$$
$$
+ (1 - \varphi_4)\left(\beta\frac{G^\alpha}{K^{1-\beta}} - \frac{\delta_K}{1-\tau}\right) + \frac{C}{K} + \delta_K - \frac{G^\alpha}{K^{1-\beta}}
$$
$$
+ \tau\left(\varphi_2 + \varphi_3(1-\varphi_0)\right)\left(\frac{G^\alpha}{K^{1-\beta}} + \frac{B}{K}\left(\beta\frac{G^\alpha}{K^{1-\beta}} - \frac{\delta_K}{1-\tau}\right)\right) \tag{6.12}
$$

$$
\frac{\dot{x}}{x} = \varphi_3(1-\varphi_0)\tau\left(\frac{K^\beta}{G^{1-\alpha}} + \beta\frac{G^\alpha}{K^{1-\beta}}\frac{B}{G} - \frac{B}{G}\frac{\delta_K}{1-\tau}\right) - \delta_G + \frac{C}{K} + \delta_K
$$
$$
- \frac{G^\alpha}{K^{1-\beta}} + \tau\left(\varphi_2 + \varphi_3(1-\varphi_0)\right)\left(\frac{G^\alpha}{K^{1-\beta}} + \frac{B}{K}\left(\beta\frac{G^\alpha}{K^{1-\beta}} - \frac{\delta_K}{1-\tau}\right)\right). \tag{6.13}
$$

For $\beta = 1 - \alpha$, (6.11)–(6.13) is an autonomous system of differential equations in the variables c, b, and x. The local dynamics of the model can then be analyzed by calculating the eigenvalues of the Jacobian matrix of (6.11)–(6.13). That matrix, however, is very complicated, and we cannot determine stability properties for the analytical model. Therefore, we employ numerical computations and simulations.

In the numerical examples we restrict our analysis to regimes A1, A2, and B1.[13] For parameters, we take $\sigma = 2$, $\rho = 0.1$, and α is set to $\alpha = 0.25$, which is the same value Barro (1990) used in his example. φ_1 and φ_2 are fixed at $\varphi_1 = 0.3$ and $\varphi_2 = 0.35$, which are about the values for Germany for the mid-1980s (see Sachverständigenrat 1993, table 38). The depreciation rates are $\delta_K = 0.2$ and $\delta_G = 0.05$, and $n = 0.02$. Those parameter values are left unchanged throughout the simulations. First, we analyze regime A1. To do so we set $\varphi_4 = 1$ and $\varphi_3 = 1.5$. Analyzing our model with those parameter values, we see that there are two rest points for system (6.11)–(6.13). The first, however, yields a negative growth rate, $g < 0$. That latter equilibrium is locally determinate; that is, two eigenvalues are positive and one is negative. This means that there exist

---

[13] Note that in our numerical examples we also have restricted the parameters of the production function so that we have $\beta = (1 - \alpha)$.

TABLE 6.4
Eigenvalues of the Jacobian for Regime A1

τ	λ_1	λ_2	λ_3
0.15	−3.47	0.83	−0.56
0.17	−3.14	0.82	−0.51
0.19	−2.86	0.81	−0.46
0.20	−2.73	0.81	−0.44
0.21	−2.62	0.80	−0.42
0.22	−2.50	0.80	−0.40
0.23	−2.40	0.80	−0.38
0.24	−2.30	0.79	−0.36
0.25	−2.21	0.79	−0.34
0.26	−2.22	0.78	−0.32
0.30	−1.80	0.77	−0.26
0.35	−1.48	0.75	−0.20

unique values $C(0)$ and $B(0)$, which can be chosen freely by the household and by the government respectively, such that the economy converges to that equilibrium.[14] The second equilibrium point implies a positive endogenous growth rate that depends on the tax rate τ. The maximum balanced growth rate is $g = 0.056$, which is obtained for $\tau = 0.23$. That BGP is locally indeterminate (two negative eigenvalues, one positive). Table 6.4 gives the eigenvalues $\lambda_{1,2,3}$.

Setting $\varphi_4 = 0.9$, we get regime A2. Like regime A1, there are two BGPs, of which the first gives a negative balanced growth rate and is locally determinate, that is, has one negative and two positive eigenvalues. The eigenvalues for the second BGP are given in table 6.5, showing that this path is again locally indeterminate.

Reducing φ_4, we observed that for $\varphi_4 \leq 0.8$ a BGP no longer exists. For $\varphi_4 \leq 0.05$ there again exists a BGP, which, however, is accompanied by a negative government debt. Further, this path is globally indeterminate; that is, there exist two BGPs. One of them is locally indeterminate; the other, however, is completely unstable (three positive

[14] This implies that the government can control $B(0)$. If $B(0)$ is taken as given, the economy is determinate with two negative eigenvalues and unstable, except for a one-dimensional stable manifold, with one negative eigenvalue.

TABLE 6.5
Eigenvalues of the Jacobian for Regime A2

τ	λ_1	λ_2	λ_3
0.15	−3.28	0.90	−0.28
0.17	−2.95	0.88	−0.26
0.19	−2.67	0.86	−0.24
0.20	−2.55	0.86	−0.23
0.21	−2.44	0.85	−0.21
0.22	−2.34	0.84	−0.20
0.23	−2.25	0.84	−0.19
0.24	−2.16	0.83	−0.18
0.25	−2.08	0.83	−0.17
0.26	−2.01	0.82	−0.15
0.30	−1.78	0.81	−0.11
0.35	−1.66	0.80	−0.05

TABLE 6.6
Eigenvalues of the Jacobian for Regime B1

τ	λ_1	λ_3	λ_2
0.15	1.49	−1.29	0.86
0.17	1.41	−1.12	0.72
0.19	1.34	−0.98	0.73
0.21	1.29	−0.86	0.73
0.22	1.27	−0.81	0.74
0.23	1.25	−0.76	0.74
0.24	1.23	0.74	−0.71
0.25	1.22	0.73	−0.67
0.26	1.20	0.73	−0.63
0.27	1.19	0.73	−0.59
0.30	1.16	0.72	−0.50
0.35	1.13	0.70	−0.37

eigenvalues) and yields a negative growth rate. This result also holds for regime B2.

Let us next analyze the dynamics for regime B1. In that regime, we have global indeterminacy, where one BGP is locally determinate and gives a positive endogenous growth rate of around 2.5 percent per year. The second path yields a negative endogenous growth rate and is again completely unstable. Table 6.6 gives the eigenvalues of the Jacobian with $\varphi_4 = 0$ and $\varphi_3 = 0.35$.

These examples demonstrate that all regimes are globally indeterminate. However, one of the BGPs always gives a negative growth rate and does not make sense from the economic point of view. The economically reasonable BGP is always locally indeterminate in regimes A1 and A2, that is, two negative eigenvalues and one positive. For regime B1, the feasible BGP is locally determinate, that is, one negative and two positive eigenvalues.

6.3 THE ESTIMATION OF THE GROWTH MODEL

We employ time series data on consumption, public debt, and public capital stock to estimate our model for the U.S. and German economies after World War II. All variables are defined relative to the private capital stock. That is, we use the following new variables introduced in the last section:

$$c \equiv \frac{C}{K}, \quad b \equiv \frac{B}{K}, \quad x \equiv \frac{G}{K}.$$

Deriving these new variables with respect to time gives

$$\frac{\dot{c}}{c} = \frac{\dot{C}}{C} - \frac{\dot{K}}{K}, \quad \frac{\dot{b}}{x} = \frac{\dot{B}}{B} - \frac{\dot{K}}{K}, \quad \frac{\dot{x}}{x} = \frac{\dot{G}}{G} - \frac{\dot{K}}{K} \tag{6.14}$$

In the following, we will estimate this system empirically using the GMM, which is described in detail in the technical appendix at the end of the book.

The set of orthogonal conditions for our GMM estimation is now given by our dynamic system (6.14), which can be written as follows:

$$E\left[\tilde{c} - f_1\left(c(\psi), x(\psi), b(\psi)\right)\right] = 0 \tag{6.15}$$

$$E\left[\tilde{b} - f_2\left(c(\psi), x(\psi), b(\psi)\right)\right] = 0 \tag{6.16}$$

$$E\left[\tilde{x} - f_3\left(c(\psi), x(\psi), b(\psi)\right)\right] = 0 \tag{6.17}$$

where $f_i(\cdot), i = 1, 2, 3$ are the right-hand side of (6.11)–(6.13) and depend on the parameter set $\psi = (\rho, \sigma, \alpha)$. The terms $\tilde{c}, \tilde{b}, \tilde{x}$ represent the deviation of the actual growth rates from their trend values at time period t.[15] The sample moments can be computed using (6.15), (6.16), and (6.17). The numerical minimization of the distance function was again solved by using the simulated annealing algorithm (for details of this algorithm see the technical appendix at the end of the book).

Next, we need to discuss the data set for the U.S. and German economies. The time series are quarterly data for the United States from 1960.4 to 1992.1. The consumption series is from OECD (1998). Total government debt, federal, state, and local, is taken from OECD (1999). The series for the private capital stock was obtained from quarterly investment by applying the perpetual inventory method with a quarterly discount rate of 0.075/4. The data for investment were taken from OECD (1998). For the public capital stock we take the gross nonmilitary capital stock as reported in Musgrave (1992), table 13, which includes federal, state, and local public capital stock (equipment and structures). Since these data are available only annually, we generated quarterly data by linear interpolation. For the computation of the income tax rate and budgetary regime parameters $\varphi_0, \varphi_1, \varphi_2, \varphi_3, \varphi_4$ we have computed average values using OECD (1999), the *Economic Report of the President* (1994), and Citibase (1992).

For Germany we employ the same ratios as for the United States. The data are again quarterly and cover the period from 1966.1 to 1995.1. Private consumption and public gross debt are from OECD (1998, 1999). The private capital stock is again obtained from quarterly investment data (from OECD 1998) by using the perpetual inventory method with a quarterly depreciation rate of 0.075/4. The quarterly public capital stock was computed from annual data by linear interpolation. The data are from Statistisches Bundesamt (1991, 1994b, 1995). The data to compute the parameters $\varphi_0, \varphi_1, \varphi_2, \varphi_3$ and φ_4 are from Statistisches Bundesamt (1984) and Sachverständigenrat (1995). The tax rate is the ratio of taxes and social contributions to GDP. The GDP is from Statistisches Bundesamt (1974, 1995).

The next tables report the results of our empirical estimations. Table 6.7 shows the GMM estimation for the U.S. economy assuming regime A2. For the United States, the deficit has been larger than public investment but

---

[15] In order to avoid detrending through procedures such as the Hodrick-Prescott (HP) filter that may bias the estimation results, we here use a formulation in terms of growth rates as suggested by our model (6.14). However, we also undertook the estimation with HP-detrended data. The results turned out to be less reasonable than the reported results using growth rates.

TABLE 6.7
Results of the GMM Estimation for U.S. Time Series, 1960.4–1992.1, with $(\tau, \varphi_0, \varphi_1, \varphi_2, \varphi_3, \varphi_4) = (0.32, 0.815, 0.4, 0.35, 1.3, 0.9)$ from Empirical Data

	ρ	σ	$1 - \alpha$
Estimated Parameters	0.061	0.053	0.244
(standard errors)	(75,096)	(614,621)	(0.0179)

smaller than the sum of public investment plus interest payments on public debt, so it can be described by our regime A2. The quarterly depreciation parameters are set as follows: $\delta_K = 0.075/4$ and $\delta_G = 0.05/4$, and the population growth is $n = 0.015/4$.

The private capital share $1 - \alpha$ is statistically significant and about 25 percent, which seems a bit low. Normally, one would expect a capital share of about 0.3. This low value implies that the share of the public capital stock is extremely high, namely about $\alpha = 0.75$. We think that this is an implausibly high value since it would imply that the elasticity of aggregate per capita output with respect to public capital is 75 percent. This may hold for underdeveloped countries with a low level of public infrastructure capital. However, in developed economies with a relatively large infrastructural capital stock, an additional unit of public capital is expected to have a smaller output effect. In empirical studies that evaluate the contribution of public capital to aggregate output, results vary to a great degree, but are in general lower than 30 percent, which is also regarded as implausible by some economists (see Sturm, Kuper, and de Haan 1998).

The high public capital share is, of course, due to our specification of the aggregate production function, which has constant returns to scale in private and public capital. Thus, all factors contributing to economic growth in the United States are summarized in either private or public capital, so it is not possible to get reasonable values for both of these parameters. Therefore, our empirical estimation is limited in detecting the share of public capital in the aggregate production function. Here, other procedures are more appropriate (for a detailed survey see Sturm, Kuper, and de Haan 1998).

As concerns the two other structural parameters, ρ and σ, table 6.7 shows that the standard errors are extremely high, such that these estimates are not reliable. We assume that this is due to the fact that ρ and σ only appear in the equation $\dot{c}/c$ but not in the equations $\dot{x}/x$ and $\dot{b}/b$. Therefore, a deviation from the estimated values of ρ and σ will not

TABLE 6.8
Results of the NLLS Estimation of $\dot{c}/c$ for U.S.
Time Series, 1960.4–1992.1, with α Set to the
Value in Table 6.7

	ρ	σ
Estimated Parameters	0.052	0.192
(standard errors)	(0.0006)	(0.0066)

change the objective function, which is to be minimized, to a great degree. To get reliable values for ρ and σ, we take the estimated value of the parameter α from table 6.7 and insert it in the equation $\dot{c}/c$. Then we estimate $\dot{c}/c$ with nonlinear least squares (NLLS) to obtain ρ and σ. The result is presented in table 6.8.

Table 6.8 shows that we now get reliable estimates for both the rate of time preference, ρ, and the inverse of the intertemporal elasticity of substitution, σ. The intertemporal elasticity of substitution is about 5, which seems to be very high. Here we should like to point out that our theoretical model, which considers only public and private capital as affecting economic growth, cannot yield the same structural parameters obtained in the other chapters.

Next, we estimate our model for Germany. Table 6.9 reports the estimation results for the German economy assuming that fiscal regime A1 prevailed in Germany with the same depreciation parameters as for the United States but a zero population growth rate, that is, $n = 0$.

As in the case of the United States, only the private capital share, $1 - \alpha$, is reliable, while the standard errors of both ρ and σ are extremely high, so that these cannot be relied upon. Again, we suppose that this is due to the fact that these parameters only appear in the equation $\dot{c}/c$, as in the case of the United States. Therefore, we again take the estimated parameter for α from table 6.9 and estimate equation $\dot{c}/c$ with NLLS to obtain values for ρ and σ. The result is shown in table 6.10.

TABLE 6.9
Results of the GMM Estimation for German Time Series,
1966.1–1995.1, with $(\tau, \varphi_0, \varphi_1, \varphi_2, \varphi_3, \varphi_4) = (0.4, 0.945, 0.4, 0.42, 1.5, 1)$ from Empirical Data

	ρ	σ	$1 - \alpha$
Estimated Parameters	0.004	0.224	0.135
(standard errors)	(230566)	(8425716)	(0.0287)

TABLE 6.10
Results of the NLLS Estimation of $\dot{c}/c$ for German Time Series, 1966.1–1995.1, with α Set to the Value in Table 6.9

	ρ	σ
Estimated Parameters	0.0015	0.151
(standard errors)	(0.0004)	(0.0067)

Again, this procedure yields reliable estimates for ρ and σ. However, the time preference parameter, ρ, for Germany seems very low. On the other hand, the intertemporal elasticity of substitution $1/\sigma$ is very high.

In order to compare the time paths of the economic variables in both countries we consider the equations giving the growth rates of per capita GDP and of per capita consumption. The growth rate of per capita GDP is given by

$$\frac{\dot{Y}}{Y} = (1 - \alpha)\frac{\dot{K}}{K} + \alpha\frac{\dot{G}}{G}.$$

The introduction of the budgetary regimes implies, as mentioned earlier, that the ratio of public capital to private capital, B/K, enters the economy-wide resource constraint, leading to a crowding out of private capital. This, for its part, implies a lower investment share and, consequently, a lower growth rate of per capita GDP. Further, our model predicts that higher interest payments on public debt are accompanied by fewer public resources available for public investment, implying a lower growth rate of the public capital stock. Comparing the United States and Germany, one realizes that the debt ratio was higher in the United States than in Germany, while the growth rate of the public capital stock was lower over the time period we considered.[16] A lower growth rate of public capital also has a negative effect on GDP growth in our framework and, thus, contributes to the different growth experience of these two countries.

The growth rate of per capita consumption (and thus also GDP on the BGP) is given by the following equation:

$$\frac{\dot{C}}{C} = -\frac{\rho + \delta_K}{\sigma} + \frac{(1 - \tau)(1 - \alpha)x^\alpha}{\sigma}.$$

From this expression, we conclude that a higher intertemporal elasticity of substitution, $1/\sigma$, for Germany tends to raise the growth rate of private

---

[16] But it should be noted that the level of public capital relative to private capital was higher in the United States than in Germany in the considered time periods.

consumption. Empirically, a high intertemporal elasticity of consumption implies that households are more willing to forgo consumption today and shift it into future as the interest rate rises. Further, the smaller rate of time preference, ρ, in Germany also tends to raise the growth rate of consumption. That is, a high intertemporal elasticity of consumption has a stimulating effect on the investment share and, thus, on the growth rate of consumption. Consequently, the estimated values for the preference parameters in our model, $1/\sigma$ and ρ, tend to give a higher growth rate of consumption for Germany than for the United States over our considered time periods, which is compatible with the historical results. On the other hand, the higher tax rate, τ, as well as the lower level of public capital to private capital, x, tend to lower the German growth rate of consumption.

6.4 INTERTEMPORAL BUDGET CONSTRAINT AND ECONOMIC GROWTH

In the previous sections we have assumed that the government can also borrow from the capital market to finance its expenditures when we have studied the impact of the composition of public spending on economic growth. Yet the limits of public borrowing remained unexplored. This takes us to the question of the level of public deficit (debt) and economic growth. It is a reasonable proposition that economic growth is feasible in the long run only if intertemporal budget constraints (private as well as public) are fulfilled.

The question of how large a private individual's debt can become is usually solved by referring to the intertemporal budget constraint. Private households are subject to the borrowing constraint stating that the expected present value of expenditures must not exceed the expected present value of receipts, known as the no-Ponzi game condition. That condition means that a private household cannot continually borrow from capital markets and pay the interest by borrowing more.

Concerning government debt, that latter question remains unsettled from a theoretical point of view. If a government could borrow and pay the interest by borrowing more, any fiscal policy would be sustainable, and in some model economies that is possible. In overlapping generations models, which are dynamically inefficient, a government can borrow in order to pay interest on outstanding debt (see Diamond 1965); that is, it may run a Ponzi scheme. However, that possibility is not given any longer when the economy is dynamically efficient.[17] Then the government faces a present-value borrowing constraint stating that the current

---

[17] For an empirical study analyzing whether the U.S. economy is dynamically efficient see Abel et al. (1989).

value of public debt must equal the discounted sum of future surpluses exclusive of interest payments. McCallum (1984) has studied a perfect-foresight version of the competitive equilibrium model of Sidrauski (1967) for the possibility of maintaining a permanent budget deficit. Bohn (1995) has shown that in an exchange economy with representative agents, the government must always satisfy the no-Ponzi game condition. The idea is that an optimizing individual will not buy financial claims from an organization intending to play a Ponzi game.[18]

We leave aside the question of how to test whether private intertemporal budget constraints are fulfilled.[19] Empirical studies that help to clarify whether governments meet the intertemporal budget constraint are also desirable. For the United States there exist numerous studies, starting with the paper by Hamilton and Flavin (1986). The authors propose a framework for analyzing whether governments run Ponzi schemes or not and apply that test to the U.S. time series data. Other papers followed that also investigated that issue and partly reached different conclusions (see, e.g., Kremers 1989; Wilcox 1989; Trehan and Walsh 1991). For Germany, Boss and Lorz (1995) have analyzed the impact of public debt, but they explicitly suppose that the intertemporal budget constraint is met at any point of time.

We can refer to our growth model with the government sector and fiscal regimes for the United States and Germany and use the estimated structural parameters for those two economies to study the problems of sustainability of public debt. Our methodology permits us to explore the sustainability of public debt by employing the transversality condition. We will employ two approaches. In the first approach, we check whether the intertemporal budget constraint is fulfilled for the United States and Germany given our estimated parameters obtained above. In a second approach, we resort to another sustainability test proposed by Hamilton and Flavin (1986) and subsequent authors.

For our endogenous growth model we can compute the transversality condition at the steady state, implying that the no-Ponzi game condition holds, which amounts, in our model, to the condition

$$n\sigma - \rho + (1 - \alpha)x^{\alpha}((1 - \tau) - \sigma) + \delta_K(\sigma/(1 - \tau) - 1) < 0.$$

Computing this term with the average value of x and with the estimated parameters yields 0.006 for Germany and −0.003 for the United States. Thus, given our parameters for our growth variants estimated above, the

---

[18] The question whether debt is sustainable for given level of debt and time-varying interest rates is studied in Semmler and Sieveking (1997).

[19] For further details on this question, see Semmler and Sieveking (2000).

transversality condition would be fulfilled for the United States, while it would be violated for Germany. This result holds, however, only if the parameters remain constant over time. But in reality some parameters, the tax rate, for example, are subject to changes. Therefore, in the next section we want to perform a more direct test that does not rely on predetermined parameter values.

As for the sustainability of the government deficit and debt, starting with Hamilton and Flavin (1986) an extensive empirical literature has employed further econometric techniques such as unit root and cointegration tests. For U.S. times-series data, sustainability tests of deficit and debt have been undertaken by Kremers (1989), Trehan and Walsh (1988, 1991), Wilcox (1989), Roberds (1991), and Bohn (1998). These studies do not necessarily overturn the results of Hamilton and Flavin (1986). The results obtained by recent studies are in fact ambiguous and depend on how the public deficit and debt are measured,[20] what time periods are chosen, and what techniques are applied. While Kremers, Wilcox, and Roberds come to the conclusion that sustainability is not guaranteed (for data up to 1984), Trehan and Walsh confirm the opposite conclusion, one also reached by Hamilton and Flavin.

Before we present some empirical results, we first need to make some theoretical remarks on the measurement of the accumulation of public debt in discrete time.

The accounting identity describing the accumulation of public debt in discrete time is given by

$$B_t = B_{t-1}(1 + r_{t-1}) - S_t, \tag{6.18}$$

where B_t stands for public debt in constant terms, r_t is the real interest rate, and S_t is government surplus exclusive of interest payments in constant terms.

Let d_t denote the real discount factor from period t back to period zero, which is defined as

$$d_t = \prod_{j=0}^{t-1} (1 + r_j)^{-1}; \ d_0 = 1. \tag{6.19}$$

Multiplying both sides of (6.18) with d_t leads to

$$B_t d_t = B_{t-1} d_{t-1} - S_t d_t. \tag{6.20}$$

---

[20] Eisner, starting with his contribution in 1986, has shown in a series of papers that the public (net) debt and deficit has to be computed correctly when the sustainability of public debt is studied. Eisner (1986) does not undertake an econometric study on sustainability of public debt, however.

If we define the discounted value of public debt as $b_t \equiv B_t d_t$ and the discounted value of the surplus as $s_t \equiv S_t d_t$, we can rewrite (6.20) and get

$$b_t = b_{t-1} - s_t. \tag{6.21}$$

Equation (6.21) is a simple first-order difference equation that can be solved by recursive substitution forward, leading to

$$b_t = \sum_{j=1}^{N} s_{t+j} + b_{t+N}. \tag{6.22}$$

If the second term in (6.22), b_{t+N}, goes to zero in the limit, the current value of public debt equals the sum of the expected discounted future noninterest surpluses. Then we have

$$b_t = E_t \sum_{j=1}^{N} s_{t+j}, \tag{6.23}$$

with E_t denoting the expectations of creditors. Equation (6.23) is the present-value borrowing constraint, and we refer to a fiscal policy that satisfies that constraint as a sustainable policy. Equivalent to requiring that (6.23) must be fulfilled is that the following condition holds:

$$\lim_{N \to \infty} E_t b_{t+N} = 0. \tag{6.24}$$

That equation is usually referred to as the no-Ponzi game condition (see, e.g., Blanchard and Fischer 1989, chapter 2).

Another strategy to test whether a given public debt is sustainable is to look at the ratio of public debt to GDP. The motivation for this procedure is that economies grow over time and that the GDP can be considered a proxy for the tax base. That means that the GDP multiplied with a given maximal tax rate represents the true collateral. Hence if the discounted debt-to-GDP ratio converges to zero for $t \to \infty$, a given fiscal policy should be sustainable. This is sometimes called "effective sustainability" in contrast to "actual sustainability" when the time series in the level of public debt is investigated (see Feve and Henin 1996).

In the next section we will try to shed some light on the question of whether conditions (6.23) and (6.24) are fulfilled for the United States and Germany employing a finite data set. To do so we basically follow the so-called restricted Flood-Garber test proposed by Hamilton and Flavin (1986). The starting point of this test is the equation

$$b_t = A_0 \prod_{j=1}^{t} (1 + r_j) + E_t \sum_{j=1}^{\infty} s_{t+j} + \varepsilon_t, \tag{6.25}$$

with ε_t an error term. If $A_0 = 0$, b_t will be stationary for any stationary series of s_t and the present-value borrowing constraint holds. If $A_0 > 0$, b_t will not be stationary.

Hamilton and Flavin used (6.25) and posited that the error term is given by the white noise process $\varepsilon_t = c_5 + \varepsilon_{1t}$. Inserting this error term in (6.25) and assuming that expectations about the current surplus depend on past surpluses gives only after some modifications[21] the following two equations which are simultaneously estimated by nonlinear least square.

$$s_t = c_1 + c_2 s_{t-1} + c_3 s_{t-2} + c_4 s_{t-3} + \varepsilon_{2t} \tag{6.26}$$

$$b_t = A_0 \prod_{j=1}^{t}(1 + r_j) + c_5 + \frac{(c_2 a + c_3 a^2 + c_4 a^3)s_t}{1 - c_2 a - c_3 a^2 - c_4 a^3}$$

$$+ \frac{(c_3 a + c_4 a^2)s_{t-1}}{1 - c_2 a - c_3 a^2 - c_4 a^3} + \frac{(c_4 a)s_{t-2}}{1 - c_2 a - c_3 a^2 - c_4 a^3} + \varepsilon_{1t}. \tag{6.27}$$

The term $a = 1/(1 + r)$ is based on a constant interest rate.[22] Hamilton and Flavin (1986) employ time series data from an earlier period, 1960–1984, for the United States and get results as reported in table 6.11.[23]

TABLE 6.11
Sustainability Test of Public Debt,
United States, 1960–1984

Param.	Estim.	t-Statistic
A_0	−61.52	−0.12
c_1	0.90	0.25
c_2	0.15	0.78
c_3	−0.47	−2.10
c_4	−0.51	−2.50
c_5	241.51	−3.50

[21] For details, see Hamilton and Flavin (1986), p. 817.

[22] In fact, for the time period Hamilton and Flavin (1986) consider, they take $r = 0.0112$. In later studies a time-varying interest rate has been suggested.

[23] Note that those results are undertaken for earlier periods. Including a more recent period might be more interesting. We reiterate the test by Hamilton and Flavin (1986) here for methodological purposes.

In order to create nonsustainability of public debt the parameter A_0 should be positive and statistically significant, as mentioned earlier. Consequently, this test does not suggest that the intertemporal budget constraint for the United States was violated. A_0 is a bubble term, and a positive value of this coefficient implies that b_{t+N} in (6.22) does not go to zero, thus violating equation (6.23). Since in the 1990s the U.S. fiscal debt was decreasing due to budget surpluses, the result would not change; that is, sustainability of public debt would certainly be met if we included that period (see, e.g., Bohn 1998).

Therefore, we focus on Germany, as one of the core countries of the European Union. Undertaking the sustainability test for Germany, we have computed net debt.[24] Like Hamilton and Flavin, we use annual data. For public net debt we employ total gross public debt minus public tangible assets. The term $a = 1/(1 + r)$ is as in Hamilton and Flavin (1986). We have taken for r the average real rate of return on long-term government bonds in Germany. The average real interest rate for the time period 1955–1994 was 0.041.[25] The results with the data for Germany from 1955 to 1994 are reported in table 6.12.

Again, nonstationarity of public net debt requires the parameter A_0 be positive and significantly different from zero. As the coefficient A_0 indicates, German public debt is not sustainable if one considers the time period from 1955 to 1994.

One might argue that the large increase in government debt caused by the unification of East and West Germany in 1990 marked a change in regime and that the no-Ponzi game condition would probably hold if

TABLE 6.12
Restricted Flood-Garber Test, 1955–1994

Param.	Estim.	Std. Error	t-Statistic
A_0	0.6889	0.3193	2.1572
c_1	9.63e-04	0.0137	−0.0704
c_2	1.4441	0.1187	12.17
c_3	−0.7011	0.192	−3.6516
c_4	0.2411	0.1240	1.944
c_5	−0.2996	1.4445	−0.2074

[24] For a justification of using net debt see Eisner and Pieper (1984).
[25] A description of the data is in the appendix to this chapter.

TABLE 6.13
Restricted Flood-Garber Test, 1955–1989

Param.	Estim.	Std. Error	t-Statistic
A_0	0.8049	0.5477	1.4698
c_1	3.04e-03	0.0153	0.1985
c_2	1.5076	0.1304	11.5638
c_3	−0.802	0.2095	−3.8286
c_4	0.2776	0.1356	2.0471
c_5	−0.5603	2.1327	−0.2627

we take data for the period 1955–1989. Therefore, we have studied that period. The results are reported in table 6.13.

As the results from table 6.13 indicate, the coefficient A_0 is still positive, but it is no longer statistically significant. That is, the hypothesis that German public debt was sustainable for the time period from 1955 to 1989 cannot be rejected. This suggests that the huge increase in German public debt due to German unification made German public debt unsustainable.[26]

Applying the methodology of Hamilton and Flavin, we could show that there are likely to be regime changes in the sustainability of public debt (at least for the German case). Although our results on the sustainability of debt are already informative, further research taking into account criticism of such methods seems to be necessary.[27]

6.5 CONCLUSION

This chapter has presented and estimated an endogenous growth model with public capital and government capital market borrowing. Our study shows that a stricter budgetary regime, in which public deficit is allowed only for public investment, appears to have a higher growth rate and a lower debt-to-private-capital ratio. But as to the growth effects of

[26] More tests that confirm this view are undertaken in Greiner and Semmler (1999).

[27] Bohn (1995), for example, examines the theoretical foundations of these studies and concludes that the existing empirical models are still not sufficiently theoretically founded, so the validity of those tests cannot be guaranteed. Semmler and Sieveking (2000) also consider the theoretical foundation of the studies on debt sustainability.

a debt-financed increase in public investment, we saw that less strict budgetary regimes do not necessarily show worse performance. Yet the numerical study revealed that less strict budgetary regimes are in general associated with higher debt-to-private-capital ratios, which again can offset the positive growth effect. Further, if too large a fraction of interest on the public debt is paid by issuing new debt, sustained per capita growth may not be feasible. We also have studied the transitional dynamics and the problem of indeterminacy of the growth path.

In the empirical part, we used an estimation strategy similar to the one employed in the previous chapter. The model suggests an explanation for the different growth performance of Germany and the United States in the postwar period. However, it must also be stated that the estimated parameters are partly out of line. Thus, this model performs worse than the models in chapters 3–5. But this is in part due to the theoretical model that postulates an endogenous growth model with only private and public capital. In our simplified model, all factors generating economic growth are summarized in private and public capital, while other important factors such as human capital, accumulation of knowledge, or positive externalities of investment are not explicitly taken into account.

Nevertheless, it is important to study the effects of fiscal policy on the growth rates of economies assuming that public expenditures can have productive effects. Indeed, there is sufficient evidence that public spending may have growth-stimulating effects (see the survey by Sturm, Kuper, and de Haan 1998). Therefore, theoretical endogenous growth models with productive government spending are worth studying.

In the framework of this model we also have studied the problem of the link of growth to debt sustainability. For Germany we have shown that the intertemporal budget constraint has been violated, mainly due to the unification, whereas it is fulfilled for the United States, given our estimated parameters. As regards more direct tests, we can draw from our time series studies the conclusion that the intertemporal budget constraint of the government has not been met for Germany if we include the time period after 1989. Yet, as our test showed, the hypothesis of stationarity in the discounted net debt cannot be rejected if we take the time period up to 1989. It is, however, difficult to reach a clear conclusion concerning sustainability of net debt with a time series that is as short as ours.[28] In fact, there may be a small sample bias.

Nevertheless, the study of the relationship among economic growth, public spending, and sustainability of public debt is important because

[28] Note that Hamilton and Flavin (1986), Wilcox (1989), and Trehan and Walsh (1991) used annual data from 1960 to 1984.

it helps to clarify whether public infrastructure spending can add to economic growth and whether given fiscal policies fulfill the intertemporal budget constraint and are sustainable.

APPENDIX

1. Derivations of Some Theoretical Results

Here we briefly sketch the derivation of the system of differential equations that describes our economy as well as the derivation of our comparative statics results.

To solve the optimization problem of the household we define $S = K + B$.[29] The flow budget constraint can be rewritten as

$$\dot{S} = -C - (\delta_K + n)K - nB + (w + r_1 K + r_2 B)(1 - \tau) + T_p.$$

and the current-value Hamiltonian is written as

$$H(\cdot) = L_0 u(C) + \gamma_1 ((w + r_1 K + r_2 B)(1 - \tau) + T_p - C - nB$$
$$- (\delta_K + n)K) + \gamma_2 (S - K - B)$$

where γ_1 is the shadow value (costate variable) of the total asset and γ_2 is a Lagrangian multiplier. Differentiating $H(\cdot)$ with respect to the control C and setting the derivative equal to zero gives

$$L_0 u'(C) = \gamma_1.$$

The evolution of γ_1 is given by

$$\dot{\gamma_1} = (\rho - n)\gamma_1 - \gamma_2.$$

Combining those two equations gives

$$\frac{\dot{C}}{C} = -\frac{1}{\sigma}\left(\rho - n - \frac{\gamma_2}{\gamma_1}\right). \tag{6.28}$$

---

[29] On this procedure see Mino (1996).

Moreover, the limiting transversality condition for the household

$$\lim_{t \to \infty} e^{-(\rho - n)t} \gamma_1 S = 0$$

must hold.

The necessary conditions for an optimum are completed by

$$\gamma_2 = \gamma_1 \left((1 - \tau) r_1 - (n + \delta_K) \right)$$

$$\gamma_2 = \gamma_1 \left((1 - \tau) r_2 - n \right).$$

Combining those two equations yields

$$\frac{\gamma_2}{\gamma_1} = \left((1 - \tau) r_1 - (n + \delta_K) \right) = \left((1 - \tau) r_2 - n \right). \tag{6.29}$$

This equation is the no-arbitrage condition between holding physical capital K and government bonds B; that is, the after-tax net rate of return to physical capital must be equal to the after-tax net rate of return to government bonds. That equation also gives the return on government bonds as $r_2 = r_1 - \delta_K / (1 - \tau)$. Taking (6.28) and (6.29) and using the marginal conditions for the firm, which state that the wage rate and the return on private capital equal the marginal product of labor and capital respectively, then gives the growth rate of consumption, $\dot{C}/C$, as a function of parameters and of the marginal product of private capital. The economy-wide resource constraint, $\dot{K}/K$, is obtained by combing the budget constraint of the household with the budget constraint of the government, where we used the definition of I_p and C_p. $\dot{G}/G$ is obtained from $\dot{G} = \varphi_3(1 - \varphi_0)T - (n + \delta_G)G$, with $T = \tau(w + r_1 K + r_2 B)$ and the marginal conditions and no-arbitrage condition giving w, r_1, and r_2. $\dot{B}/B$, finally, is an immediate consequence of the budgetary regime.

To derive the comparative statics results along a BGP we first state that the balanced growth rate is given by $\dot{C}/C$, which merely depends on the endogenous variable on the BGP $x^* = G^*/K^*$ and on exogenously given parameters. Further, fiscal policy in our model implies a change in the parameters $\varphi_1, \varphi_2, \varphi_3$, and φ_4 respectively. To analyze how x^* reacts to changes in those parameters, we compute c^* from[30] $\dot{c}/c = 0$ and insert that c^* in $\dot{b}/b$ and $\dot{x}/x$. Further, the constraint $C_p + T_p + \varphi_4 r_2 B = \varphi_0 B$ makes φ_0 an endogenous variable, which depends on $b, \varphi_1, \varphi_2, \varphi_4, \tau$, and α. Inserting that φ_0 in $\dot{b}/b$ and $\dot{x}/x$ and setting the left-hand side equal to zero then implicitly describes b^* and x^* along the BGP, and variations of x^* can be obtained by implicit differentiation.

---

[30] Note that we exclude the economically meaningless stationary point $c = b = x = 0$ such that we can consider our system in the rates of growth.

Defining $\dot{b}/b = 0 \equiv q(x, b, \varphi_0; \cdot)$ and $\dot{x}/x = 0 \equiv q_1(x, b, \varphi_0; \cdot)$, and implicitly differentiating these two equations with respect to the parameters leads to

$$\begin{bmatrix} \partial b/\partial z \\ \partial x/\partial z \end{bmatrix} = -\frac{1}{\det M} \begin{bmatrix} \partial q_1(\cdot)/\partial x & -\partial q(\cdot)/\partial x \\ -\partial q_1(\cdot)/\partial b & \partial q(\cdot)/\partial b \end{bmatrix} \begin{bmatrix} \partial q(\cdot)/\partial z \\ \partial q_1(\cdot)/\partial z \end{bmatrix}.$$

M is given by

$$M = \begin{bmatrix} \partial q(\cdot)/\partial b & \partial q(\cdot)/\partial x \\ \partial q_1(\cdot)/\partial b & \partial q_1(\cdot)/\partial x \end{bmatrix}$$

and z stands for the parameters φ_1, φ_2, φ_3, and φ_4.

2. Description of the Data Used in Section 6.4

For the net debt we have taken total gross public debt (local, state, and federal, excluding mutual indebtedness and excluding social insurance) minus public assets (local, state, and federal, excluding social insurance). Data for public debt are from Sachverständigenrat (1995); data for public assets are from Deutsche Bundesbank (1983, 1994, 1996).

Surplus exclusive of interest payments is defined as total consolidated receipts (*bereinigte Einnahmen*) minus total consolidated expenditures (*bereinigte Ausgaben*) plus interest payments (excluding social insurance, respectively). Those data were taken from Statistisches Bundesamt (1960, 1985, 1992, 1995).

To get real data we divided all data by the consumer price index with $1991 = 100$. Data for the consumer price index were taken from Sachverständigenrat (1995) and from Statistisches Bundesamt (1994a).

For the long-term interest rate we have taken the yield of long-term (three years or more) government bonds. Those data were taken from

TABLE 6.14
Computation of Discounted Real Public Net Debt

nominal public gross debt
− nominal public assets
= nominal public net debt
÷ consumer price index
= real public net debt
× discount factor ($d_t = \prod_{j=0}^{t-1}(1 + r_j)^{-1}$; $d_0 = 1$)
= discounted real public net debt

TABLE 6.15
Computation of Discounted Real Surplus Exclusive of
Interest Payments

total nominal public receipts
− total nominal public expenditures
= nominal public surplus inclusive of interest payments
− nominal interest payments
= nominal public surplus exclusive of interest payments
÷ consumer price index
= real public surplus exclusive of interest payments
× discount factor $(d_t = \prod_{j=0}^{t-1}(1 + r_j)^{-1};\ d_0 = 1)$
= discounted real public surplus exclusive of interest payments

Sachverständigenrat (1995) and from OECD (1973). The real long-term interest rate is defined as the interest rate minus inflation rate, with the inflation rate calculated from the consumer price index.

Finally, all data were discounted back to the year 1955 using the real long-term interest rate. Tables 6.14 and 6.15 give a survey of those computations.

CHAPTER 7

Economic Growth and Income Inequality

Not all countries grow at the same rate, and the gains from growth are not equally distributed. To investigate the reasons for these differences, we next consider the relation between economic growth and income distribution. Before we study this problem in the context of a more specific growth model, we give a brief survey of previous literature.

7.1 EARLIER THEORIES

Theories attempting to explain the distribution of income are as old as economics as a science. The classical economists Adam Smith, David Ricardo, and Karl Marx gave explanations of which part of national income goes to owners of capital, workers, and landlords, respectively.[1] Ricardo, for example, based his theory on the Malthusian idea of an unlimited supply of labor that brings down the wage rate to its subsistence level in the long run, due to decreasing returns in agriculture. The landlords consume their rent incomes, and only the owners of capital save a part of their profits, which is invested and generates economic growth.

The modern theory of income distribution begins after World War II with work by Kaldor (1956, 1961), Pasinetti (1962), Kalecki (1971), and others. Kaldor proposed a distribution theory based on Keynesian ideas. He presumes that owners of capital and workers have different propensities to save, with the latter's propensity being lower than the former's, an assumption that is necessary for the model to be stable. Further, in the work by Kaldor investment drives savings and the investment share, that is, the ratio of investment to GDP, is given exogenously. Because aggregate savings must equal aggregate investment, these two assumptions imply a certain distribution of income between capitalists and workers that may vary over the business cycle. Kaldor assumes that workers save, but he does not recognize that, as a consequence, they receive capital income. This omission was criticized by Pasinetti (1962), who extended the Kaldor model by taking this capital income into account.[2]

---

[1] An extensive treatment of the classical theory is given in Foley and Michl (1999).
[2] See also the model by Samuelson and Modigliani (1966).

Kalecki's (1971) model assumes that the degree of monopoly determines the mark-up in the product market and thereby the income distribution in an economy. Kalecki considers the market concentration and the degree of monopoly as a variable affecting the dominance of firms in the distribution of income. The degree of monopoly is defined not as the ratio of the price to marginal costs but rather as the ratio of sales to direct costs, which are composed of wages and material costs. As a result, Kalecki determines that the wage share depends only on the degree of monopoly and on the ratio of the material costs to the labor costs. The higher those two parameters, the lower the wage share in the economy. Over time, the wage share is roughly constant, yet the degree of monopoly rises while the ratio of material costs to labor costs declines.

Other theories that attempt to explain the distribution of income start from the neoclassical theory of factor income and attempt to give it a microeconomic foundation. Best known is the human capital approach. In this line of research it is assumed that economic decisions of individuals about their individual investments in the formation of human capital determine the income distribution. The question of what the income distribution looks like is answered in two steps: First, the optimal decision of the individual is derived, giving the amount of the individual's investment in skill formation. Second, the implications of the former solution for the income distribution are derived. Those implications depend on parameters such as the inherited skills or the age of a population. Taking these parameters from real-world economies is then supposed to explain the observed spread in incomes. The human capital approach goes back to the work by Mincer (1958) and Becker (1962). More up-to-date versions have been presented by Stiglitz (1975) and Riley (1976). The human capital approach is also relevant to the new growth theory (as demonstrated in this book in chapter 4). It is indeed an important factor affecting not only economic growth but also the distribution of income.

These theories, however, do not say anything about the relation between the state of development and the equality of income distribution. An important contribution to this field of research, still the subject of empirical debate, was made by Kuznets (1955). Kuznets argued that in the early stages of development, the rich accumulate more wealth than the poor. As a consequence, the income distribution becomes more unequal. Only when the level of aggregate income has reached a certain threshold is the trend reversed. Then the income distribution becomes more equal because lower-income groups gain more political influence, which tends to equalize income distribution. This relation between the degree of development and the distribution of income forms an inverted U-shaped function, known as the Kuznets curve, relating the level of GDP to some measure of inequality. Whether the Kuznets curve is confirmed by empirical data has not yet been resolved. Numerous studies have reached different conclusions (cf. Anand and Kanbur 1993; Ogwang 1995).

7.2 RECENT THEORIES

With the rise of the new growth theory, the relation between income distribution and economic growth has again attracted the attention of economists.[3] However, the issue of whether income distribution affects the growth rate or the causality runs the other way has not yet been resolved. This is a difficult problem because both the growth rate and income distribution are seen as endogenous variables. The recent theories on the interrelation of growth and income distribution can be classified roughly into three approaches.

In the first, income distribution affects the growth rate by determining the outcome of political elections and by affecting the efficiency with which resources are employed. The idea that income distribution affects economic growth via political elections goes back to work by Alesina and Rodrik (1994), Bertola (1993), Perotti (1993), and Persson and Tabellini (1994). The approach stating that inequality has effects on the efficient use of resources if capital markets are not perfect goes back to Galor and Zeira (1993) and Benabou (1995, 1996).

The second line of research assumes that wage differentials in industrialized countries are due to international trade, in particular due to imports of goods from less-developed countries. This is emphasized by Richardson (1995) and Wood (1995), among others.

The third approach focuses on education and technical change as causes for inequality. It particularly stresses the relation of technical change and supply and demand of groups with different skills. In Murphy, Riddell, and Romer (1998), for example, it is endogenous technical progress that leads to economic growth, but also generates wage inequality between low- and high-skilled workers. This literature will be further discussed in section 7.3.

In order to demonstrate the connection between the distribution of capital, the outcome of political elections, and the process of growth, we will give a brief sketch of the model by Alesina and Rodrik (1994).

Alesina and Rodrik assume an aggregate production function with private capital and labor as input factors. In addition to those factors, productive public investment also affects aggregate output. This public input is financed by an income tax, and it is assumed that the government

---

[3] For a survey of the literature on inequality and economic growth see Aghion, Caroli, and García-Peñalosa (1999).

runs a balanced budget at any moment in time. The households in this economy are identical with respect to their preferences but differ in capital endowment. The households receive labor and capital income and are assumed to maximize the discounted stream of utilities arising from consumption.

If we analyze this model, it turns out that a growth-maximizing income tax rate exists, just as in the model in chapter 6. This is not too surprising because productive public spending is financed by tax revenue. This demonstrates that the income tax rate affects the growth rate. For this model, one can also calculate the second-best income tax rate maximizing the utility function of the i-th household. The solution depends on the relative endowment of the household with capital, and the income tax rate is higher the poorer in capital endowment the household is. The reason is that the wage rate positively depends on the income tax rate because a higher income tax rate implies more public investment, which has a stimulating effect on the marginal product of labor, that is, on the wage rate. An interesting result is obtained when the household does not work but receives interest income from its capital endowment. In this case, the growth-maximizing income tax rate coincides with the rate the household would choose. However, if the household also gets labor income, then it chooses an income tax rate that exceeds the growth-maximizing rate.

The tax rate in the economy is set by the party that represents the median voter. Consequently, the tax rate that is most favorable for the median voter will be implemented. In reality, the distribution of capital is such that the median's capital share is lower than the average. Further, the difference between the median and the average is larger the more unequal the distribution is. As a consequence, economies with an unequal distribution of capital end up with a higher income tax rate, which has negative effects on economic growth. It should also be mentioned that this result can be generalized to the income distribution. In that case, a more unequal distribution of income leads to a higher tax rate and, as a consequence, to lower growth. This generalization can be made because labor is assumed to be homogeneous and all households have the same amount available, implying that a higher relative capital labor share goes along with a higher income.

This model demonstrates that the income distribution determines the growth process through the political process. A more unequal society tends to choose a higher income tax rate, which negatively affects economic growth.

The starting point of the approach emphasizing the importance of credit markets and inequality is the idea that an unequal distribution of income and wealth, together with incomplete capital markets, leads to an inefficient use of resources. To illustrate this idea we refer to the model presented by Benabou (1996).

An important assumption in this model is that human capital is formed as by-product of investment. This means that any unit of investment increases both physical capital and the efficiency of labor, as in the model presented in chapter 3. Another important assumption is that the aggregate production function in this economy is characterized by decreasing returns to scale. Individuals in this economy differ with respect to their initial human capital, which can be invested or consumed. Further, individuals can borrow on the capital market, but this market may be incomplete. This means that not every individual has the opportunity to get a loan. Redistribution in this economy is achieved by taxing individuals with higher initial capital and by redistributing tax revenue to those individuals who have smaller stocks of human capital.

If credit markets are incomplete, investment differs between individuals because they have different stocks of human capital. In general, individuals invest more the larger their stock of human capital. Further, poor individuals invest more the greater the amount of capital that is redistributed. However, with greater redistribution, rich individuals invest less. But the additional output of poor individuals, as a result of redistribution, is larger than the loss in output due to richer individuals being taxed because the production function has decreasing returns. Therefore, redistribution increases investment and leads to a higher growth rate.

If capital markets are complete, every individual can borrow the same amount independent of his or her initial condition. This implies that the growth rate is independent of the distribution of human capital. As a consequence, redistribution does not affect the growth rate if capital markets are complete. The reason is that, in this case, the unequal distribution of resources is compensated by individuals getting credit. To summarize, redistribution increases economic growth if credit markets are incomplete but does not have growth effects if an economy is characterized by complete credit markets.

The negative correlation between inequality and economic growth also seems to be compatible with empirical observations. We do not go into the details of the empirical literature but mention the studies by Persson and Tabellini (1994) and by Perotti (1996). Perotti estimates an equation with the GDP growth rate as the dependent variable, which is explained by the variable equality and by other variables for a sample of sixty-seven countries. He finds that there is a positive and statistically significant correlation between economic growth and income distribution. The more equal income distribution is, the higher the growth rate. Further, this result is robust, meaning that the correlation is not caused by outliers or by heteroscedasticity. Basically the same outcome is obtained by Persson and Tabellini (1994), who use data from fifty-six countries from 1960 to 1985. These authors also find that in the countries they consider, the growth rate is higher the more equal the income distribution.

Another channel through which wage differentials can be affected is international trade. This has been pointed out by Richardson (1995) and Wood (1995), among others. The starting point of the theoretical analysis is the Heckscher-Ohlin theory, in which trade and wages are linked only through changes in product prices. If the domestic price of a high-technology good rises relative to the price of a low-technology good, the wages of the skilled workers will rise relative to those of the unskilled. This linkage is known as the Stolper-Samuelson theorem. It holds true because the Heckscher-Ohlin theory assumes a fixed relationship between output and input factors, which implies a similarly fixed relationship between the prices of goods and factor payments.

It should be noted that such a change in product prices is brought about by exogenous factors. One possibility for a change in the prices of products is a reduction of trade barriers, such as a decrease in transport costs or in tariffs. This will drive a wedge between the price of the high-technology good and the low-technology good, with the latter becoming relatively cheaper in the developed country. The second possibility that could affect product prices is a change in relative supplies of skilled and unskilled workers. For example, an increase in unskilled workers in the developing countries increases the output of the low-technology good and, consequently, reduces its relative price on the world market.

The exogenously induced change in the price of the low-quality good affects the wage differential between skilled and unskilled workers. As a consequence, the relative wage of the unskilled workers declines. It should be noted that this decrease in the relative wage of the unskilled workers is also feasible if the supply of unskilled workers rises and if the labor demand curve has a finite elasticity, without changing the price of the good. However, if the labor demand curve is infinitely elastic, an increase in the labor supply, as long as it does not alter the price of the two types of goods, will only change the composition of the output, not the relative wage. This is called the "pure Rybczynski" case. An objection to this line of reasoning is that the level of imports of manufactured goods is small. For example, the United States imported less than 3 percent of GDP from low-wage countries in 1990.

An argument against this objection is provided by calculating the factor content of the impacts of trade. This shows to what extent skilled and unskilled workers are used in the production of a country's exports and how much they would have been used if it had produced its imports by itself rather than imported them. The differences between exports and imports are then seen as the effects of trade on the employment of unskilled and skilled labor, in comparison to the situation without trade. An example of this method is provided by Sachs and Shatz (1994), who use it to find the effect of the change in trade between 1978 and 1990 on the demand for production and nonproduction workers in manufacturing in the United States. The outcome of their study is that trade with developing countries diminished the employment of unskilled workers in the United States because the reduction in output was concentrated primarily in sectors with relatively few skilled workers.

Wood (1995) argues that many of the factor content calculations in the literature are biased downward because of the way they calculate the labor content of imported goods. The factor content method implicitly assumes that the goods exported contain as much skilled and unskilled labor as the goods imported. This, however, does not hold true. Instead, developed countries specialize in the production of skill-intensive goods, while they import unskilled-labor-intensive goods. Given this situation, producing all of the imports at home implies that more unskilled workers are needed than obtained by assuming that the exports are just as unskilled-labor-intensive as the imports. As a consequence, Wood (1995) obtains higher estimates of the decline in the number of unskilled workers caused by trade with low-wage countries than do Sachs and Shatz (1994).

7.3 TECHNOLOGICAL CHANGE AND WAGE INEQUALITY

Here we present a growth model that brings into focus the interrelation of education, technical change, and wage inequality. The model builds on an idea presented by Murphy, Riddell, and Romer (1998). Those authors assume that technical progress leads to wage differentials between high-skilled workers and unskilled workers.[4] As technical progress occurs, the relative marginal productivity of different inputs changes. Moreover, if there is sufficient complementarity between skills and new technology, the demand for more educated employees rises, which also may permit an increase in their wages relative to those of unskilled workers.

However, the work by Murphy, Riddell, and Romer (1998) is not the only contribution analyzing the relationship between technical change and income inequality. Galor and Tsiddon (1997), for example, examine the interaction among technical progress, wage inequality, intergenerational earnings mobility, and economic growth. They demonstrate that earnings mobility determines the speed of technical progress and economic growth, while technical progress determines wage inequality and intergenerational

---

[4] However, in contrast to Krusell et al. (2000), they do not consider substitution between unskilled labor and capital.

earnings mobility. Acemoglu (1998) underlines the importance of high-skilled labor in generating technical progress. On the one hand, a greater supply of high-skilled workers depresses the wages of high-skilled workers simply because high-skilled labor becomes less scarce. On the other hand, more high-skilled labor leads to new technologies that increase the demand for high-skilled workers and, as a consequence, to higher wages for high-skilled workers. Thus, an increase in the number of high-skilled workers does not necessarily imply lower wages for high-skilled workers. Galor and Moav (2000) also emphasize the role of skill-biased technical change in explaining the evolution of technology, educational attainment, and wage inequality. They assert that faster technical change increases the return to ability and increases wage inequality between, and also within, groups of high-skilled and unskilled workers. Further, faster technical change also leads to an increase in educational attainment and to higher average wages of skilled workers but to temporarily lower average wages of unskilled workers. Acemoglu, Aghion, and Violante (2001) in addition emphasize the role of unions in determining the wage premium to high-skilled workers. These authors argue that wage inequality and deunionization are related and that skill-biased technical change has been an important factor in deunionization and in the rise in wage inequality in the United States and United Kingdom over the last twenty-five years. The argument is that skill-biased technical change leads to deunionization because it increases the outside option of high-skilled workers and lowers the solidarity between high-skilled and low-skilled workers. Deunionization is not the cause but amplifies the increase in wage inequality, which is an immediate consequence of technical change.

The Model

Murphy, Riddell, and Romer (1998), however, do not model inequality in the context of an endogenous growth model. To achieve this, we start with the endogenous Romer (1990) growth model presented in chapter 5. Additionally, we assume that the number of capital goods, the designs A, positively affects the efficiency of both unskilled and skilled labor input. That is, we assume that capital is associated with positive externalities. We do this because technical progress is embodied in new capital goods. Therefore, installing a new machine does not just increase the capital stock but also increases the productivity of the labor input. That is, any worker is expected to produce more output with the new machine compared to the old machine (for the empirical relevance of this point, see the studies mentioned in chapter 3).

The structure of the productive sector is the same as in the basic model presented in chapter 5. Therefore, we will only briefly sketch the derivation of the equations. To integrate our idea in the Romer (1990) growth model, we first have to introduce the modified Cobb-Douglas production function

$$
Y = K^{1-\alpha} A^\alpha \eta^{\alpha-1} \left\{ \gamma_1 \left[A^\xi (H - H_A) \right]^{\frac{\sigma_p-1}{\sigma_p}} + (1 - \gamma_1) \left[A^\epsilon L \right]^{\frac{\sigma_p-1}{\sigma_p}} \right\}^{\frac{\alpha \sigma_p}{\sigma_p-1}},
$$

$$(7.1)$$

with K physical capital, H_Y high-skilled employees producing output, and H_A high-skilled employees engaged in R&D. $H = H_Y + H_A$ gives the total number of high-skilled workers in the economy. L gives the number of low-skilled workers, who produce only output. σ_p, finally, gives the elasticity of substitution between H_Y and L. As in Acemoglu (2002), we say that skilled and unskilled workers are gross substitutes when $\sigma_p > 1$ and gross complements when $\sigma_p < 1$. ξ and ϵ measure the impact of the external effect (the knowledge spillover), that is, the impact of technical progress, on H_Y and L. We may speak of skill-biased technical change if $\xi > \epsilon$ holds because in this case technical change increases labor productivity of high-skilled employees to a greater degree than labor productivity of low-skilled workers. η gives the units of forgone output that are needed to produce one unit of an intermediate good (see chapter 5).

Thus, the capital accumulation equation can be written as

$$
\dot{K} = K^{1-\alpha} A^\alpha \eta^{\alpha-1} \{X\}^{\frac{\alpha \sigma_p}{\sigma_p-1}} - C,
$$

$$(7.2)$$

with

$$
X = \gamma_1 \left[A^\xi (H - H_A) \right]^{\frac{\sigma_p-1}{\sigma_p}} + (1 - \gamma_1) \left[A^\epsilon L \right]^{\frac{\sigma_p-1}{\sigma_p}}.
$$

$$(7.3)$$

The firms in the final-good sector behave competitively. The solution to their optimization problem again gives the inverse demand function for the intermediate good $x(i)$. With the production function (7.1) it is given by

$$
p(i) = X^{\frac{\alpha \sigma_p}{\sigma_p-1}} (1 - \alpha) K^{-\alpha} \eta^{-\alpha} A^\alpha.
$$

$$(7.4)$$

The intermediate firm that produces $x(i)$ takes this function as given in solving its optimization problem. The solution to this problem gives the interest rate as

$$
r = (1 - \alpha)^2 \eta^{\alpha-1} K^{-\alpha} A^\alpha X^{\frac{\alpha \sigma_p}{\sigma_p-1}}.
$$

$$(7.5)$$

Neglecting depreciation of knowledge, the differential equation describing the evolution of the stock of knowledge or the number of designs, A, is given by

$$\dot{A} = \mu H_A^\gamma A^\phi, \tag{7.6}$$

with $\gamma, \phi \in (0, 1)$ (cf. chapter 5).

The differential equation describing the evolution of H_A over time is also obtained as in chapter 5. First, one uses the fact that the price of knowledge at time t, $P(t)$, is equal to the present value of the stream of profits, π, of each intermediate firm because the research sector behaves competitively. This leads to the differential equation

$$\dot{P}_A = r P_A - \pi, \tag{7.7}$$

with $\pi = r x \eta \alpha / (1 - \alpha)$. Second, the rental rate of human capital in the final-good sector and in the research sector must be equal. This fact gives rise to the following differential equation

$$\frac{\dot{P}_A}{P_A} = \left(\frac{\alpha \, \sigma_p}{\sigma_p - 1} - 1\right) \frac{\dot{X}}{X} + (1 - \alpha)\frac{\dot{K}}{K} + \left(\frac{\sigma_p - 1}{\sigma_p} - 1\right) \frac{\dot{H} - \dot{H}_A}{H - H_A}$$
$$+ (1 - \gamma)\frac{\dot{H}_A}{H_A} + \left(\alpha - \phi + \xi \frac{\sigma_p - 1}{\sigma_p}\right)\frac{\dot{A}}{A}. \tag{7.8}$$

Dividing (7.7) by P_A, setting the resulting expression equal to (7.8), and solving for $\dot{H}_A$ yields

$$\dot{H}_A = Z^{-1} \cdot \left[\left(\frac{\gamma}{\gamma_1}\right)(1 - \alpha)\mu X H_A^{\gamma-1}(H - H_A)^{\frac{1+\sigma_p}{\sigma_p}} A^{\phi-1+\xi\frac{1-\sigma_p}{\sigma_p}} \right.$$

$$- (1 - \alpha)(H - H_A)\frac{C}{K} + \left(\frac{\sigma_p - 1}{\sigma_p} - 1\right)n_H H$$

$$+ \left(\alpha - \phi + \xi\frac{\sigma_p - 1}{\sigma_p}\right)\mu H_A^\gamma A^{\phi-1}(H - H_A)$$

$$+ X^{-1}\left(\frac{\alpha\sigma_p}{\sigma_p - 1} - 1\right)\frac{\sigma_p - 1}{\sigma_p}\gamma_1\left(A^\xi(H - H_A)\right)^{\frac{\sigma_p-1}{\sigma_p}}$$

$$\cdot \left(\xi\mu H_A^\gamma A^{\phi-1}(H - H_A) + H n_H\right)$$

$$+ (H - H_A)\alpha(1 - \alpha)\eta^{\alpha-1}K^{-\alpha}A^\alpha X^{\alpha\sigma_p/(1-\sigma_p)}$$

$$+ X^{-1}\left(\frac{\alpha\sigma_p}{\sigma_p - 1} - 1\right)\frac{\sigma_p - 1}{\sigma_p}(1 - \gamma_1)\left(A^\epsilon L\right)^{\frac{\sigma_p-1}{\sigma_p}}(H - H_A)$$

$$\left. \cdot \left(\epsilon\mu H_A^\gamma A^{\phi-1} + n\right)\right], \tag{7.9}$$

with

$$Z = \left(\frac{\sigma_p - 1}{\sigma_p}\right) - (1 - \gamma)\frac{H - H_A}{H_A}$$

$$+ \gamma_1 \left(\frac{\sigma_p - 1}{\sigma_p}\right)X^{-1}\left(\frac{\alpha\sigma_p}{\sigma_p - 1}\right)\left(A^\xi (H - H_A)\right)^{\frac{\sigma_p - 1}{\sigma_p}}.$$

n_H and n give the growth rate of the total stock of human capital or skilled labor H and the growth rate of labor supply L, that is,

$$\dot{H} = Hn_H, \tag{7.10}$$

$$\dot{L} = Ln. \tag{7.11}$$

The model is completed by modeling the household sector. The household sector consists of two representative households. The first supplies skilled labor H; the second supplies unskilled labor L. The optimization problems of the households are given by

$$\max_{C_j} \int_0^\infty e^{-\rho t} u_j(C_j(t))dt, \quad j = H, L, \tag{7.12}$$

subject to the budget constraints. It should be noted that the following identities hold, $K_H + K_L = K$ and $C_H + C_L = C$, that is, the total aggregate capital stock and consumption equal the sum of the capital stocks and consumption of both households.

The optimization problem gives the growth rates of consumption as

$$\frac{\dot{C}_j}{C_j} = -\frac{\rho_j - r}{\sigma_j}, \quad j = H, L, \tag{7.13}$$

with $1/\sigma_j$ the constant intertemporal elasticity of substitution of consumption between two points in time of household j, $j = H, L$, and ρ_j the subjective rate of time preference of household j, $j = H, L$.

The system to be estimated, which contains only observable variables, is then given by equations (7.2), (7.6), (7.9), (7.10), (7.11), and (7.13), with the interest rate r given by (7.5). It must be noted that in estimating (7.13) we cannot identify whether we estimate (σ_L, ρ_L) or (σ_{Hy}, ρ_{Hy}). This holds because no data are available for the level of consumptions of households supplying skilled labor H_Y or unskilled labor L. Therefore, we have to employ aggregate data.

Our economy is completely described by equations (7.2), (7.6), (7.9), (7.10), (7.11), and (7.13), with the interest rate r given by (7.5). A BGP for this model is derived as for the semiendogenous growth model with R&D in chapter 5. Again, we define a BGP as a path with a constant output/capital ratio, Y/K, and where all variables grow at constant but not necessarily equal rates. This implies

$$\frac{\dot{Y}}{Y} = \frac{\dot{K}}{K} = \frac{\dot{C}}{C} = \frac{\dot{C}_H}{C_H} = \frac{\dot{C}_L}{C_L}.$$

It should be noted that a common growth rate of consumption of the two households implies that aggregate consumption grows at the same rate. That holds because of

$$\frac{\dot{C}}{C} = \frac{\dot{C}_H}{C_H}\frac{C_H}{C} + \frac{\dot{C}_L}{C_L}\frac{C_L}{C} = g\left(\frac{C_H}{C} + \frac{C_L}{C}\right) = \frac{\dot{C}_j}{C_j} = -\frac{\rho_j - r}{\sigma_j}, \quad j = H, L,$$

with $g = \dot{C}_H/C_H = \dot{C}_L/C_L$.

The intertemporal elasticity of substitution of the two households and the subjective rate of time preference need not necessarily be equal but may differ to a certain degree. However, for a common growth rate of consumption to exist, those parameters cannot take arbitrary values. This holds because a common growth rate for C_H and C_L implies that

$$\frac{\sigma_L}{\sigma_H} = \frac{\rho_L - r}{\rho_H - r}$$

must always be fulfilled.

Further, using $d/dt\,(\dot{A}/A) = 0$ and $d/dt\,(\dot{K}/K) = 0$ yields

$$\frac{\dot{A}}{A} = \frac{\gamma}{1 - \phi}n_{H_A}, \quad \frac{\dot{K}}{K} = \frac{\gamma}{1 - \phi}n_{H_A} + \frac{\sigma_p}{\sigma_p - 1}\frac{\dot{X}}{X},$$

where we define $n_{H_A} = \dot{H}_A/H_A$. If the growth rates of A and H_Y are constant, it can easily be shown that the following relation holds concerning the growth rate of X:

$$\lim_{t \to \infty} \frac{\dot{X}}{X} = \frac{\sigma_p - 1}{\sigma_p}\left(\xi n_A + n_{H_Y}\right), \quad \text{for} \quad (\epsilon\, n_A + n) \le (\xi\, n_A + n_{H_Y}),$$

with n and n_i denoting the growth rate of L and of variable i, $i = A, H_Y$ respectively. The condition $(\epsilon\, n_A + n) \le (\xi\, n_A + n_{H_Y})$ does not pose a true limitation of our model. This holds because, on the one hand, the growth rate of high-skilled labor in the final-goods sector, n_{H_Y}, has been larger than the growth rate of unskilled labor, n, in the industrialized countries in the recent decades. On the other hand, it is to be expected that the external effect associated with new machines, that is, with a rise in A, is greater for skilled labor than for unskilled labor, implying $\xi > \epsilon$. Moreover, dividing (7.7) by P_A and setting it equal to (7.8) shows that on a BGP, H_A and H_Y must grow at the same rate.[5] This fact, together with the constraint $H_A + H_Y = H$, implies that H also grows at the rate with which H_A and H_Y grow on the BGP; that is, we have $n_{H_A} = n_{H_Y} = n_H$. Thus, on a BGP we have

$$\frac{\dot{K}}{K} - n_H - n = n_H \frac{\gamma}{1 - \phi} (1 + \xi) - n. \tag{7.14}$$

This equation demonstrates that a sufficient and necessary condition for the growth rate of aggregate variables to exceed the growth rate of skilled and unskilled labor is

$$n_H \frac{\gamma}{1 - \phi} (1 + \xi) > n. \tag{7.15}$$

If the growth rate of human capital (high-skilled labor) equals zero, the growth rate of aggregate variables is smaller than the growth rate of labor input in the long run, just as in the modified Romer model (cf. chapter 5). Then on the BGP, aggregate output, aggregate physical capital, and aggregate consumption grow at the same rate as labor input. Looking at condition (7.15) one sees that it is more likely to be fulfilled the more productive human capital in the research process is, that is, the higher γ, and the larger the positive externality of new designs, that is, the higher ξ.

However, as in the modified R&D model of chapter 5, sustained per capita growth occurs only if the growth rate of human capital is positive, that is, if $n_H > 0$. Thus, we again get a semiendogenous growth model in which conventional government policies cannot affect the long-run balanced growth rate. In the next section we will discuss the implications of parameters values for the wage premium, assuming competitive labor markets.

The Wage Premium

The wage premium is defined as the ratio of the wages earned by high-skilled workers to the wages earned by low-skilled workers. This variable is of potential interest to economists because it can be seen as a measure for the flexibility of the labor market, which has repercussions for the unemployment rate in an economy. For example, a low rate of change of the wage premium may indicate a relatively large increase in low-skilled wages, which has negative effects on overall employment.[6]

---

[5] It can be shown that for $(\epsilon\, n_A + n) > (\xi\, n_A + n_{H_Y})$ no BGP with constant and positive per capita growth exists.

[6] In our model we do not explicitly take into consideration unemployment.

Further, the wage premium reflects the inequality between high-skilled and low-skilled workers. If the wage premium rises, the gap between employees getting high wages and employees getting low wages widens, which tends to make the income distribution more unequal. If the wage premium falls, the reverse holds.

According to Acemoglu (1998) the wage premium is determined by two factors. First, an increase in the supply of high-skilled workers reduces the wage rate for this kind of work and tends to reduce the wage premium. Second, a rise in the number of high-skilled workers implies that the profitability of technologies that are complementary to high-skilled labor increases. This has a positive effect on the wages of high-skilled workers and, consequently, increases the wage premium. It should be noted that an increase in the supply of high-skilled workers may also be the result of government policies. If a government increases expenditures for education, the number of high-skilled workers is expected to rise over time. If it reduces public spending for education, the converse holds.

To derive the wage premium, we first recall that the production function is given by

$$Y = K^{1-\alpha} A^{\alpha} \eta^{\alpha-1} \{X\}^{\frac{\alpha \sigma_p}{\sigma_p-1}}, \tag{7.16}$$

with

$$X = \gamma_1 \left[A^{\xi} (H - H_A) \right]^{\frac{\sigma_p-1}{\sigma_p}} + (1 - \gamma_1) \left[A^{\epsilon} L \right]^{\frac{\sigma_p-1}{\sigma_p}}$$

and $H - H_A = H_Y$. If we assume competitive markets, the wage rates of the high- and low-skilled employees are equal to the marginal products of high- and low-skilled work in the production sector. This gives

$$w_H = \alpha \gamma_1 \eta^{\alpha-1} K^{1-\alpha} A^{\alpha} X^{\frac{\alpha \sigma_p}{\sigma_p-1}-1} A^{\frac{\xi(\sigma_p-1)}{\sigma_p}} H_Y^{-\frac{1}{\sigma_p}}, \tag{7.17}$$

$$w_L = \eta^{\alpha-1} \alpha (1 - \gamma_1) K^{1-\alpha} A^{\alpha} X^{\frac{\alpha \sigma_p}{\sigma_p-1}-1} A^{\frac{\epsilon(\sigma_p-1)}{\sigma_p}} L^{-\frac{1}{\sigma_p}}. \tag{7.18}$$

The ratio of the marginal products of the two types of labor, the wage premium w_p, is given by

$$w_p \equiv \frac{w_H}{w_L} = \frac{\gamma_1}{1-\gamma_1} \left[\frac{A^{\xi}}{A^{\epsilon}} \right]^{\frac{\sigma_p-1}{\sigma_p}} \left[\frac{H_Y}{L} \right]^{-\frac{1}{\sigma_p}} \tag{7.19}$$

This result is similar to the one obtained by Murphy, Riddell, and Romer (1998). The major difference is that in our model the external effect of technical change, ξ and ϵ, appears in the wage premium.

Defining

$$A_{w_p} \equiv \frac{A^\xi}{A^\epsilon}, \; L_{w_p} \equiv \frac{H_Y}{L}. \tag{7.20}$$

we can derive a differential equation describing the evolution of the ratio w_p, which is

$$\frac{\dot{w}_p}{w_p} = \left(\frac{\sigma_p - 1}{\sigma_p}\right) \frac{\dot{A}_{w_p}}{A_{w_p}} - \left(\frac{1}{\sigma_p}\right) \frac{\dot{L}_{w_p}}{L_{w_p}}. \tag{7.21}$$

From the definitions of A_{w_p} and L_{w_p} we get

$$\frac{\dot{A}_{w_p}}{A_{w_p}} = (\xi - \epsilon)\frac{\dot{A}}{A}, \tag{7.22}$$

$$\frac{\dot{L}_{w_p}}{L_{w_p}} = \frac{\dot{H}_Y}{H_Y} - \frac{\dot{L}}{L}. \tag{7.23}$$

Looking at the wage premium, equation (7.19), we see that four main factors determine this variable.

First is the quotient of the productivity parameters $\gamma_1/(1 - \gamma_1)$. If γ_1 is close to zero, the wage premium will have a small value too. A small value for γ_1 means that low-skilled workers contribute more to output than high-skilled workers and have a higher productivity. Consequently, the wage of the low-skilled workers is relatively high and the wage premium is relatively low. If γ_1 is large, say close to 1, the reverse holds. That is, the productivity of the high-skilled workers is relatively high, and, as a consequence, their wage rate and the wage premium are high, too.

Second, the ratio A^ξ/A^ϵ affects the wage premium. A high (low) value for ξ relative to ϵ means that the positive external effect of technical change affects high-skilled workers to a greater (lesser) degree than low-skilled workers. That is, technical change, an increase in A, leads to a greater (smaller) increase in the productivity of high-skilled workers than low-skilled workers. As a consequence, the larger the positive difference $\xi - \epsilon$, the higher the wage premium, provided skilled and unskilled labor are gross substitutes, that is, for $\sigma_p > 1$. In this case technical change, that is, an increase in A, raises the wage premium. If skilled and unskilled labor are gross complements ($\sigma_p < 1$), technical change, that is, an increase in A, leads to a decline in the wage premium. This holds because in this case skilled and unskilled labor are gross complements, and therefore the relative increase in the labor productivity of skilled labor also increases the demand for unskilled labor, such that the latter increase exceeds the increase in demand for skilled labor.

Third, the number of high-skilled workers relative to the number of low-skilled workers determines the wage premium. If this ratio is high, the supply of high-skilled workers is relatively large. As a consequence, the wage premium will take on a low value.

The fourth factor that affects the wage premium is the elasticity of substitution between high-skilled and low-skilled workers, σ_p. To find the effect of σ_p on the wage differential, we rewrite (7.19) and get

$$w_p = \frac{w_H}{w_L} = \frac{\gamma_1}{1 - \gamma_1} A^{\xi - \epsilon} \left[A^{\epsilon - \xi} \left(\frac{L}{H_Y} \right) \right]^{\frac{1}{\sigma_p}}. \tag{7.24}$$

Differentiating that expression with respect to σ_p gives

$$\frac{\partial w_p}{\partial \sigma_p} = -\frac{\gamma_1}{1 - \gamma_1} A^{\xi - \epsilon} \left[A^{\epsilon - \xi} \frac{L}{H_Y} \right]^{\frac{1}{\sigma_p}} \sigma_p^{-2} \ln \left[A^{\epsilon - \xi} \left(\frac{L}{H_Y} \right) \right]. \tag{7.25}$$

This expression is positive (negative) for $A^{\epsilon - \xi}(L/H_Y) < (>) 1$. This implies that a higher elasticity of substitution increases (reduces) the wage differential if the ratio (L/H_Y) is relatively small (large), that is, if it is smaller (larger) than the threshold level $A^{\xi - \epsilon}$. That means if the supply of high-skilled workers is relatively large, an increase in the elasticity of substitution between high-skilled and low-skilled workers increases the wage differential. If the supply of high-skilled workers is small, a higher elasticity of substitution between high-skilled and low-skilled workers reduces the wage differential.

The growth rate of the wage differential is given by equation (7.21) together with (7.22) and (7.23). It crucially depends on the elasticity of substitution between high-skilled and low-skilled workers, that is, on σ_p. The effect of σ_p on the growth rate of the wage differential is obtained by differentiating (7.21) with respect to σ_p. This gives

$$\frac{\partial (\dot{w}_p / w_p)}{\partial \sigma_p} = \frac{1}{\sigma_p^2} \left[\frac{\dot{A}_{w_p}}{A_{w_p}} + \frac{\dot{L}_{w_p}}{L_{w_p}} \right]. \tag{7.26}$$

If the sum in brackets is positive, an increase in the elasticity of substitution raises the growth rate of the wage differential. This means that the difference between high-skilled and low-skilled wages rises with a higher elasticity of substitution, provided the term in brackets is positive. This latter expression is composed of two parts. First is the difference between the growth rates of the labor productivity of high-skilled and low-skilled workers. A positive difference tends to make the expression in brackets positive. Second is the difference between the growth rates of high-skilled workers and low-skilled workers. If this expression is positive, the term in brackets tends to be positive, too.

Thus, we can state that an increase in the elasticity of substitution between high- and low-skilled workers raises the growth rate of the wage differential if there is skill-biased technical change and if the growth rate of high-skilled labor exceeds the growth rate of low-skilled labor. If high-skilled and low-skilled labor grow at the same rate, only the skill bias $(\xi - \epsilon)$ affects equation (7.26). Then the growth rate of the wage differential is higher the higher the elasticity of substitution between high-skilled and low-skilled workers, provided that skill-biased technical change $(\xi - \epsilon > 0)$ is a given. If the labor productivity of low-skilled workers grows faster than that of high-skilled workers as a consequence of technical change, that is, if $\xi < \epsilon$, the reverse holds. In that case, an increase in the elasticity of substitution reduces the growth rate of the wage differential; that is, the difference between high-skilled and low-skilled wages becomes smaller over time.

Some Empirical Results on Wage Inequality

In this section we look at the evolution of the wage differential between high-skilled and low-skilled workers in the United States and in Germany. First, we state some stylized facts and then look at empirical estimates of the parameters determining the wage differential.

FACTS ON THE WAGE PREMIUM

Before undertaking empirical estimations one should consider some facts on inequality. Figure 7.1 presents the pattern of wage premiums for four OECD member countries: Germany, the United Kingdom, France, and the United States. It should be mentioned that, particularly in the case of Germany and the United States, different measures of wage inequality are compared. The data of wage differentials are taken from the OECD *Employment Outlook* (1993–1996). In this source, wage inequality is measured by the ratios of the 10th (D1) and 50th (D5) percentile to the 90th (D9) percentile of wage earners.[7] Taking into account that the 90th percentile of the income distribution shows the wages earned almost entirely by high-skilled workers, whereas the 10th percentile shows the wages for low-skilled workers, it can be shown that the median income of different skill groups increases with the level of education.

---

[7] See, e.g., Katz and Autor (1999); and Murphy, Riddell, and Romer (1998) for similar approaches.

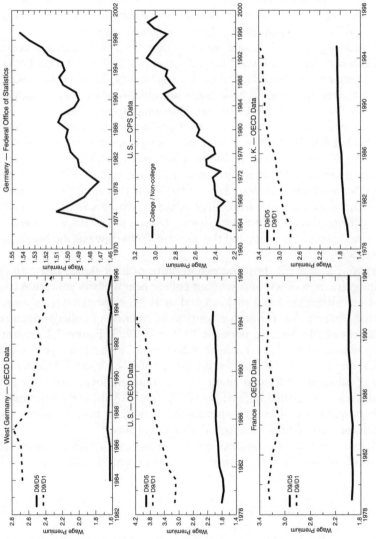

Figure 7.1. Patterns of wage premiums.

For the United States and Germany we also employ different sources. Long time series for U.S. wage data are taken from the U.S. Bureau of the Census (1998, 2000). For Germany a separate time series of wage inequality is constructed by taking data of the *Fachserie 16* published by Statistisches Bundesamt (Federal Office of Statistics). In this case, we compare wages earned by employees at supervisory job positions to wage earners at lower job positions in thè manufacturing sector.[8]

Considering figure 7.1, one observes that the D9/D5 ratios increase moderately or remain constant for each country. Furthermore, the D9/D1 ratios, derived from the OECD data, increase sharply for the United States and the United Kingdom. For Germany one observes a decreasing pattern, while for France the D9/D1 ratio remains roughly constant.

Concentrating on Germany and having a look at the data taken from Statistisches Bundesamt, we observe increasing inequality for the employees in the West German manufacturing sector. In particular, we observe a sharp increase of the wage premium since the middle 1990s. For the United States, Census Bureau data (1998) show that until the end of the 1970s the wage premium for college-educated workers over those without a college education increases slowly. During the 1980s we observe a sharp increase in this ratio, and the increase slows down at the beginning of the 1990s.[9]

Figures 7.2 and 7.3 show increasing ratios of high-skilled labor and a declining fraction of workers without college or university education (the ratios are normalized to 1 in 1963 and in 1979, respectively). In particular, we observe that for both countries the fraction of college-educated employees nearly doubled between 1979 and 1999. Figure 7.2 presents college-educated workers (bachelor's degree and higher) as a percentage of total employees (solid line) for the United States. Figure 7.3 shows the ratio of university-educated employees to total employees for Germany (solid line). The dashed lines of figures 7.2 and 7.3 show the fraction of workers without college or university education. In both countries the fraction of "low-skilled" workers declines over time.[10]

We can conclude that figures 7.2 and 7.3 indicate a rising demand for high-skilled labor in both countries.[11] This argument could be related,

---

[8] It should be mentioned that we concentrate on West German time series only. Time series for reunified Germany are not taken into account because of outliers and measurement errors. See the appendix for our computations.

[9] Sources of data for figure 7.1 are OECD (1993, 1996); Statistisches Bundesamt (1978–2000); and U.S. Bureau of the Census (1998).

[10] Data for figure 7.2 are taken from U.S. Bureau of the Census (1998) and our own calculations. Data for figure 7.3 are from Statistisches Bundesamt (1978–2000) and our own calculations.

[11] See Katz and Murphy (1992) for a supply-and-demand explanation of wage inequality.

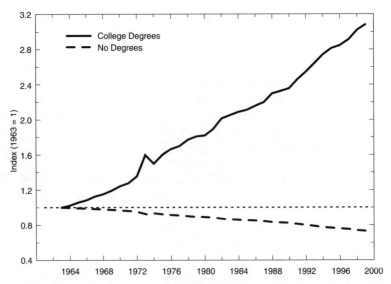

Figure 7.2.   High- and low-skilled employment, United States, 1963–1999
(Index 1963 = 1)

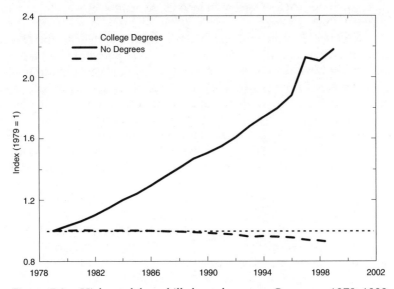

Figure 7.3.   High- and low-skilled employment, Germany, 1979–1999
(Index 1979 = 1)

at least in the case of the United States, to the increasing wage premium. For Germany this argument does not seem to be convincing because we observe, at least in the aggregate, no increase in the wage premium.

One explanation for this observation is provided by Acemoglu (1998). Acemoglu assumes that an increase in the number of high-skilled workers first leads to a decline in the wage premium. The rise in the amount of qualified labor generates skill-biased technical progress, which, for its part, leads to a higher demand for skilled labor, generating an increase in the wage differential. The latter increase is larger than the initial decrease in the wage premium, so in the long run the wage premium rises, although it falls in the short run. This explanation can also account for the oscillations in the wage premium in the United States, observable in figure 7.1. In light of our model, skill-biased technical change implies that it affects the labor productivity of high-skilled workers to a greater degree than labor productivity of low-skilled workers, that is, $\xi > \epsilon$ holds.

A similar explanation is offered by Murphy, Riddell, and Romer (1998). They estimate an equation that is basically the same as our equation (7.19). They conclude that the growth rate of productivity has decreased since the 1970s, but the rate of change in the skill bias in technology has not changed, which has fostered the demand for high-skilled labor. Further, they compare the United States to Canada and conclude that public policies in Canada facilitated substantial growth in postsecondary education over the last two decades. This sharp rise in higher education prevented an increase in income inequality, as was the case for the United States.

In Germany the labor market is more regulated than in the United States, and German trade unions have been an important factor in determining the growth rates of wages. Since an important goal of trade unions has been to reduce wage inequality, the wage premium in Germany does not react to the supply and demand of labor as it does in the United States. This important factor must be taken into account when looking at the evolution of the wage differential in Germany. An additional explanation may simply be that the increase in high-skilled labor in Germany has been sufficient to prevent the wage premium from rising as it did in the United States.

DATA SOURCES AND COMPUTATIONS

Considering equation (7.21), we need data for H_Y, L, and A. H_Y represents employed civilian labor force at a higher educational level, for example, those who have earned a college degree (bachelor's degree and higher). L denotes the number of employees at a lower educational level. (Details of the data sources are given in the appendix.) For the United States the data are taken from the U.S. Bureau of the

Census, *Annual Statistical Abstract* (various issues since 1965) and the U.S. Bureau of the Census (1998, 2000). The German series are taken from Statistisches Bundesamt (1978–2000). The time series of median wages and wage dispersions are taken from the U.S. Bureau of the Census (1998, 2000) and from the *Fachserie 16* published by Statistisches Bundesamt. We must point out that the applied German data represent only wages and employees of the West German manufacturing sector.[12]

A primary problem is to construct a reliable measure of the stock of knowledge, A, for which various measures exist (see also the discussion in chapter 5). A measure should include innovative investments, a measurable output of knowledge production, and the flow of information. As an approximation of the first two measures we take R&D investment and the number of national patent grants. The third item is difficult to approximate. It could include trade flows of technology, the number of Internet connections, or the number of scientific workshops and conferences. To be consistent with the theoretical model, a closed economy without foreign trade is assumed. Furthermore, taking the growing number of Internet connections into account, one might assume that the information flow across industrialized countries such as the United States and Germany is the same. Therefore, we apply three different approximations of the growth rate of knowledge in our estimations. First, we take the growth rate of total R&D expenditures as a percentage of GDP. Second, we constructed a series by calculating the mean growth rate of the R&D intensity and the growth rate of national patent grants. This measure represents an inventive input (R&D expenditures) and a possible output of such investments.[13] Our third method builds on the concept we used in chapter 5, where we constructed a stock of knowledge by applying the perpetual inventory method.[14] In this case the stock of knowledge, A, is approximated through cumulated real R&D expenditure. Table 7.1 summarizes the construction of our time series data.

Before concentrating on the parameter estimations, we present some main properties of our constructed time series data. For the United States we concentrate on two different kinds of wage premiums. First, we calculate the wage premium to employees with college education over employees without college education. This time series is called "wage premium." Second, we calculate a series in which we compare the wages of employees with some college degree over employees with high school

---

[12] Note, however, that the manufacturing sector in Germany represents a large fraction of GDP, roughly 50 percent.

[13] See Siegel (1999) for a brief survey of similar approaches to approximating the stock of knowledge.

[14] Also see chapter 3 for a brief description of the perpetual inventory method.

TABLE 7.1
Data Computations

Variable	Data
$\hat{w}_p$	Time series of wage differentials Growth rate of R&D intensities
g_A	Mean growth rate of R&D intensity and patents Growth rate of the stock of knowledge (A)
g_H	Employees with college or higher education
g_L	Employees without college or higher education

education. Following Murphy, Riddell, and Romer (1998), we call this series "college premium." Table 7.2 shows some characteristics of the applied U.S. data. It should be noted that, according to table 7.1 and equation (7.21), each variable is measured in growth rates.

For the United States we observe a small mean growth rate of the wage and college premiums. Furthermore, the growth rate of technological change seems to be small, too. The mean growth rate of A and the ratios of high-skilled labor to the labor with lower skills (see lines 3 and 4) are positive, too.

Comparing the results for the United States with the German data (see table 7.3), we observe that the mean growth rate of wage inequality in the United States is four times higher than in Germany. Furthermore, table 7.3 shows that the mean growth rate of the R&D intensity is low;

TABLE 7.2
Time Series Properties, U.S. Data (1964–1999)

Variable	Mean	Std. Dev.
Wage premium	0.0078	0.0258
College premium	0.0089	0.0226
$\dfrac{\text{bach. degree}}{\text{no bach.}}$	0.0400	0.0377
$\dfrac{\text{bach. degree}}{\text{high school}}$	0.0215	0.0277
R&D intensity	−0.0005	0.0306
R&D + patents	0.0110	0.0360
Stock of knowl. (A)	0.0262	0.0081

TABLE 7.3
Time Series Properties, German Data (1974–1998)

Variable	Mean	Std. Dev.
Wage premium	0.0019	0.0068
Higher educ. / Lower educ.	0.0111	0.0231
R&D intensity	0.0028	0.0365
R&D + patents	0.0098	0.0192
Stock of knowl. A	0.0431	0.0139

in the case of the United States, it is negative. Yet for both countries we observe significantly positive growth rates of A. It is interesting to note that for most of the variables, the U.S. time series exhibit a higher standard deviation. This holds in particular for the wage premium, apparently reflecting the well-known differences in the mobility of labor of the two countries.

ESTIMATION RESULTS

Before we estimate the parameters in the equation giving the wage premium, we want to examine simple correlations between the wage premium and the main variables, such as the stock of knowledge and the relative supply of skilled workers. We employ ordinary least squares (OLS) regressions for the wage premium and the other variables. The results are summarized in table 7.4. As one would expect, most of our proxies of knowledge show a positive influence of knowledge on the wage premium. This seems to hold for the United States as well as for Germany. Results of the literature on skill-biased technological change seem to be supported

TABLE 7.4
Sign of Correlations

Country	Variable			
	R&D Intensity	R&D + Patents	g_A	$g_H - g_L$
U.S. wage premium	+	+	+	+
U.S. college premium	+	+	+	+
Germany wage prem.	+	+	−	−

by the results of table 7.4. Whereas the relative increase of high-skilled labor compared to low-skilled labor does not make the wage premium in the United States fall—but rather rise—in Germany one observes the opposite result.

The results of table 7.4 indicate positive technology effects and, except for the United States, negative supply effects. Therefore, we conclude that in the United States skilled workers are scarcer than in Germany, giving rise to an increasing wage premium in contrast to Germany.

Next we estimate the parameters of the wage premium, given by equation (7.21). Because of the structure of equation (7.21), it seems sufficient to apply OLS estimation in a first step. Consistent with the equation (7.21) and the work of Katz and Murphy (1992) and Murphy, Riddell, and Romer (1998), the regression equation

$$\hat{w}_p = \beta_1 + \beta_2 g_A - \frac{1}{\beta_3} g_{HL} + \varepsilon \tag{7.27}$$

is estimated by OLS. Here $g_A = \frac{\dot{A}}{A}$ and $g_{HL} = (g_{H_Y} - g_L)$. We want to mention that β_1 represents an arbitrary constant that captures other variables influencing the wage premium (e.g., the role of trade unions). The parameters β_2 and β_3 represent the so-called technology effect and the elasticity of substitution.[15]

In the first step, not reported here, we have employed OLS regressions. For almost all of the regressions for both the United States and Germany we obtained the expected sign, but the parameters were insignificant. The time series are characterized by strong outliers. We therefore undertook regressions by a procedure that gives less weight to outliers. We employed a nonlinear estimation technique that gives greater weight to values close to the mean and less weight to values far from it. For the United States we obtained the results in table 7.5.

The regression coefficients have the expected sign, and most of them are significant. The results for the German economy are presented in table 7.6.

Almost all of the parameters have the expected sign and are significant. The main difference between the results for the United States and Germany is that for Germany the elasticity of substitution is lower than for the United States, which has dampening effects on the wage premium.

In both countries the knowledge variable has a positive effect, and a larger growth rate of skilled compared to unskilled labor has a negative effect on the wage premium. On the other hand, the value of the

---

[15] Note that β_2 represents

$$\beta_2 = \frac{\sigma_p - 1}{\sigma_p}(\xi - \varepsilon) \Rightarrow (\xi - \epsilon) \approx \frac{\beta_3}{(\beta_3 - 1)}\beta_2.$$

TABLE 7.5
Estimation of Equation (7.27), United States (1964–1999)

Proxy for Knowl.	U.S. Wage Premium			U.S. College Premium		
	β_1	β_2	β_3	β_1	β_2	β_3
R&D Intens.	0.0207	0.0720	2.7716	0.0166	0.2959	2.6621
std. error	0.0069	0.1586	0.9879	0.0574	0.1375	1.3149
R&D + Patents	0.0212	0.0066	2.7229	0.0169	0.1645	2.6602
std. error	0.0071	0.1330	0.9412	0.0062	0.1256	1.4131
A	0.0177	0.1278	2.7506	0.0118	0.2226	2.8822
std. error	0.0177	0.5936	0.9698	0.0189	0.6125	1.8292

TABLE 7.6
Estimation of Equation (7.27), Germany (1974–1998)

Approx. of Knowl.	β_1	β_2	β_3
R&D Intens.	0.0097	0.1271	1.7536
std. error	0.0019	0.0475	0.2505
R&D + Patents	0.0122	−0.1139	1.6965
std. error	0.0024	0.0595	0.2586
A	0.0067	0.2165	1.9261
std. error	0.0022	0.0940	0.3143

elasticity of substitution between the two types of labor also affects the growth rate of the wage premium in addition to the growth rates of the supply of skilled and unskilled labor. The higher the elasticity of substitution between the two types of labor, the smaller is the growth rate of the wage premium. In other words, if there had been a larger growth rate of unskilled labor and a high elasticity of substitution, the income distribution would have been strongly skewed toward skilled labor.[16]

7.4 CONCLUSION

After reviewing earlier and more recent theories on the interaction of growth and inequality, we have built up and estimated a model

[16] This is consistent with results in resource economics. Over time, the smaller the elasticity of substitution between inputs is the larger the income share the scarce resource obtains; see Scholl and Semmler (2002).

that appears to be particularly relevant for advanced countries. We have focused on the interrelation between education, technical change, and knowledge spillovers, which gives us a framework to study the determinants of wage inequality within and also between countries.

In a growth model with technical change we have shown that there are four main factors that may create wage inequality. These are the rate of technological change, the knowledge spillover effect, the relative supply of skilled and unskilled labor, and the elasticity of substitution between high- and low-skilled workers. We have shown that if technical change, the knowledge spillover effect, and the growth rate of the ratio of skilled to unskilled labor are given and positive, then the elasticity of substitution also affects wage inequality. In the presence of skill-biased technical change and thus an upward shift of the demand for high-skilled labor, a low elasticity of substitution may reduce wage inequality if the growth rate of the ratio of skilled to unskilled labor is positive.[17] On the other hand, with high elasticity of substitution, the wage inequality is less corrected and the degree of wage inequality may be higher in the long run.

Both our model and our estimates for the U.S. and European time series data allow a coherent interpretation of the trends in wage inequality. We undertake time series estimates for the United States and Germany. In the case of the United States, the elasticity of substitution is greater than 1 and larger than that for Germany. For Germany, the stylized facts show that there is less wage inequality, and one can observe that the reduction of inequality arising from a positive growth rate of skilled to unskilled labor will occur to a higher degree due to the lower elasticity of substitution in Germany compared to the United States. Yet, overall we want to point out that in Europe and particularly in Germany, other forces, for example the trade union wage-setting policies, and welfare state measures have also reduced wage inequality over time. We have not taken into account those forces, which may explain a part of the trend in the wage premium in the United States as compared to Europe. As the stylized facts showed, it is only in recent times that wage inequality has tended to rise in Europe.

Another important influence assumed to increase wage inequality is international trade.[18] In particular, if an industrialized country increases its exports of skill-intensive goods and increases its imports of labor-intensive goods, production will shift to skill-intensive goods, which increases the skill-biased wage inequality. Yet, in the long run the rising wage inequality may lead to a reduction of the ratio of high-skilled

---

[17] See also Acemoglu (2002).
[18] See also section 7.2.

to low-skilled workers. However, Krugman (1994) has argued that if international trade were the main force behind growing wage inequality, this would lead to two observable facts: first, a declining ratio of skilled to unskilled employment because unskilled labor becomes relatively cheaper and, second, a substantial shift of employment toward skill-intensive industries. Krugman demonstrates, however, that both propositions fail to hold and that wage differentials and the relative demand for skilled people has increased because of some "common factors that affect all sectors" (1994, p. 36).[19] We thus want to argue that our model of economic growth and inequality can be used as a reasonable device to capture the trends of inequality in advanced countries.

Yet, in spite of arguing that our growth model of the interaction of education, technical change, knowledge externalities, and inequality may be a useful model for advanced countries to study wage inequality within and across countries, we are aware that there may be deeper underlying microeconomic mechanisms that allow for such inequalities. In this respect, specifically for the United States, particularly relevant may be the membership theory of inequality and poverty (Brock and Durlauf 2000a, 2000b; Durlauf 1996a, 1996b, 2000), which maintains that the composition and behavior of the groups of which a person is a member play an important role in socioeconomic outcomes. Based on this approach, one can spell out numerous observable and nonobservable factors such as family, neighborhood, peer group, and so on that affect children's education and skill potentials (Brock and Durlauf 2000a, 2000b). This approach can explain substantial immobility, social lock-in phenomena concerning economic status across generations, and a lack of education and formation of human skills for certain socioeconomic groups.

In the approach taken here, persistent inequality is seen to arise from the forces of economic growth. We have argued that inequality, beyond that already generated by education, can be substantially affected by the growth of knowledge, technical change, and the interaction and spillover effects in production activities. Recent literature on education, skill-biased technical change, and skill formation in the workplace (see Acemoglu 2002 and Aghion 2002) and our approach here have stressed the latter view. This type of work demonstrates that there are factors at work, for example spillover effects in production activities, that can considerably add to education-based inequalities. The present chapter has considered some of the relevant mechanisms that may give rise to such persistent inequalities.

---

[19] For views skeptical that the openness of the economy and trade has increased wage inequality in advanced industrial countries, see Aghion, Caroli, and García-Peñalosa (1999) and Aghion (2002).

APPENDIX: DATA COMPUTATIONS

1. U.S. Data

For the United States, the number of more-educated workers consists of the sum of male and female employees who earned college degrees (bachelor's degree and higher). The number of less-educated employees consists of the sum of employees who earned high school degrees or less. In particular, the U.S. Bureau of the Census distinguishes between less than the nineth grade, the nineth to tenth grade, and the high school degree.

Calculating the wage premiums, the wage of high-skilled labor is approximated by the median of wages of male and female employees with college education. The wage of low-skilled labor is given by the median of wages earned by less-educated male and female employees. For the United States we distinguish between so-called college premiums and wage premiums:

$$\text{wage premium} = \frac{\text{median wages college education}}{\text{median wages noncollege education}}$$

$$\text{college premium} = \frac{\text{median wages college education}}{\text{median wages high school education}}$$

Main data source: U.S. Bureau of the Census (1998, 2000).

2. German Data

In contrast to the United States, for Germany we employ data for the manufacturing sector only. The available data are for both male and female blue- and white-collar workers at different job positions. Because of the German education system, we treat blue- and white-collar workers in supervisory job positions as high-skilled labor. In particular, such workers are educated at school for at least twelve years; furthermore, they normally get a practical education (apprenticeship). Similarly, we treat employees at lower job positions and, therefore, at a lower educational level as low-skilled labor. The numbers of employees and the wages for the German economy are calculated analogously to the United States.

$$\text{wage premium} = \frac{\text{median wages at supervisory job positions}}{\text{median wages at lower job positions}}$$

Data source: Statistisches Bundesamt, *Fachserie 16* (various issues since 1978).

CHAPTER 8

Conclusions

This book has studied economic growth from a time series perspective. As we have argued, the essential forces of growth are not the same in all times and in all countries. Prior studies have demonstrated that time series studies may be preferable because cross-country studies miss certain characteristics of particular stages of growth. If countries differ considerably in their state of development and per capita income, they may be characterized by different models or different technology or preferences parameters. It is also to be expected that different institutional conditions and social infrastructure in the countries make them heterogeneous. Indeed, all our empirical investigations confirm this time series perspective. In our time series studies for different countries, we clearly obtain different estimates for the technology and preference parameters of the models for the countries under consideration. We also have indicated that even for one country, the technology and preference parameters may have changed over time.

Brock and Durlauf (2001) have also argued that cross-country studies tend to fail because they do not admit model uncertainty and parameter heterogeneity. Moreover, a large body of recent literature goes even further and maintains that there are groups of countries that converge to different per capita incomes in the long run. More particularly, there are thresholds in development and growth. A large number of countries tend to stay below some threshold, at low per capita income, and other countries above the threshold tend to move to high per capita income. Thus, one expects a bimodal distribution of per capita income in the long run. Quah (1996) and Kremer, Onatski, and Stock (2001) predict twin peaks in the per capita income distribution, with poor and rich countries at the end of the distribution.

In order to take this criticism of the cross-country studies seriously, we have pursued a time series perspective. We started our study on economic growth in chapter 2 by presenting stylized time series facts and confronting them with growth models. We show that no one model fits all countries and all stages of growth. In order to fit the theory to the data, we need different variants of growth models for different time periods. In chapter 3 we showed that in earlier stages of growth, or in catch-up periods, learning from others, externalities, and increasing returns have been major sources of economic growth. At a later stage, schooling, education, and buildup of human capital have been important. Growth effects are visible that appear to be proportional to the educational effort. Such scale effects of education and human capital may not hold for later stages of development, as Krüger and Lindahl (2001) have shown. There seem to be nonlinearities at work, since educational efforts show less than proportional effects on growth rates in advanced countries. The modified Uzawa-Lucas model, presented and estimated in chapter 4, might be the appropriate model to describe the stage of development at which the creation of human capital is effective in increasing per capita income.

In a later stage, in addition to the creation of human capital, the creation and diffusion of knowledge and new technology through R&D spending and a high proportion of scientists and engineers in the total working population seem to become important. Only countries that are at the forefront of technological change may be successful in keeping growth rates high. The Romer model, presented and estimated in chapter 5, seems to better describe this stage. In fact, as we have argued, the problem of endogenous growth can be modeled for advanced countries best not by the Uzawa-Lucas model, but by a Romer-type model that includes both human capital and knowledge accumulation. Time series data by and large support the latter model for advanced industrial countries when, again, nonlinearities in the production of knowledge are taken into account.

Finally, social and public infrastructure appear to be important for all stages of growth, yet each stage may need specific social and public infrastructure. The relation of public infrastructure and economic growth has been treated theoretically and empirically in chapter 6.

While treating growth from a time series perspective, we have seen that two major growth models, the Uzawa-Lucas and Romer models, exhibit scale effects—models in which the level of a variable has a direct effect on per capita growth. They can be made compatible with long-run time series data only when we remove the direct scale effects from the models. In both of our original growth models we introduce nonlinearities that show us that the long-run growth path is leveling off as level variables, representing forces of growth, rise. The modified Uzawa-Lucas model reveals positive per capita growth only on the transition path when there is a persistent increase in the time spent on education, but the Romer model shows that there can still be persistent long-run per capita growth if human capital grows. The other two endogenous growth models, the model with positive externalities of chapter 3 and the model with public infrastructure in chapter 6, do not contain such scale effects, and the empirical verification of these models using time series data is easier. However, the latter two models are highly stylized in the sense that they lack important variables determining economic growth, among them human capital, knowledge accumulation, and new technology.

On the other hand, the model with positive externalities of investment is certainly relevant and can explain, as we have shown, the time paths of some economies, in particular at early stages of growth or in transition stages. In that model, we presumed that technical progress is incorporated in investment goods, which has stimulating growth effects. But the model does not indicate how this technical progress is achieved, and one would be interested in a model that contains this mechanism in more detail. A similar argument holds for the model with public infrastructure stimulating economic growth; human capital and the level of technology are not modeled explicitly. Although the modeling of forces of growth is incomplete, this type of model is useful because it indicates how a government's fiscal policies can affect economic growth. Thus, on the whole, growth models incorporating the formation of human capital, knowledge accumulation, and new technology are more promising. Yet, as we have shown, these models exhibit scale effects and can be reasonably estimated only after removing those scale effects and introducing nonlinearities.

As concerns economic policy in the modified Uzawa-Lucas model, where scale effects have been eliminated, the long-run balanced growth rate becomes exogenously determined and public policies can affect the growth rate only on the transition path or when the government succeeds in raising educational effort. The modified Romer model is a growth model where the long-run balanced growth rate depends on the growth rate of human capital and on parameters of the knowledge production function. Policies that have a stimulating effect on those factors raise economic growth.

Last, we want to note that countries can also improve growth rates by attempting to move as close as possible to the world technology frontier by enjoying spillover benefits and externalities through learning from others and investment in the adoption of new technologies, as well as by government policies, public infrastructure, and institutions that enhance growth by approaching the world technological frontier. As we have seen, knowledge is nonrivalrous, and thus spillover effects and increasing returns are likely to enhance economic growth. This process has helped countries with low per capita income to enjoy high per capita growth and sometimes growth miracles. Such rapid learning from others and moving close to the world technological frontier is characteristic of a number of countries in recent times. However, other countries and regions have not taken off but have rather remained impoverished. In the last two decades some countries have experienced high positive growth rates, other countries small or even negative growth rates. This seems to have caused, as much recent work states,[1] an increase in the inequality of per capita income across countries.

As concerns the inequality within countries, we could show that the gains from growth are also not equally distributed. We have sketched—for advanced industrial countries—a growth model with human capital and knowledge accumulation that helps us to understand how the forces of growth can generate inequality. Along the line of other recent work, we have examined in particular to what extent modern knowledge-based production activities may give rise to wage and income inequality. We focus on wage inequality for high- and low-skilled workers, which has increased in the past decades as empirical work has shown.

Allowing for different types of households with different skill characteristics, our growth model shows that general knowledge accumulation and spillover effects can lead to an increase in wage inequality, in particular between high-skilled and low-skilled labor. In our view, externalities from knowledge accumulation and spillover play major roles. In addition, the general growth rate of knowledge, the relative supply of skilled and unskilled labor, and the elasticity of substitution between those two types of labor are relevant factors in explaining why the wage premium for skilled relative to unskilled labor has risen, in particular in the United States during the last decades. These four factors also allow us to give a quantitative assessment of the causes of cross-country differences in wage inequality. Although, for example, a faster increase in the supply of high-skilled labor relative to low-skilled labor tends to reduce the price of high-skilled labor and, thus, wage differentials, historically the opposite has been observed for the United States. As Murphy, Riddell, and Romer (1998) conclude, this increase has not been sufficient to satisfy the increased demand for high-skilled labor in the United States. Yet as we have shown, the relative supply of different skill groups is only one factor that determines wage inequality.

We also must add, with respect to such trends, that there appear to be noticeable differences between the United States and European economies. As compared to the United States, there are differences in some European countries, especially in Germany and France, where wage differentials have remained roughly constant over the last twenty years. In addition to the above-mentioned factors, the impact of welfare state measures on wage income, and trade unions in Europe, aiming at reducing the wage differential between different groups, are also important factors

---

[1] See Jones (2002), which gives a full account of the diverse performance of countries in recent times. See also the work on the twin peaks distribution of per capita income cited at the beginning of this chapter.

in explaining the evolution of wage inequality in the United States as compared to European countries.[2]

Overall we want to stress that although we have analytically and econometrically studied a variety of different growth models and their fit with the data, all the models share common features. In all of our models, physical capital, human capital, and accumulated knowledge, together with some externalities and public infrastructure, affect the output and productivity of the economy. All of those forces of growth affect the per capita growth rate of the economy. It would thus have been challenging to develop a model encompassing all the different forces of growth. Yet, as we have argued in section 1.3, the complexity of the analytical solution and time series estimate of such models would make such an effort theoretically as well as empirically impractical. We thus focused in our modeling strategy on a few forces of growth at a time.

[2] Acemoglu, Aghion, and Violante (2001) show that deunionization, which has occurred in the United States and the United Kingdom since the 1980s, has amplified the effect of skill-biased technical change on inequality.

Technical Appendix

1. SOME BASICS OF DYNAMIC OPTIMIZATION

For a variety of growth models we have presumed intertemporal behavior and dynamic optimization of economic agents. We here present some basics of the method of dynamic optimization using Pontryagin's maximum principle and the Hamiltonian.

Let an intertemporal optimization problem be given by

$$\max_{u(t)} J(x(0), 0), J(\cdot) \equiv \int_0^\infty e^{-\rho t} F(x(t), u(t)) dt \tag{A.1}$$

subject to

$$\frac{dx(t)}{dt} \equiv \dot{x}(t) = f(x(t), u(t)), x(0) = x_0 \tag{A.2}$$

with $x(t) \in \mathbb{R}^n$ the vector of state variables at time t and $u(t) \in \Omega \subseteq \mathbb{R}^m$ the vector of control variables at time t and $F : \mathbb{R}^n \times \mathbb{R}^m \to \mathbb{R}$ and $f : \mathbb{R}^n \times \mathbb{R}^m \to \mathbb{R}^n$. ρ is the discount rate and $e^{-\rho t}$ is the discount factor. $F(x(t), u(t))$, $f_i(x(t), u(t))$ and $\partial f_i(x(t), u(t))/\partial x_j(t)$, $\partial F(x(t), u(t))/\partial x_j(t)$ are continuous with respect to all $n+m$ variables for $i, j = 1, \ldots, n$. Further, $u(t)$ is said to be admissible if it is a piecewise continuous function on $[0, \infty)$ with $u(t) \in \Omega$.

Define the current value Hamiltonian $H(x(t), u(t), \theta(t), \theta_0)$ as follows:

$$H(x(t), u(t), \theta(t), \theta_0) \equiv \theta_0 F(x(t), u(t)) + \theta(t) f(x(t), u(t)) \tag{A.3}$$

with $\theta_0 \in \mathbb{R}$ a constant scalar and $\theta(t) \in \mathbb{R}^n$ the vector of costate variables or shadow prices. $\theta_j(t)$ gives the change in the optimal objective functional J^* resulting from an increment in the state variable $x_j(t)$. If $x_j(t)$ is a capital stock, $\theta_j(t)$ gives the marginal value of capital at time t. Assume that there exists a solution for (A.1) subject to (A.2). Then, we have the following theorem.

THEOREM 1

Let $u^\star(t)$ be an admissible control and $x^\star(t)$ is the trajectory belonging to $u^\star(t)$. For $u^\star(t)$ to be optimal, it is necessary that there exist *a continuous vector function* $\theta(t) = (\theta_1(t),\ldots,\theta_n(t))$ *with piecewise continuous derivatives and a constant scalar* θ_0 *such that:*

(a) $\theta(t)$ *and* $x^\star(t)$ *are solutions of the canonical system*

$$\dot{x}^\star(t) = \frac{\partial}{\partial\theta}H(x^\star(t),u^\star(t),\theta(t),\theta_0)$$

$$\dot{\theta}(t) = \rho\theta(t) - \frac{\partial}{\partial x}H(x^\star(t),u^\star(t),\theta(t),\theta_0),$$

(b) *For all* $t \in [0,\infty)$ *where* $u^\star(t)$ *is continuous,* $H(x^\star(t),u^\star(t),\theta(t),\theta_0) \geq H(x^\star(t),u(t),\theta(t),\theta_0)$ *must hold,*

(c) $(\theta_0,\theta(t)) \neq (0,0)$ *and* $\theta_0 = 1$ *or* $\theta_0 = 0$.

REMARKS:

1. If the maximum with respect to $u(t)$ is in the interior of Ω, $\partial H(\cdot)/\partial u(t) = 0$ can be used as a necessary condition for a local maximum of $H(\cdot)$.
2. It is implicitly assumed that the objective functional remains bounded, i.e., $\int_0^\infty e^{-\rho t}F(x^\star(t),u^\star(t)) < \infty$. If $x^\star$ and $u^\star$ grow without an upper bound, $F(\cdot)$ must not grow faster than ρ.

Theorem 1 provides us only with necessary conditions. The next theorem gives sufficient conditions.

THEOREM 2

If the Hamiltonian with $\theta_0 = 1$ *is concave in* $(x(t),u(t))$ *jointly and if the transversality condition* $\lim_{t\to\infty} e^{-\rho t}\theta(t)(x(t) - x^\star(t)) \geq 0$ *holds, conditions (a) and (b) from Theorem 1 are also sufficient for an optimum. If the Hamiltonian is strictly concave in* $(x(t),u(t))$, *the solution is unique.*

REMARKS:

1. If the state and costate variables are positive, the transversality condition can be written as stated in earlier chapters.[1]
2. Given some technical conditions, it can be shown that the transversality condition is also a necessary condition.

These two theorems demonstrate how optimal control theory can be applied to solve dynamic optimization problems. The main role is played by the Hamiltonian (A.3). It should be noted that in most economic applications, as in this book, interior solutions are optimal, so $\partial H(\cdot)/\partial u(t) = 0$ can be presumed. For further reading and more details concerning optimal control theory, see the books by Feichtinger and Hartl (1986) or Seierstad and Sydsæter (1987) or other books dealing with an introduction to optimal control theory.

---

[1] Note that in the book we did not indicate optimal values by $\star$.

2. THE GENERALIZED METHOD OF MOMENTS (GMM)

The GMM estimation employed here starts with a set of orthogonal conditions, representing the population moments established by a theoretical model:

$$E[g(y_t, \psi)] = 0 \tag{A.4}$$

where y_t is a $p \times 1$ vector of observed variables at date t, ψ is a $q \times 1$ vector of unknown parameters to be estimated, and $g(\cdot)$ is a $r \times 1$ vector mapping from R^T. Let T denote the sample size. The sample moments of $g(\cdot)$ can then be written as

$$g_T(\psi) = \frac{1}{T} \sum_{t=1}^{T} g(y_t, \psi). \tag{A.5}$$

The idea of the GMM estimator is to choose an estimated ψ that matches the sample moments $g_t(\psi)$ and the population moments given by (A.4) as closely as possible. To achieve this, one needs to define a distance function by which that closeness can be judged. Hansen (1982) suggested a distance function:

$$J(\psi) = [g_T(\psi)]' W_T [g_T(\psi)], \tag{A.6}$$

where W_T, called the weighting matrix, is $r \times r$, symmetric, and positive definite. Thus, the GMM estimator is the value of ψ, denoted as $\hat{\psi}$, that minimizes (A.6). From the results established in Hansen (1982), a consistent estimator of the variance-covariance matrix of $\hat{\psi}$ is given by

$$\text{Var}(\hat{\psi}) = \frac{1}{T}(D_T)^{-1} W_T (D_T')^{-1},$$

where $D_T = \partial g_T(\hat{\psi})/\partial \psi'$. There is great flexibility in the choice of W_T for constructing a consistent and asymptotically normal GMM estimator. In this book, we adopt the method of Newey and West (1987), who suggested that

$$W_t^{-1} = \hat{\Omega}_0 + \sum_{j=1}^{m} w(j, m)(\hat{\Omega}_j + \hat{\Omega}_j'), \tag{A.7}$$

with $w(j,m) \equiv 1-j/(1+m)$, $\hat{\Omega}_j \equiv (1/T) \sum_{t=j+1}^{T} g(y_t, \hat{\psi}^*) g(y_{t-j}, \hat{\psi}^*)$, and m to be a suitable function of T.[2] Here $\hat{\psi}^*$ is required to be a consistent estimator of ψ. Thus two-step estimation is suggested as in Hansen and Singleton (1982). First, one chooses a suboptimal weighting matrix to minimize (A.6) and hence obtains a consistent estimator $\hat{\psi}^*$. One then uses the consistent estimator obtained in the first step to calculate the optimum W_T through which (A.6) is reminimized.

For example, for the preliminary estimation of the modified Uzawa-Lucas I model, the set of orthogonal conditions (A.5) for our GMM estimation is given by the two equations (4.46) and (4.47).

Generally, the estimation is undertaken in two steps. In a first step the weighting matrix (A.7) used in the distance function (A.6) will be approximated by an arbitrary weighting matrix in order to get an initial estimate of the parameter set ψ. In a second step the estimated parameter set from the first step is employed and the weighting matrix (A.7) and the function (A.6) are recomputed. For our applications, a computer algorithm, written in Gauss, is designed to solve the optimization problem (A.6) using simulated annealing. A sketch of the simulated annealing algorithm is given later in this appendix. The computer program consists of an outer algorithm that computes the endogenous variable for a given parameter set and an inner algorithm, the simulated annealing algorithm, that searches for the parameter set in order to minimize the distance function (A.6). Both algorithms are iteratively connected.

3. ESTIMATING NONLINEAR MODELS WITH AUTOCORRELATION
   OF THE DISTURBANCE TERM

Suppose the model we estimate takes the form

$$f(y_t, x_t, \theta) = u_t \tag{A.8}$$

Here $f(\cdot)$ could be a vector-valued function. In this case, we shall always assume that there is no cross-correlation between different elements of u_t. If u_t is *i.i.d.*, the moment restriction for the GMM estimation takes the form

$$E[f(y_t, x_t, \theta)] = 0 \tag{A.9}$$

---

[2] According to our sample size, we choose $m = 3$. This is based on the consideration that $m(T)$ takes the form of $T^{1/5}$, which satisfies the requirement on $m(T)$ as indicated in Theorem 2 of Newey and West (1987).

while the objective for NLLS estimation is to

$$\min_{\theta} \sum_{t=1}^{T} f(y_t, x_t, \theta)' \cdot f(y_t, x_t, \theta) \tag{A.10}$$

where T is the number of observations.

Suppose now that u_t follows an $AR(p)$ process:

$$u_t = \rho_1 u_{t-1} + \rho_2 u_{t-2} + \cdots + \rho_p u_{t-p} + \epsilon_t \tag{A.11}$$

where ϵ_t is *i.i.d.* Then it must be true that

$$f^*(y_t, y_{t-1}, \ldots, y_{t-p}, x_t, x_{t-1}, \ldots, x_{t-p}, \theta^*) = \epsilon_t \tag{A.12}$$

where θ^* is the set of structural parameters that include the original θ as well as $\rho_1, \rho_2, \ldots, \rho_p$, and

$$f^*(\cdot) = f(y_t, x_t, \theta) - \rho_1 f(y_{t-1}, x_{t-1}, \theta) - \rho_2 f(y_{t-2}, x_{t-2}, \theta)$$
$$- \cdots - \rho_p f(y_{t-p}, x_{t-p}, \theta) \tag{A.13}$$

Therefore, the moment restriction for GMM estimation should be written as

$$E\left[f^*(\cdot)\right] = 0 \tag{A.14}$$

while the objective for NLLS estimation is to

$$\min_{\theta^*} \sum_{t=1}^{T} f^*(\cdot)' \cdot f^*(\cdot) \tag{A.15}$$

Note that the above approach to dealing with the problem of the autocorrelation in the disturbance will lose the first p observations in the sample. If our sample is large, this will not be a big problem.

4. A SKETCH OF THE SIMULATED ANNEALING ALGORITHM

The subsequently introduced global optimization algorithm, algorithm simulated annealing, moves uphill and downhill and operates with a varying step size and a random search so as to escape local optima. The step size is narrowed and the random search confined to an ever smaller region when the global maximum is approached in the computation of the parameter set. The algorithm is applied to solve the GMM estimation as described earlier. The procedure amounts to the search of a set of parameters that minimizes the distance function (A.6). The problem is to search for that set in an appropriate order and within an appropriate space. Conventional algorithms[3] for such groping are generally suited for cases where there is only one optimum. Given the fact that the model to be estimated is nonlinear in parameters, this is unlikely in our case. We thus employ the simulated annealing algorithm, since it is particularly suitable to escaping local optima. Detailed descriptions of its mathematical features are given in Corana et al. (1987) and Goffe, Ferrier, and Rogers (1994).

Let $f(x)$, for example, be a function that is to be maximized and $x \in S$, where S is a subspace in R^n. This subspace S should be defined from the economic viewpoint and by computational convenience. In our case, we assume $-5 < x_i < 5$ for all i ($i = 1, 2, \ldots, n$). The algorithm starts with an initial parameter vector x^0. Its function value $f^0 = f(x^0)$ is calculated and recorded. One sets the optimum x and $f(x)$, denoted by x_{opt} and f_{opt} respectively, equal to x^0 and $f(x^0)$. Other initial conditions include the initial step-length (a vector with the same dimension as x) denoted by v^0 and an initial temperature (a scalar) denoted by T^0.

The new variable, x', is chosen by varying the i-th element of x^0 such that

$$x'_i = x^0_i + r \cdot v^0_i \tag{A.16}$$

where r is a uniformly distributed random number in $[-1, 1]$. If x' is not in S, repeat (A.16) until x' is in S. The new function value $f' = f(x')$ is then computed. If f' is larger than f^0, x' is accepted. If not, the Metropolis criterion,[4] denoted as p, is used to decide on acceptance, where

$$p = e^{(f'-f)/T^0} \tag{A.17}$$

This p is compared to p', a uniformly distributed random number from $[0, 1]$. If p is greater than p', x' is accepted. Besides, f' should also be compared to the updated f_{opt}. If it is larger than f_{opt}, both x_{opt} and f_{opt} are replaced by x' and f'.

The above steps (starting with (A.16)) should be undertaken and repeated N_S times[5] for each i. Subsequently, the step-length is adjusted. The i-th element of the new step-length vector (denoted as v'_i) depends on

---

[3] An extensive review of traditional algorithms can be found in Judge et al. (1988).
[4] Motivated by thermodynamics.
[5] N_S is suggested to be 20 by Corana et al. (1987).

its number of acceptances (denoted as n_i) in its last N_S times of the above repetition and is given by

$$
v_i' = \begin{cases} v_i^0[1 + c_i(n_i/N_S - 0.6)/0.4] & \text{if } n_i > 0.6N_S; \\ \dfrac{v_i^0}{[1+c_i(0.4-n_i/N_S)/0.4]} & \text{if } n_i < 0.4N_S; \\ v_i^0 & \text{if } 0.4N_S \le n_i \le 0.6N_S \end{cases} \tag{A.18}
$$

where c_i is suggested to be 2 by Corana et al. (1987) for all i. With the new selected step-length vector, one goes back to (A.16) and hence starts a new round of iteration. After another N_S repetitions, the step-length will be readjusted again. These adjustments as to each v_i should be performed N_T times.[6] We then come to adjust the temperature. The new temperature (denoted as T') will be

$$
T' = R_T T^0 \tag{A.19}
$$

with $0 < R_T < 1$.[7] With this new temperature T', we should go back again to (A.17). But this time, the initial variable x^0 is replaced by the updated x_{opt}. Of course, the temperature will be reduced further after an additional N_T times of adjusting the step-length of each i.

For convergence, the step-length in (A.16) is required to be very small. In (A.18), whether the new selected step-length is enlarged or not depends on the corresponding number of acceptances. The number of acceptances n_i is not only determined by whether the new selected x_i increases the value of the objective function, but also by the Metropolis criterion, which itself depends on the temperature. Thus a convergence will ultimately be achieved with the continuous reduction of the temperature. The algorithm will end by comparing the value of f_{opt} for the last N_ϵ times (suggested to be 4) when readjustment of the temperature is attempted.

[6] N_T is suggested to be 100 by Corana et al. (1987).
[7] R_T is suggested to be 0.85 by Corana et al. (1987).

Data Sources

Bundesministerium für Bildung und Forschung (BMBF). 1996. *Bundesbericht Forschung 1996*. Bonn, CD-ROM, August.
———. 2000. *Grund- und Strukturdaten 1999/2000*. Bonn.
Citibase. 1992. *Database*. New York.
Deutsche Bundesbank. 1983. *Revidierte Ergebnisse der gesamtwirtschaftlichen Finanzierungsrechnung für die Jahre 1950 bis 1959*. Frankfurt am Main.
———. 1994. *Ergebnisse der gesamtwirtschaftlichen Finanzierungsrechnung für Westdeutschland 1960 bis 1992*. Frankfurt am Main.
———. 1996. *Ergebnisse der gesamtwirtschaftlichen Finanzierungsrechnung für Deutschland 1990 bis 1995. Statistische Sonderveröffentlichung 4*. Frankfurt am Main.
Economic Report of the President. 1994. Washington, D.C.: U.S. Government Printing Office.
Institut der Deutschen Wirtschaft. 2000. *Zahlen zur wirtschaftlichen Entwicklung der BRD*. Cologne.
Musgrave, J. C. 1992. "Fixed Reproducible Wealth in the United States, Revised Estimates." *Survey of Current Business* 72: 106–137.
National Science Foundation (NSF). 1996, 1998, 2000. *Science and Engineering Indicators*. Washington, D.C.: U.S. Government Printing Office. Internet source http://www.nsf.gov/.
———. 1998. *National Patterns of R&D—Resources*. Washington, D.C.: U.S. Government Printing Office. Internet source http://www.nsf.gov/.
Office for National Statistics. 1965–1998. *Annual Abstract of Statistics*. London.
Organization for Economic Cooperation and Development (OECD). 1973. *Main Economic Indicators, 1955–1973*. Paris: OECD.
———. 1980–1998a. *Main Science and Technology Indicators*. Paris: OECD.
———. 1993, 1996. *Employment Outlook*. Paris: OECD.
———. 1998. *Statistical Compendium, CD-ROM 1998, National Accounts I + II*. Paris: OECD.
———. 1999. *Statistical Compendium, CD-ROM 1999, National Accounts I + II*. Paris: OECD.
Sachverständigenrat zur Begutachtung der gesamtwirtschaftlichen Lage. 1993. *Zeit zum Handeln—Antriebskräfte stärken, Jahresgutachten 1993/94*. Stuttgart: Metzler-Poeschel.
———. 1994. *Den Aufschwung sichern—Arbeitsplätze schaffen. Jahresgutachten 1994/95*. Stuttgart: Metzler-Poeschel.
———. 1995. *Im Standortwettbewerb. Jahresgutachten 1995/96*. Stuttgart: Metzler-Poeschel.
———. 1998. *Vor weitreichenden Entscheidungen. Jahresgutachten 1998/99*. Stuttgart: Metzler-Poeschel.

Statistisches Bundesamt. 1960. *Staatsfinanzen, Fachserie L, Reihe 1.* Stuttgart: Metzler-Poeschel.

———. 1974. *Lange Reihen zur Wirtschaftsentwicklung.* Stuttgart: Verlag W. Kohlhammer.

———. 1977, 1990–1999. *Statistisches Jahrbuch für die Bundesrepublik Deutschland.* Stuttgart: Metzler-Poeschel.

———. 1978–2000, various issues. *Bevölkerung und Erwerbstätigkeit, Fachserie 1, Reihe 4.2.1, Struktur der Arbeitnehmer.* Wiesbaden: Metzler-Poeschel.

———. 1978–2000, various issues. *Löhne und Gehälter, Fachserie 16, Reihe 2.2 und 2.1.* Wiesbaden: Metzler-Poeschel.

———. 1984. *Volkswirtschaftliche Gesamtrechnungen. Fachserie 18, Reihe S. 7.* Stuttgart: Metzler-Poeschel.

———. 1985. *Finanzen und Steuern, Fachserie 14, Reihe 3.1.* Stuttgart: Metzler-Poeschel.

———. 1991. *Volkswirtschaftliche Gesamtrechnungen. Fachserie 18, Reihe S. 17.* Stuttgart: Metzler-Poeschel.

———. 1992. *Finanzen und Steuern, Fachserie 14, Reihe 3.1.* Stuttgart: Metzler-Poeschel.

———. 1994a. *Volkswirtschaftliche Gesamtrechnungen. Fachserie 17, Reihe 7.* Stuttgart: Metzler-Poeschel.

———. 1994b. *Volkswirtschaftliche Gesamtrechnungen. Fachserie 18, Reihe 1.3.* Stuttgart: Metzler-Poeschel.

———. 1995. *Volkswirtschaftliche Gesamtrechnungen. Fachserie 18, Reihe 1.2.* Stuttgart: Metzler-Poeschel.

Summers, R., and A. Heston. 1991. "The Penn World Table (Mark 5): An Expanded Set of International Comparisons, 1950–1988." *Quarterly Journal of Economics* 106: 327–368. (PWT Mark 5.6, released 1995, contains data up to 1992 and is available on the Internet: http://datacentre.chass.utoronto.ca: 5680/pwt/)

U.S. Bureau of the Census. 1965–present, various issues. *Annual Statistical Abstract of the United States.* Washington, D.C.: U.S. Government Printing Office.

———. 1998. *Measuring 50 Years of Economic Change Using the March Current Population Survey.* Current Population Reports P60-203. Washington, D.C.: U.S. Government Printing Office, September.

———. 2000. *Money Income in the United States: 1999.* Current Population Reports P60-209. Washington, D.C.: U.S. Government Printing Office.

Bibliography

Abel, A., G. N. Mankiw, L. H. Summers, and R. Zeckhauser. 1989. "Assessing Dynamic Efficiency." *Review of Economic Studies* 56: 1–20.

Abramovitz, M. 1986. "Catching Up, Forging Ahead, and Falling Behind." *Journal of Economic History* 46: 385–406.

———. 1994. "Catch-Up and Convergence in the Postwar Growth Boom and After." In *Convergence of Productivity: Cross-National Studies and Historical Evidence*, ed. W. J. Baumol, R. R. Nelson, and E. N. Wolff, pp. 86–125. Oxford: Oxford University Press.

Acemoglu, D. 1998. "Why Do New Technologies Complement Skills? Directed Technical Change and Wage Inequality." *Quarterly Journal of Economics* 113: 1055–1089.

———. 2002. "Technical Change, Inequality and the Labor Market." *Journal of Economic Literature* 40: 7–72.

Acemoglu, D., P. Aghion, and G. L. Violante. 2001. "Deunionization, Technical Change and Inequality." MIT, Cambridge, MA. Mimeograph.

Aghion, P. 2000. "Technical Change, Institutions, and the Dynamics of Inequality." University College, London, and EBRD. Mimeograph.

———. 2002. "Schumpeterian Growth Theory and the Dynamics of Income Inequality." *Econometrica* 70, no. 3: 855–882.

Aghion, P., E. Caroli, and C. García-Peñalosa. 1999. "Inequality and Economic Growth: The Perspective of the New Growth Theories." *Journal of Economic Literature* 37: 1615–1660.

Aghion, P., and P. Howitt. 1992. "A Model of Growth through Creative Destruction." *Econometrica* 60: 323–351.

———. 1998. *Endogenous Growth Theory*. Cambridge, MA: MIT Press.

Alesina, A., and D. Rodrik. 1994. "Distributive Politics and Economic Growth." *Quarterly Journal of Economic Growth* 109: 465–490.

Altug, S. 1989. "Time to Build and Aggregate Fluctuations: Some New Evidence." *International Economic Review* 30: 889–920.

Amano, R. A., and T. S. Wirjanto. 1998. "Government Expenditure and the Permanent-Income Model." *Review of Economic Dynamics* 1: 719–730.

Anand, S., and S. M. R. Kanbur. 1993. "The Kuznets Process and the Inequality Development Relationship." *Journal of Development Economics* 40: 25–52.

Arrow, K. J. 1962. "The Economic Implications of Learning by Doing." *Review of Economic Studies* 29: 155–173.

Arrow, K., and M. Kurz. 1970. *Public Investment, the Rate of Return, and Optimal Fiscal Policy*. Baltimore: John Hopkins University Press.

Asada, T., W. Semmler, and A. Novak. 1998. "Endogenous Growth and the Balanced Growth Equilibrium." *Research in Economics* 52: 189–212.

Aschauer, D. A. 1989. "Is Public Expenditure Productive?" *Journal of Monetary Economics* 23: 177–200.

Azariadis, C., and A. Drazen. 1990. "Threshold Externalities in Economic Development." *Quarterly Journal of Economics* 105, no. 2: 501–526.

Barro, R. J. 1979. "On the Determination of Public Debt." *Journal of Political Economy* 87: 940–971.

———. 1990. "Government Spending in a Simple Model of Endogenous Growth." *Journal of Political Economy* 98: S103–S125.

Barro, R. J., and J.-W. Lee. 1993. "International Comparisons of Educational Attainment." *Journal of Monetary Economics* 32: 363–394.

———. 2000. "International Data on Educational Attainment: Updates and Implications." Working paper no. 7911, National Bureau of Economic Research.

Barro, R. J., and X. Sala-i-Martin. 1992. "Public Finance in Models of Economic Growth." *Review of Economic Studies* 59: 645–661.

———. 1995. *Economic Growth.* New York: McGraw-Hill.

Baxter, M., and R. King. 1993. "Fiscal Policy in General Equilibrium." *American Economic Review* 83: 315–335.

Becker, G. S. 1962. "Invstment in Human Capital." *Journal of Political Economy* 70: S9–S49.

Benabou, R. 1995. "Unequal Societies." Working paper no. 5583, National Bureau of Economic Research.

———. 1996. "Inequality and Growth." Working paper no. 5658, National Bureau of Economic Research.

Benhabib, J., and R. Farmer. 1994. "Indeterminacy and Increasing Returns." *Journal of Economic Theory* 63: 19–41.

———. 1995. "Indeterminacy and Sector Specific Externalities." Working paper, New York University.

Benhabib, J., and R. Perli. 1994. "Uniqueness and Indeterminacy." *Journal of Economic Theory* 63: 113–142.

Benhabib, J., R. Perli, and D. Xie. 1994. "Monopolistic Competition, Indeterminacy, and Growth." *Ricerche Economiche* 48: 279–298.

Bernard, A. B., S. N. Durlauf. 1995. "Convergence in International Output." *Journal of Applied Econometrics* 71: 161–174.

Bertola, G. 1993. "Market Structure and Income Distribution in Endogenous Growth Models." *American Economic Review* 83: 1184–1199.

Beyn, W.-J., T. Pampel, and W. Semmler. 2002. "Dynamic Optimization and Skiba Sets in Economic Examples." *Optimal Control Applications and Methods* 22, no. 5–6: 251–280.

Blanchard, O. J., and S. Fischer. 1989. *Lectures on Macroeconomics.* Cambridge, MA: MIT Press.

Blinder, A. S., R. M. Solow. 1973. "Does Fiscal Policy Matter?" *Journal of Public Economics* 2: 291–337.

Bohn, H. 1995. "The Sustainability of Budget Deficits in a Stochastic Economy." *Journal of Money, Credit, and Banking* 27: 257–271.

———. 1998. "The Behaviour of U.S. Public Debt and Deficits." *Quarterly Journal of Economics* 113: 952–963.

Boldrin, M., and A. Rustichini. 1994. "Growth and Indeterminacy in Dynamic Models with Externalities." *Econometrica* 62: 323–342.

Boskin, M. J. 1978. "Taxation, Saving, and the Rate of Interest." *Journal of Political Economy* 86: S3–S27.

Boss, A., and O. J. Lorz. 1995. "Die oeffentliche Verschuldung in der Bundesrepublik Deutschland. Ausmaß und Belastungswirkung." *Jahrbuch für Wirtschaftswissenschaften* 46: 152–183.

Breiman, L., J. H. Friedman, R. A. Olshen, and C. J. Stone. 1984. *Classification and Regression Trees.* New York: Chapman and Hall.

Brock, W. A., and S. Durlauf. 2000a. "Growth Economics and Reality." University of Wisconsin, Madison. Mimeograph.

———. 2000b. "Interactions-Based Models." University of Wisconsin, Madison. Mimeograph. Also forthcoming in *Handbook of Econometrics 5*, ed. J. Heckman and E. Leamer. Amsterdam: North-Holland.

———. 2001. "Growth Empirics and Reality." SSRI Working paper no. 2024R, University of Wisconsin, Madison.

Caballe, J., and M. S. Santos. 1993. "On Endogenous Growth with Physical Capital and Human Capital." *Journal of Political Economy* 101: 1042–1067.

Campbell, J. Y., A. W. Lo, and A. C. MacKinlay. 1997. *The Econometrics of Financial Markets.* Princeton, NJ: Princeton University Press.

Cass, D. 1965. "Optimum Growth in an Aggregative Model of Capital Accumulation." *Review of Economic Studies* 32: 233–240.

Chari, V., L. Christiano, and P. Kehoe. 1994. "Optimal Policy in a Business Cycle Model." *Journal of Political Economy* 102: 617–652.

Chow, G. 1993. "Statistical Estimation and Testing of a Real Business Cycle Model." Econometric Research Program, Research memorandum no 365, Princeton University.

Christiano, L., and M. Eichenbaum. 1992. "Current Real Business Cycle Theories and Aggregate Labor Market Fluctuation." *American Economic Review* 82: 431–472.

Coe, D. T., and E. Helpman. 1995. "International R&D-Spillovers." *European Economic Review* 39: 859–887.

Cooley, J. F., J. Greenwood, and M. Yorukoglu. 1997. "The Replacement Problem." *Journal of Monetary Economics* 40: 457–499.

Corana, A., M. Marchesi, C. Martini, and S. Ridella. 1987. "Minimizing Multimodal Functions of Continuous Variables with the Simulated Annealing Algorithm." *ACM Transactions on Mathematical Software* 13: 262–280.

DeLong, B. J., L. H. Summers. 1991. "Equipment Investment and Economic Growth." *Quarterly Journal of Economics* 106: 445–502.

Diamond, P. 1965. "National Debt in a Neoclassical Growth Model." *American Economic Review* 55: 1126–1150.

Dinopoulos, E., and P. Thompson. 1999. "Reassessing the Empirical Validity of the Human Capital Augmented Neoclassical Growth Model." *Journal of Evolutionary Economics* 9: 135–154.

Domar, E. D. 1946. "Capital Expansion, Rate of Growth and Employment." *Econometrica* 14: 137–147.

———. 1957. *Essays in the Theory of Economic Growth.* London: Macmillan.

Durlauf, S. 1996a. "Neighborhood Feedbacks, Endogenous Stratification, and Income Inequality." In *Dynamic Disequilibrium Modelling,* ed. W. Barnett, G. Gandolfo, and C. Hilllinger, New York: Cambridge University Press.

Durlauf, S. 1996b. "A Theory of Persistent Income Inequality." *Journal of Economic Growth* 1: 75–93.

———. 2000. "The Membership Theory of Poverty: The Role of Group Affiliations in Determining Socio-Economic Outcomes." Dept. of Economics, University of Wisconsin, Madison. Mimeograph.

Durlauf, S. N., and P. A. Johnson. 1995. "Multiple Regimes and Cross-Country Growth Behavior." *Journal of Applied Econometrics* 10: 365–384.

Durlauf, S. N., and D. T. Quah. 1999. "The New Empirics of Economic Growth." In *Handbook of Macroeconomics,* ed. J. B. Taylor, and M. Woodford, vol. 1A, pp. 235–308, Amsterdam: Elsevier.

Eisner, R. 1986. *How Real Is the Federal Deficit?* New York: Free Press.

Eisner, R., and P. J. Pieper. 1984. "A New View of the Federal Debt and Budget Deficits." *American Economic Review* 74: 11–29.

Erenburg, S. J. 1993. "The Relationship between Public and Private Capital." Working paper no. 85, Jerome Levy Institute.

Ewijk, C. van 1991. *On the Dynamics of Growth and Debt.* Oxford: Oxford University Press.

Ewijk, C. van, and T. van de Klundert. 1993. "Endogenous Technology, Budgetary Regimes and Public Policy." In *The Political Economy of Government Debt,* ed. H. A. A. Verbon, and A. A. M. Van Winden Frans, pp. 113–136. Amsterdam: North-Holland.

Feichtinger, G., and R. F. Hartl. 1986. *Optimale Kontrolle ökonomischer Prozesse.* Berlin: DeGruyter.

Feve, P., and P.-Y. Henin. 1996. "Assessing Maastricht Sustainability of Public Deficits in a Stochastic Environment." CEPREMAP, Paris. Mimeograph. Paper presented at the CEEA Symposium on Problems of European Monetary Union, Frankfurt, November 1996.

Flaschel, P., R. Franke, and W. Semmler. 1997. *Dynamic Macroeconomics: Instability, Fluctuations and Growth in Monetary Economies.* Cambridge, MA: MIT Press.

Foley, D., and T. Michl. 1999. *Growth and Distribution.* Cambridge, MA: Harvard University Press.

Futagami, K., Y. S. Morita, and A. Shibata. 1993. "Dynamic Analysis of an Endogenous Growth Model with Public Capital." *Scandinavian Journal of Economics* 95: 607–625.

Galor, O., and O. Moav. 2000. "Ability-Based Technological Transition, Wage Inequality, and Economic Growth." *Quarterly Journal of Economics* 115: 469–497.

Galor, O., and D. Tsiddon. 1997. "Technological Progress, Mobility, and Economic Growth." *American Economic Review* 87: 363–382.

Galor, O., and J. Zeira. 1993. "Income Distribution and Macroeconomics." *Review of Economic Studies* 60: 35–52.

Glomm, G., and B. Ravikumar. 1994. "Public Investment in Infrastructure in a Simple Growth Model." *Journal of Economic Dynamics and Control* 18: 1173–1187.

Goffe, W., G. Ferrier, and J. Rogers. 1994. "Global Optimization of Statistical Functions with Simulated Annealing." *Journal of Econometrics* 60: 65–99.

Greenwood, J., Z. Hercowitz, and P. Krusell. 1997. "Long-Run Implications of Investment-Specific Technological Change." *American Economic Review* 87: 342–362.

Greiner, A. 1996. "Endogenous Growth Cycles: Arrow's Learning by Doing Reconsidered." *Journal of Macroeconomics* 18: 587–604.

Greiner, A., and W. Semmler. 1996. "Multiple Steady States, Indeterminacy and Cycles in a Basic Model of Endogenous Growth." *Journal of Economics* 63: 79–99.

———. 1999. "An Inquiry into the Sustainability of German Fiscal Policy: Some Time Series Tests." *Public Finance Review* 27: 220–236.

———. 2000. "Endogenous Growth, Government Debt and Budgetary Regimes." *Journal of Macroeconomics* 22: 363–384.

Grossman, G. M., and E. Helpman. 1991. *Innovation and Growth in the Global Economy.* 2nd edition. Cambridge, MA: MIT Press.

Hall, R. 1988. "Intertemporal Substitution in Consumption." *Journal of Political Economy* 96: 339–357.

Hall, R. E., and C. I. Jones. 1999. "On the Limitations of Government Borrowing: A Framework for Empirical Testing." *Quarterly Journal of Econmics* 114: 83–116.

Hamilton, J. D. 1994. *Time Series Analysis.* Princeton, NJ: Princeton University Press.

Hamilton, J., and M. Flavin. 1986. "On the Limitations of Government Borrowing: A Framework for Empirical Testing." *American Economic Review* 76: 808–819.

Hamilton, J. D., and J. Monteagudo. 1998. "The Augmented Solow Model and the Productivity Slowdown." *Journal of Monetary Economics* 42: 495–509.

Hansen, L. P. 1982. "Large Sample Properties of Generalized Method of Moments Estimators." *Econometrica* 50: 1029–1054.

Hansen, L. P., and K. J. Singleton. 1982. "Generalized Instrumental Variables Estimation of Nonlinear Rational Expectations Models." *Econometrica* 50: 1269–1286.

Hanushek, E. A., and D. D. Kimko. 2000. "Schooling, Labor Force Quality, and the Growth of Nations." *American Economic Review* 90: 1184–1208.

Harrod, R. F. 1939. "An Essay in Dynamic Economic Theory." *Economic Journal* 49: 14–33.

———. 1948. *Towards a Dynamic Economics.* London: Macmillan.

Jones, C. I. 1995a. "R&D-Based Models of Economic Growth." *Journal of Political Economy* 103: 759–784.

———. 1995b. "Time Series Tests of Endogenous Growth Models." *Quarterly Journal of Economics* 110: 495–525.

———. 1997. *The Upcoming Slowdown in U.S. Economic Growth*. New York: W. W. Norton.

———. 1998. *Introduction to Economic Growth*. New York: W. W. Norton.

———. 2002. "Sources of U.S. Economic Growth in a World of Ideas." *American Economic Review* 92, no. 1: 220–239.

Jorgenson, D. W., F. M. Gollop, and B. M. Fraumeni. 1987. *Productivity and U.S. Economic Growth*. Cambridge, MA: Harvard University Press.

Judge, G. G., R. C. Hill, W. E. Griffiths, H. Luetkepohl, and T.-C. Lee. 1988. *Introduction to the Theory and Practice of Econometrics*. 2nd edition. New York: John Wiley and Sons.

Kaldor, N. 1956. "Alternative Theories of Distribution." *Review of Economic Studies* 23: 83–100.

———. 1961. "Capital Accumulation and Economic Growth." In *The Theory of Capital: Proceedings of a Conference Held by the International Economics Association*, ed. F A. Lutz and D. C. Hague, pp. 177–222. New York: St. Martin's Press.

———. 1966. *Essays on Value and Distribution*. London: Duckworth.

Kalecki, M. 1971. *Selected Essays on the Dynamics of the Capitalist Economy 1933–1970*. Cambridge: Cambridge University Press.

Katz, L. F., and D. H. Autor. 1999. "Changes in the Wage Structure and Earnings Inequality." In *Handbook of Labor Economics*, ed. O. Ashenfelter and D. Card, vol. 3, pp. 1463–1555. Amsterdam: Elsevier.

Katz, L. F., and K. M. Murphy. 1992. "Changes in Relative Wages, 1963–1987: Supply and Demand Factors." *Quarterly Journal of Economics* 107: 35–78.

Kendrick, J. W. 1976. *The Formation and Stocks of Total Capital*. New York: Columbia University Press.

Keynes, J. M. 1936. *The General Thoery of Employment, Interest and Money*. London: Macmillan.

Klenow, P. J., and A. Rodriguez-Clare. 1998. "The Neoclassical Revival in Growth Economics: Has It Gone Too Far?" In *NBER Macroeconomics Annual*, ed. B. S. Bernanke and J. J. Rotemberg, pp. 73–103. Cambridge, MA: MIT Press.

Koopmans, T. C. 1965. "On the Concept of Optimal Economic Growth." In *The Econometric Approach to Development Planning*, pp. 225–300. Amsterdam: North-Holland.

Kremer, M., A. Onatski, and J. Stock. 2001. "Searching for Prosperity." Working paper no. 8250, National Bureau of Economic Research.

Kremers, J. M. 1989. "U.S. Federal Indebtedness and the Conduct of Fiscal Policy." *Journal of Monetary Economics* 23: 219–238.

Krüger, A. B., and M. Lindahl. 2001. "Education for Growth: Why and for Whom?" *Journal of Economic Literature* 39: 1101–1136.

Krugman, P. 1994. "Past and Prospective Causes of High Unemployment." *Federal Reserve Bank of Kansas City Economic Review* (fourth quarter): 23–43.

Krusell, P., L. E. Ohanian, J. V. Rios-Rull, and G. L. Violante. 2000. "Capital-Skill Complementarity and Inequality: A Macroeconomic Analysis." *Econometrica* 68: 1029–1053.

Kuznets, S. 1955. "Economic Growth and Income Inequality." *American Economic Review* 45: 1–28.

———. 1973. "Modern Economic Growth: Findings and Reflections." *American Economic Review* 63: 247–258.

Levhari, D. 1966. "Extensions of Arrow's Learning by Doing." *Review of Economic Studies* 33: 117–131.

Levine, R., and D. Renelt. 1992. "A Sensitivity Analysis of Cross-Country Growth Regression." *American Economic Review* 82: 942–963.

Lucas, R. E. 1988. "On the Mechanics of Economic Development." *Journal of Monetary Economics* 22: 3–42.

———. 1990. "Supply-Side Economics: An Analytical Review." *Oxford Economic Papers* 42: 293–316.

Maddison, A. 1994. "Explaining the Economic Performance of Nations, 1820–1989." In *Convergence of Productivity: Cross-National Studies and Historical Evidence*, ed. W. J. Baumol, R. R. Nelson, and E. N. Wolff, pp. 20–61. Oxford: Oxford University Press.

———. 2001. *The World Economy: A Millenial Perspective*. Paris: Organization for Economic Cooperation and Development.

Mankiw, N. G., D. Romer, and D. N. Weil. 1992. "A Contribution to the Empirics of Economic Growth." *Quarterly Journal of Economics* 107: 407–437.

Marx, K. 1967. "Capital: A Critique of Political Economy." In *The Process of Capitalist Production as a Whole*, vol. 3. New York: International Publishers.

McCallum, B. T. 1984. "Are Bond-Financed Deficits Inflationary? A Ricardian Analysis." *Journal of Political Economy* 92: 123–135.

Mill, J. S. 1900. Principles of Political Economy. New York: Colonial Press.

Mincer, J. 1958. "Investment in Human Capital and Personal Income Distribution." *Journal of Political Economy* 66: 281–302.

Mino, K. 1996. "Analysis of a Two-Sector Model of Endogenous Growth with Capital Income Taxation." *International Economic Review* 37, no. 1: 227–251.

Mulligan, C. B, and X. Sala-i-Martin. 1993a. "Some Evidence on the Links between Aggregate Income and Human Capital." University of Chicago. Mimeograph.

———. 1993b. "Transitional Dynamics in Two-Sector Models of Endogenous Growth." *Quarterly Journal of Economics* 108: 737–773.

Murphy, K. M., W. C. Riddell, and P. M. Romer. 1998. "Wages, Skills, and Technology in the United States and Canada." In *General Purpose Technologies and Economic Growth*, ed. E. Helpman, pp. 283–309. Cambridge, MA: MIT Press.

Nehru, V., E. Swanson, and A. Dubey. 1995. "A New Database on Human Capital Stock in Developing and Industrial Countries: Sources Methodology and Results." *Journal of Development Economics* 26: 379–401.

Newey, W. K., and K. D. West. 1987. "A Simple, Positive-Definite, Heteroskedasticity and Autocorrelation Consistent Covariance Matrix." *Econometrica* 55: 703–708.

Ogwang, T. 1995. "The Economic Development–Income Inequality Nexus: Further Evidence on Kuznets' U-Curve Hypothesis." *American Journal of Economics and Sociology* 54: 1–2.

Paap, R., and H. K. van Dijk. 1998. "Distribution and Mobility of Wealth of Nations." *European Economic Review* 42: 1269–1293.

Park, W. G. 1995. "International R&D Spillovers and OECD Economic Growth." *Economic Inquiry* 33: 571–591.

Pasinetti, L. L. 1962. "Rate of Profit and Income Distribution in Relation to the Rate of Economic Growth." *Review of Economic Studies* 29: 267–279.

Perotti, R. 1993. "Political Equilibrium, Income Distribution, and Growth." *Review of Economic Studies* 60: 755–776.

———. 1996. "Growth, Income Distribution, and Democracy: What the Data Say." *Journal of Economic Growth* 1: 149–187.

Persson, T., and G. Tabellini. 1994. "Is Inequality Harmful for Economic Growth?" *American Economic Review* 84: 600–621.

Psacharopoulos, G., and A. M. Arriagada. 1986. "The Educational Composition of the Labor Force: An International Comparison." *International Labor Review* 125: 561–574.

Quah, D. T. 1996. "Empirics for Economic Growth and Convergence." *European Economic Review* 40: 1353–1375.

Ricardo, D. 1951. "Principles of Political Economy and Taxation." In *Works and Correspondence*, ed. P. Straffa with M. Dobb, vol. 1. Cambridge: Cambridge University Press.

Richardson, D. J. 1995. "Income Inequality and Trade: How to Think, What to Conclude." *Journal of Economic Perspectives* 9: 33–55.

Riley, J. G. 1976. "Information, Screening and Human Capital." *American Economic Association, Papers and Proceedings* 66: 254–260.

Rivera-Batiz, L., and P. Romer. 1991. "Economic Integration and Endogenous Growth." *Quarterly Journal of Economics* 106: 531–555.

Roberds, W. 1991. "Implications of Expected Present Value Budget Balance: Application to Postwar U.S. Data." In *Rational Expectations Econometrics*, ed. L. Hanson and T. Sargent, pp. 163–175. Boulder: Westview Press.

Romer, P. M. 1986. "Increasing Returns and Long-Run Growth." *Journal of Political Economy* 94: 1002–1037.

———. 1990. "Endogenous Technological Change." *Journal of Political Economy* 98: S71–S102.

Ryder, H. E., and G. M. Heal. 1973. "Optimal Growth with Intertemporally Dependent Preferences." *Review of Economic Studies* 40: 1–31.

Sachs, J. D., and H. J. Shatz. 1994. "How Trade Hurt Unskilled Workers." *Brookings Papers on Economic Activity* 1: 1–84.

Sala-i-Martin, X. 1997. "I Just Ran Two Million Regressions." *American Economic Association Papers and Proceedings* 87: 1325–1352.

Samuelson, P. A., and F. Modigliani. 1966. "The Pasinetti Paradox in Neo-Classical and More General Models." *Review of Economic Studies* 33: 269–303.

Scholl, A., and W. Semmler. 2002. "Sustainable Economic Growth and Exhaustible Resources: A Model and Estimation for the U.S." *Discrete Dynamics in Nature and Society* 7, no. 2: 79–92.

Schumpeter, J. A. 1935. *Theorie der wirtschaftlichen Entwicklung*. 4th edition. Munich: Duncker & Humblot.

Segerstrom, P. S. 1998. "Endogenous Growth without Scale Effects." *American Economic Review* 88: 1290–1310.

Seierstad, A., and K. Sydsæter. 1987. *Optimal Control Theory with Economic Applications*. Amsterdam: North-Holland.

Semmler, W., and G. Gong. 1996a. "Estimating Parameters of Real Business Cycle Models." *Journal of Economic Behavior and Organisation* 30: 301–325.

———. 1996b. "Parameter Estimation and Moment Evaluation of Business Cycle Models." Department of Economics, New School University, New York. Mimeograph.

Semmler, W., and M. Sieveking. 1997. "Using Vector Field Analysis for Studying Debt Dynamics." Paper prepared for the winter meeting of the Econometric Society, Chicago, January 1998.

———. 2000. "Critical Debt and Debt Dynamics." *Journal of Economic Dynamics and Control* 24: 1121–1144.

Shell, K. 1967. "A Model of Inventive Activity and Capital Accumulation." In *Essays on the Theory of Optimal Economic Growth*, ed. K. Shell, pp. 67–85. Cambridge, MA: MIT Press.

Sheshinski, E. 1967. "Optimal Accumulation with Learning by Doing." In *Essays on the Theory of Optimal Economic Growth*, ed. K. Shell, pp. 31–52. Cambridge, MA: MIT Press.

Sidrauski, M. 1967. "Rational Choice and Patterns of Growth in a Monetary Economy." *American Economic Association, Papers and Proceedings* 57: 534–544.

Siegel, D. S. 1999. "Skill-Biased Technological Change." Upjohn Institute for Employment Research, Kalamazoo, Michigan.

Skiba, A. K. 1978. "Optimal Growth with Convex-Concave Production Function." *Econometrica* 46: 527–539.

Smith, A. 1976. "An Inquiry into the Nature and Causes of the Wealth of Nations." In *The Glasgow Edition of Works and Correspondence of Adam Smith*, ed. R. H. Cambell and A. S. Skinner, vol. 2. Oxford: Clarendon Press.

Solow, R. M. 1956. "A Contribution to the Theory of Economic Growth." *Quarterly Journal of Economics* 70: 65–94.

———. 1957. "Technical Change and the Aggregate Production Function." *Review of Economics and Statistics* 39: 312–320.

———. 2003. "General Comments on Part IV." In *Knowledge, Information and Expectations in Modern Macroeconomics*, ed. P. Aghion, R. Frydman, J. Stiglitz and M. Woodford, pp. 546–549. Princeton, NJ: Princeton University Press.

Stiglitz, J. E. 1975. "The Theory of Screening, Education, and the Distribution of Income." *American Economic Review* 65: 283–300.

Sturm, J. E., G. H. Kuper, and J. de Haan. 1998. "Modelling Government Investment and Economic Growth on a Macro Level." In *Market Behaviour and Macroeconomic Modelling*, ed. S. Brakman, H. van Ees, and S. K. Kuipers, pp. 359–406. London: Macmillan/St. Martin's Press.

Summers, R., and A. Heston. 1991. "The Penn World Table (Mark 5): An Expanded Set of International Comparisons, 1950–1988." *Quarterly Journal of Economics* 106: 327–368.

Swan, T. V. 1956. "Economic Growth and Capital Accumulation." *Economic Record* 32: 334–361.

Trehan, B., and C. E. Walsh. 1988. "Common Trends, the Government Budget Constraint, and Revenue Smoothing." *Journal of Economic Dynamics and Control* 12: 425–444.

———. 1991. "Testing Intertemporal Budget Constraints: Theory and Applications to U.S. Federal Budget and Current Account Deficits." *Journal of Money, Credit, and Banking* 23: 206–223.

Turnovsky, S. J. 1995. *Methods of Macroeconomic Dynamics*. Cambridge, MA: MIT Press.

Uzawa, H. 1965. "Optimum Technical Change in an Aggregative Model of Economic Growth." *International Economic Review* 6: 18–31.

———. 1968. "Time Preference, the Consumption Function and Optimum Asset Holdings." In *Value, Capital and Growth: Papers in Honour of Sir John Hicks*, ed. J. N. Wolfe, pp. 485–504. Edinburgh: University of Edinburgh Press.

Wan, H. Y. 1970. "Optimal Saving Programs under Intertemporally Dependent Preferences." *International Economic Review* 11: 521–547.

Ward, M. 1976. "The Measurement of Capital." Organization for Economic Cooperation and Development, Paris.

Wilcox, D. W. 1989. "The Sustainability of Government Deficits: Implications of the Present-Value Borrowing Constraint." *Journal of Money, Credit, and Banking* 21: 291–306.

Wolff, E. N. 1996. "The Productivity Slowdown: The Culprit at Last? Follow-up on Hutten and Wolff." *American Economic Review* 86: 1239–1252.

Wood, A. 1995. "How Trade Hurt Unskilled Workers." *Journal of Economic Perspectives* 9: 57–80.

Xie, D. 1991. "Increasing Returns and Increasing Rates of Growth." *Journal of Political Economy* 99: 429–435.

Young, A. 1995. "The Tyranny of Numbers: Confronting the Statistical Realities of the East Asian Growth Experience." *Quarterly Journal of Economics* 110: 641–680.

Index